Defenders *of* Reason *in* Islam

Other books on Islamic Studies published by Oneworld:

City of Wrong: A Friday in Jerusalem, M. Kamel Hussein (trans. Kenneth Cragg), ISBN 1-85168-072-1

Companion to the Qur'án, William Montgomery Watt, ISBN 1-85168-036-5

The Event of the Qur'án: Islam in its Scripture, Kenneth Cragg, ISBN 1-85168-067-5

The Faith and Practice of Al-Ghazálí, William Montgomery Watt, ISBN 1-85168-062-4

Islam and the West, Norman Daniel, ISBN 1-85168-129-9

Jesus in the Qur'án, Geoffrey Parrinder, ISBN 1-85168-094-2

Muhammad: A Short Biography, Martin Forward, ISBN 1-85168-131-0

Muslim Devotions: A Study of Prayer-Manuals in Common Use, Constance E. Padwick, ISBN 1-85168-115-9

On Being a Muslim: Finding the Religious Path in the Modern World, Farid Esack, ISBN 1-85168-146-9

The Qur'án and its Exegesis: Selected Texts with Classical and Modern Muslim Interpretations, Helmut Gätje, ISBN 1-85168-118-3

Qur'án, Liberation and Pluralism, Farid Esack, ISBN 1-85168-121-3

Rabi'a: The Life and Work of Rabi'a and Other Women Mystics in Islam, Margaret Smith, ISBN 1-85168-085-3

Rúmi: Poet and Mystic, Reynold A. Nicholson, ISBN 1-85168-096-9

A Short History of Islam, William Montgomery Watt, ISBN 1-85168-109-4

A Short Introduction to Islamic Philosophy, Theology and Mysticism, Majid Fakhry, ISBN 1-85168-134-5

Voices of Islam, John Bowker, ISBN 1-85168-095-0

DEFENDERS *of* REASON *in* ISLAM

Mu'tazilism *from* Medieval School *to* Modern Symbol

Richard C. Martin *and* Mark R. Woodward
with Dwi S. Atmaja

ONEWORLD
OXFORD

DEFENDERS OF REASON IN ISLAM
MU'TAZILISM FROM MEDIEVAL SCHOOL
TO MODERN SYMBOL

Oneworld Publications
(Sales and Editorial)
185 Banbury Road
Oxford OX2 7AR
England

Oneworld Publications
(US Marketing Office)
PO Box 830, 21 Broadway
Rockport, MA 01966
USA

ISBN 1–85168–147-7

Cover design by Peter Maguire
Printed and bound by WSOY, Finland

For our children –

Nia, Steffi, Erik, and Taqwa Aditya

Contents

PART II HARUN NASUTION AND MODERN MU'TAZILISM

Contents

Preface

This work grew out of the authors' direction of an M.A. thesis project at Arizona State University by Mr. Dwi Surya Atmaja, now professor of Arabic at the Islamic University (I.A.I.N.) at Pontionak, Indonesia. As his advisors in the Department of Religious Studies, Mark Woodward and I had for several years enjoyed wide-ranging conversations on theological developments in the modern Muslim world, particularly in Egypt and Southeast Asia – our own respective areas of primary interest. With his arrival as a graduate student in the Department of Religious Studies in the early 1990s, Dwi's voice was added to those conversations. All three of us shared the conviction that contemporary theological issues and discussions in the Islamic world could not be understood by non-Muslims – or for that matter, Muslims – who were innocent of adequate knowledge of the theological disputes and schools that arose in the first five centuries of Islam. This conviction suggested the thesis project undertaken by Mr. Atmaja: a translation of a Mu'tazili treatise on the rational foundations of theology, with a brief commentary on the implications of the text for discussions going on among Muslim groups and intellectuals in Indonesia today. The text that I suggested Mr. Atmaja translate was by Qadi 'Abd al-Jabbar (d. 1024), *Kitab al-usul al-khamsa*. A retranslation of that text appears in chapter 5 below.

Several stages marked the development of the project that produced this book following Dwi Atmaja's return to Indonesia in the summer of 1992. First, Woodward and I, in consultation with Atmaja, decided that I should revise and polish the translation of 'Abd al-Jabbar's text to make it available to students in religious and Islamic studies in some sort of published form. That eventually entailed the preparation of textual commentary and background for the modern educated reader who might be unfamiliar with the history, content, and genre of the text. Next, the Indonesian connection was deemed important enough for Woodward to develop further, as a way of demonstrating the modern relevance of the Mu'tazili theological school. In the process of research and writing on the influence of Mu'tazili thought in contemporary Indonesia, Woodward discovered a text by the modern Indonesian Mu'tazilite Harun Nasution. A translation of that text and new background chapters were subsequently added. This now gave the project two exemplars of Mu'tazili thought to be explained and interpreted – one from the medieval Islamic Middle Eastern heartlands and the other from modern Asia. Beyond the two texts and the chapters of background and commentary they required, the twentieth-century discovery of numerous Mu'tazili manuscripts in places like Yemen seemed to be an important part of the story of Mu'tazilism. That entailed writing a discussion of the roles of Orientalism and *Religionswissenschaft* in the modern textual and interpretive history of Mu'tazilism. That in turn brought attention to numerous discussions of Mu'tazilism by modern Muslim authors writing in the Middle East and the West.

The discovery of the need to add new dimensions to the work often resulted from sharing findings with colleagues in religious and Islamic studies. Bruce Lawrence had read an early draft of the Introduction and suggested the title "Critical Islam," because of the link with the modern uses of Mu'tazilism by Muslim intellectuals, many of whom were concomitantly exploring critical theory. This important insight confirmed the authors' belief that the revival of Mu'tazilism and theological rationalism could be interpreted as a modernist countermove against what Lawrence and others have called fundamentalism. Indeed, Lawrence's book, *Defenders of God*, eventually suggested to the authors the present title for their own work, *Defenders of Reason*, to which the publisher suggested adding "in Islam." Our criticism of the thesis Lawrence has advanced in *Defenders of God: The Fundamentalist Revolt Against the Modern Age* (1989) must be seen against the background of our debt to his collegial friendship and the stimulus of his provocative essay on fundamentalism.

Several other colleagues have also made important contributions to this project along the way. Hassan Hanafi read through the English translation in chapter 5, against the Arabic edition, and made several suggestions for better and more accurate renderings. A public presentation of a version of chapter 10 was made at a Fulbright conference attended by both authors and Mr. Atmaja in Jakarta in June, 1995. Responses by Nurcholish Madjid and other Indonesian theologians were helpful to the evolution of the present work. Charles J. Adams, now a part-time colleague in the Department of Religious Studies at Arizona State University, has been an important source of information throughout this project. The authors would also like to thank several friends and colleagues who graciously listened to our ideas, read one or more chapters in various draft stages, and who were willing to offer encouragement and in some cases constructive criticism: Kristin Brustad, Paul Courtright, Richard Eaton, Josef van Ess, Wendy Farley, Wadi Haddad,

Walter Lowe, Holly Martin, Ebrahim Moosa, Abdullahi an-Na'im, Gordon Newby, Frank Reynolds, Juliane Schober, Abdulkader Tayob, Norani Uthman, and John Witte. Michael Smith took time out from a busy senior year at Emory College to aid in the preparation of the bibliography.

We are grateful to our editor and publisher, Novin Doostdar, for the efficient, professional, and user-friendly manner in which he and his colleagues at Oneworld Publications have seen this project through. Helen Coward, senior editor. and Judith Willson, project editor, have been a pleasure to work with, albeit almost entirely by Internet, in the final stages of converting the manuscript into its present book form.

We are indebted the most to Dwi Surya Atmaja. He willingly and ably took on a masters thesis suggested to him by his advisors, and in the process forced them, and himself, to think more about many of the issues raised in the present book. Dwi's studies at Arizona State in many ways embody one subject matter of the book – the challenges to young Muslim modernist intellectuals by Islamism on the one side and secularism on the other. If the central text of Dwi's thesis has been retranslated into more nuanced English theological expression and the Nasution translation and seven additional chapters have since been added, the project as a whole was nonetheless motivated by Dwi's initial contribution. We hope that Dwi Atmaja and his younger Muslim colleagues will respond critically and constructively to the book whose existence Dwi has inspired.

It should go without saying that we, the authors, are finally responsible for the book that follows. Nonetheless, we are grateful to have enjoyed such generous collegial and professional support. Our spouses are among those colleagues thanked above, but can never be thanked adequately for making such diversions as the writing of books possible. Our children also saw less of us than they should have. They are the ones to whom we dedicate this work.

Richard C. Martin
Atlanta, Georgia
May 1, 1997

Notes *on* Style

Arabic and Indonesian names, titles, and technical terms are transliterated following conventions commonly used in English-language journals. In discussions where both Arabic and Indonesian terms appear, or in cases where it has seemed appropriate to identify the language of the term, the abbreviations "Ind." and "Ar." are used. The symbol ¶ indicates paragraphs in the translation in chapter 5.

For the sake of simplicity, most extra-literal typographic symbols (such as overbars to indicate long Arabic vowels and underdots to indicate harder forms of certain Arabic consonants) have been omitted. The exception is the Arabic 'ayn ('), as in 'Abd al-Jabbar, and the Arabic *hamza* or glottal stop ('), as in Qur'an. Our assumption is that Arabists will not need the full technical markings in most cases. We apologize for confusions that may arise for linguists from simplified transliteration. Our hope is that non-Arabists and non-Indonesianists who want to learn more about Mu'tazilism and Islamic theology will have greater access to the ideas and concepts discussed in the book.

Technical terms in Arabic are normally italicized when they first appear in a chapter (e.g., *kalam*) and appear thereafter in roman type (e.g., kalam). Islamic terms that appear in *Webster's Third New International Dictionary Unabridged*, such as Qur'an, Hadith, Shari'a, Sunna, etc. are not italicized. Those same terms, like Talmud, Torah, and Bible, name sacred texts or textual processes, and hence are capitalized. Other terms, such as kalam, (theological discourse), *umma* (confessional community), and '*aql* (reason) are normally not capitalized. All such terms are introduced in context. A brief glossary also appears at the end of the book for readers who may run across an important term whose definition lies somewhere in preceding pages.

Most references to Arabic texts give volume number (if any), followed by page number and line number(s). For example, *al-Mughni* 16, 27: 3–11 refers to *Kitab al-Mughni*, volume 16, page 27, lines 3–11.

Translations of Qur'an and Hadith passages are our own unless otherwise indicated. We have often consulted the Qur'an translation by Marmaduke Pickthall, *The Meaning of the Glorious Koran*, although we have endeavored to avoid its archaic use of language.

The Western Common Era calendar is followed throughout.

Abbreviations

Full reference to works listed below may be found in the bibliography.

Ar.	Arabic
art.	article
BMO	British Museum Oriental
EI²	*Encyclopaedia of Islam, Second Edition*
EIr	*Encyclopaedia Iranica*
ER	*Encyclopedia of Religion*
Fadl	'Abd al-Jabbar, *Fadl al-i'tizal wa tabaqat al-mu'tazila*
Fihrist	Al-Nadim, *The Fihrist of al-Nadim*
fol./fols.	folio/folios
Formative Period	Watt, *The Formative Period of Islamic Thought*
GAL	Brockelmann, *Geschichte der arabischen Literatur*
GAS	Sezgin, *Geschichte des arabischen Schrifttums*
Ind.	Indonesian
Jalalayn	*Tafsir al-imamayn al-jalalayn*
Maqalat	Ash'ari, *Kitab maqalat al-islamiyin*
Al-Mughni	'Abd al-Jabbar, *al-Mughni fi abwab al-tawhid wa l-'adl*
reg.	(*regnabat*) ruled
S	Supplement
SEI	*Shorter Encyclopaedia of Islam*
Sharh	'Abd al-Jabbar, *Sharh al-usul al-khamsa*
Sharh al-'uyun	Al-Hakim al-Jushami, *Sharh al-'uyun* in 'Abd al-Jabbar, *Fadl al-i'tizal*
Tabaqat	Ibn al-Murtada, *Kitab tabaqat al-mu'tazila*
Ta'liq	Manekdim, *Ta'liq 'ala sharh al-usul al-khamsa*
Theologie	van Ess, *Theologie und Gesellschaft im 2. Und 3. Jahrhundert Hidschra*

one

Introduction
A Tale of Two Texts

I n the late 1970s, the Indonesian modernist theologian Harun Nasution published a pamphlet in defense of a medieval Muslim "rationalist" theological school known as the Mu'tazila. This was somewhat unusual. Although Mu'tazili theology is discussed, sometimes positively, by modern Muslim scholars, very few have identified themselves with Mu'tazilism to the extent that Nasution has. Mu'tazili rationalists had taught doctrines about divine unity, the historical context of revelation, and ethical answerability to God that ran counter to the religious beliefs held by most Muslims. Nonetheless, Mu'tazili intellectualism enjoyed the patronage of numerous caliphs and viziers during the first two and a half centuries of the Abbasid Age (viz. 800–1050). After the heyday of the school in the ninth and tenth centuries, Mu'tazili dominance in theological discourse (*kalam*) began to wane, giving way to more centrist and populist discourses, such as those of the Ash'ari and Maturidi theologians (*mutakallimun*), and the Hanbali, Hanafi, and Shafi'i jurisconsults (*fuquha'*).

Theological rationalism did not altogether disappear in Islamic thought, however. Shi'i theologians continued to dictate and comment on medieval Mu'tazili texts as part of their madrasa curriculum.[1] After the eleventh century and the influence of Abu Hamid al-Ghazali (d. 1111) in particular, Aristotelian philosophical method rivaled the more disputational practices of the mutakallimun. With the emergence of Islamic modernist thinking in the latter part of the nineteenth century, however, Mu'tazili rationalism began to enjoy a revival of interest among Sunni Muslim intellectuals. During this past century, the discovery of several Mu'tazili

1

manuscripts hibernating in Middle Eastern libraries has led to an increase of scholarly interest in Mu'tazili texts by both Western and Muslim scholars. The former have tended to interest themselves in Mu'tazili parallels with, and origins in, Christian and Hellenistic sources. The latter have often seen in the Mu'tazili texts an indigenous rationalism that could be revived in the service of adapting Islam to the modern world. Although both motivations are pertinent to this study, the latter comes into focus especially in Parts II and III below.

The current study is structured by two short expositions of Mu'tazili doctrine, one dictated in Arabic in Iran toward the end of the tenth century, and the other written, as we have indicated, by Harun Nasution in Bahasa Indonesia in the late 1970s. In his pamphlet on Mu'tazilism, Nasution several times cites a theologian, Qadi 'Abd al-Jabbar (d. 1024). Indeed, Nasution specifically cites a work attributed to 'Abd al-Jabbar that had been published in Egypt in 1965 under the title *Sharh al-usul al-khamsa* (Commentary on the five fundamentals [of theology]). In addition to Nasution's text, this study also presents the original treatise at the basis of the commentary, 'Abd al- Jabbar's *Kitab al-usul al-khamsa* (Book on the five fundamentals). These two texts, 'Abd al-Jabbar's original treatise and Harun Nasution's modernist commentary, form the two textual and historical foci of this study.

The identification, translation, and general significance of these two texts, considered together as examples of Mu'tazili thought and separately as discourses belonging to quite different historical moments, form the subject matter of Parts I and II (chapters 2 through 9) below. The rest of this chapter and the next set the stage for considering the specific matters of text and context by discussing the history of Mu'tazilism and, more generally, the conflict between rationalism and traditionalism in Islam. Part III considers further the archeology of Mu'tazilism by modernist Muslim intellectuals – scholars who do not necessarily refer to themselves as Mu'tazilites, as Harun Nasution does, but who nonetheless find in the rationalism for which the Mu'tazili theologians are remembered a counterpoise to Islamist, including fundamentalist, movements.

From the Project of Orientalism to the Fundamentalism Project

Harun Nasution's text, as well as the works of other modernist Muslim scholars we shall discuss in Part III below, raises the question of Orientalism – the colonial and postcolonial project to recover and reconstruct the classical religions and civilizations of colonial subjects. That Orientalist scholarship was political in motivation and effect was argued lucidly in 1963 by the Egyptian Marxist intellectual Anwar Abdel Malek.[2] Fifteen years later, criticism of Orientalism itself became a "project" that jolted academe and reverberated throughout the social sciences and humanities with the publication of Edward W. Said's *Orientalism*.[3] Said characterized the discourse of Orientalism in a well-known passage that is itself polemical and rhetorical:

> The Orientalist surveys the Orient from above, with the aim of getting hold of the whole sprawling panorama before him – culture, religion, mind, history, society. To do this he must see every detail through the device of a set of reductive categories (the Semites, the Muslim mind, the Orient, and so forth). Since these categories are primarily schematic and efficient ones, and since it is more or less assumed that no Oriental can know himself the way an Orientalist can, any vision of the Orient ultimately comes to rely for its coherence and force on the person, institution, or discourse whose property it is . . . [W]e have noted how in the history of ideas about the Near Orient in the West these ideas have maintained themselves regardless of any evidence disputing them. (Indeed, we can argue that these ideas *produce evidence that proves their validity*.)[4]

More recently, Peter van der Veer has carried the critique of the Orientalist project a step further. Speaking of the work of Sanskritists and other Orientalists working on the South Asia subcontinent, van der Veer has argued:

> Orientalists brought modern philological methods and concepts to bear on India's past. In critical editions of Hindu scriptures they replaced a fragmented, largely oral set of traditions with an unchanging, homogenized written canon. The critical editions of the Mahabharata and Ramayana as well as the ongoing Purana-projects show this process of selection and unification very well. In that way a "history," established by modern science, came to replace a traditional "past."[5]

Van der Veer makes the case that Western Orientalists working in South Asia fastened onto the Brahmanical textual tradition, thus privileging a view of South Asian religion held by the Brahmin "caste" (itself a social concept that is prominent in Orientalist scholarship). Thus, the Orientalist project in India, he concludes, was the construction of a "Hindu" historical and textual tradition. This in turn became an (unintended) scriptural focus for Hindu (and Muslim) communalism based on religious nationalism. In short, contemporary religious fundamentalism has constructed its militant "Hindu" identity in part from materials provided by Orientalist scholarship.

Is the Orientalist project similarly linked with Islamic revivalist movements (referred to in general as *usuliyun* "fundamentalists" and *islamiyun* "Islamists")? A complete analysis of that question goes beyond the scope of this book, although a brief exploration of the issue is relevant. Clearly, the debate about modern Islamic identity, which engages in critiques of Orientalism and the West more generally, also utilizes Orientalist scholarship; indeed, contemporary Islamic discourse about modernity utilizes and itself engages in the Orientalist project of renovating the Islamic past through the publication of critical editions of traditional texts. Harun Nasution's text, *The Mu'tazila and Rational Philosophy* in chapter 9 below, indicates in its footnotes not only a reliance on Orientalist editions but also includes Nasution's own scholarly approval of interpretations of the Mu'tazila by such well-known Protestant Christian Orientalists as D. B. MacDonald and A. J. Wensinck. Indeed, Muslim discourse about Islam and modernity includes both Islamist efforts to reestablish the society of the first righteous generations (*salafiya*) as well as the modernist call for adapting Islam to the exigencies of the modern age. Both aspects of this discourse are historically, if not also logically, post-Orientalist. We argue that historians of religion must then ask the question: what was the "pre-Orientalist" background or the broader intellectual context of Orientalism? This brings us from the project of Orientalism to the science of religion (*Religionswissenschaft*).

Van der Veer's characterization above of the Orientalism project as "a 'history,' established by modern science," is reminiscent of the nineteenth-century turn toward the optimism that society, culture, and religion could be studied scientifically. The anti-Orientalist criticism of Western scholarship on Islam has, from the beginning, focused a great deal of attention on philology as the discipline par excellence of Orientalism. However, to paraphrase a remark that Karl Barth made about Adolf Harnack and nineteenth-century biblical criticism, critics who look deep into the well of *Orientalismusforschung* will find the face of F. Max Müller staring back at them. The crucial decade when the "turn" took place, as Eric Sharpe has shown, was from 1859 to 1869:

> The decade began, of course, with the publication of Darwin's *Origin of Species*. Before its end, Herbert Spencer was well started on his elaborate *System of Synthetic Philosophy*, Thomas Huxley had confronted Bishop Wilberforce before the British Association in the name of science, E. B. Tylor had launched his theory of "animism" . . . and an expatriate

German philologist resident in Oxford, Friederich Max Müller, had begun to publish a definitive edition of the Sanskrit text of the *Rig Veda* . . . and suggested to the English-speaking world that, so far from science and religion being irreconcilable opposites, there might be a "Science of Religion" which would do justice to both. In short, comparative religion (at first a synonym for the science of religion) did not exist by 1859; by 1869 it did.[6]

The scholarly conceit that the study of religion consists in a science or in sciences that *explain* the "data of religion" has led communities of scholars in the academy, such as the American Academy of Arts and Sciences (and to a lesser extent the American Academy of Religion), to isolate problems in the study of religion for special attention. The "problem" to receive the most attention in the last decade has come to be known, rather uneasily, by the rubric "fundamentalism." Like Orientalism, fundamentalism is linked to colonialism. In much of the world, fundamentalism is construed as a postcolonial phenomenon and thus can be analyzed comparatively across traditions. In short, fundamentalism is now a "project" of the academy. We agree with those scholars associated with the Fundamentalism Project who hold that fundamentalist-like movements should also be compared historically with similar movements and conflicts within universal religious traditions, such as Islam. We disagree with the narrower claim that fundamentalism is primarily explicable as an intellectual and social phenomenon of modernity. The faultiness of the claim in general is that virtually no contemporary or recent social phenomena can be excluded from it, and thus it loses its explanatory power. Nonetheless, the conditions of modernity have clearly altered the rationalism/traditionalism conflict. We will describe and assess the influence of modernity on the "spirit of Mu'tazilism" and rationalism in the later chapters of this book.

What little general interest there has been in the academy in the Mu'tazila, rationalism, or Islamic modernism has been almost entirely eclipsed by journalists and scholars who like to fret in public about the causes and effects of Islamic fundamentalism. Muslim rationalist and modernist theologians, by and large, have not provided the media with sound bites and video footage for the evening news. Thus, before we attempt to discuss the complex relationship between rationalism and traditionalism, we must examine the role of Western (and Muslim) neo-Orientalism in editing out all but the Islamist movements when modern Islamic thought and movements come under discussion in Western public discourse.

Recently, scholars in religious studies have attempted to recapture ground taken by political scientists, the media, and Washington think tanks regarding the explanation and interpretation of religious fundamentalism, especially in its more violent expressions. Two of the earliest such attempts appeared in 1987 (Lionel Caplan, ed., *Studies in Religious Fundamentalism* and Richard T. Antoun and Mary Elaine Hegland, eds., *Studies in Religious Fundamentalism)*. Two years later, Bruce B. Lawrence published the first edition of his very influential study titled *Defenders of God: The Fundamentalist Revolt Against the Modern Age* (1989). The main title of Lawrence's book has inspired the title of the present volume. The greatest expression of the new scholarly focus on fundamentalism is the multi-volume Fundamentalism Project, a study involving dozens of scholars, under the auspices of the American Academy of Arts and Sciences, funded by the John D. and Catherine T. MacArthur Foundation, and edited by Chicago historian Martin E. Marty and his associate R. Scott Appleby; the first volume appeared in 1991.[7]

An important contribution of these studies is the attempt to analyze religious phenomena comparatively. The Fundamentalism Project directors, Marty and Appleby, asked contributing scholars to determine whether or not a family of resemblances existed among fundamentalist-like religious movements around the world. By the end of the first volume, the directors of the Fundamentalism Project tentatively concluded that over and against the onslaught of modernity on traditional religious worldviews and patterns of living, more or less militant movements have arisen in response. On the basis of the data collected in the first volume, they suggested constructing a model of a pure fundamentalism, against which actual cases (for example, the Islamist movements we referred to earlier) could be compared. In proposing the construction of this model, Marty and Appleby suggested that one could begin to see in fundamentalism an "ideal typical impulse" or religious idealism, in which "the transcendent realm of the divine, as revealed and made normative for the religious community, alone provides *an irreducible basis for communal and personal identity.*"[8]

In *Defenders of God*, Bruce Lawrence set out not so much to describe "fundamentalisms," as Marty and Appleby's earlier volumes were to do, but rather, to explain why, out of traditional religions in recent times – specifically Judaism, Christianity, and Islam – fundamentalist movements have emerged. One independent variable in particular appears in Lawrence's analysis, namely modernism. Fundamentalist movements among the Abrahamic faiths have one common trait, which Lawrence describes as "the hatred, which is also the fear, of modernism."[9] If we can identify modernism as the independent variable in Lawrence's explanation of the emergence of fundamentalism, the "key category" for interpreting fundamentalism is post-Enlightenment modernity. The insistent tone of Lawrence's conviction about this is worth quoting further:

> Without modernity there are no fundamentalists, just as there are no modernists. The identity of fundamentalism, both as a psychological mindset and a historical movement, is shaped by the modern world. Fundamentalists seem bifurcated between their cause and their outcome; they are at once the consequence of modernity and the antithesis of modernism.
>
> Either way, one cannot speak of premodern fundamentalists . . . To speak about fundamentalism and to trace the lineage of any cadre of fundamentalists one must begin with the specific points of connectedness to, and interaction with, the processes that heralded the global material transformation of our world that we call modernization, the result of which was modernity.[10]

Therefore, fundamentalism for Lawrence "[l]ike Calvinism" for a political scientist like Michael Walzer, "is best assessed as an ideology not a theology or philosophy," to which Lawrence adds, in the case of fundamentalism, that: "for that matter, [fundamentalism is not] a social deprivation or historical recurrence."[11]

It is precisely here that the provocative theoretical work of Bruce Lawrence in particular, and the much larger Fundamentalism Project in general, can be called into question by the textual materials we propose to present and to interpret in this volume. Our position is that Islamist and other forms of "fundamentalism" (which we agree with Lawrence and Marty is a usable comparative term) belongs to a larger discourse of which theological modernism, including neo-Mu'tazilism, is an important part. We do not wish to deny, however, that the reduction of theological discourse to ideology may yield useful insights into social and political aspects of movements like fundamentalism and Calvinism. What we do deny is that such reductions are exclusively able to provide an adequate explanation of fundamentalism.

We submit that however much Muslim fundamentalists may construct their identity in opposition to post-Enlightenment modernism, they do so through theological opposition to Islamic modernism, which in turn is a discourse on theological rationalism. Moreover, in doing so, they are following historical patterns of theological conflict that we will identify throughout this volume. Defenders of God like Hasan al-Banna' (d. 1949), the founder of the Muslim Brotherhood in Egypt, engaged in a debate with defenders of reason like Muhammad 'Abduh, and not for the first time in the history of Islamic theology. It necessarily follows that the historical nature of the theological discourse of which fundamentalism is a part must be reasserted. Muslim fundamentalists like Sayyid Qutb and Muslim modernists like Harun Nasution have been engaged in a longstanding dispute about God and His attributes, political ruptures that occurred in the first generations of Islam, and other matters that the Fundamentalist Project has all but overlooked. Understanding other dimensions of that discourse besides fundamentalism is the task ahead. This task cycles us back through the social-science base of the Fundamentalist Project agenda, to describe and explain fundamentalism, to the humanistic task of interpreting texts. Both approaches are appropriate. We want to emphasize here, however, that the study of religious discourse and the theological conflict expressed in such discourses must engage texts and their literary and social histories.

We turn now to consider theological discourse in Islam in relation to the two texts that lie ahead.

'*Ilm al-kalam*, the Discipline of Disputing Religion

Theological controversy was vigorously pursued in classical Islamicate society.[12] The term we translate as "theology" is in Arabic "kalam," meaning "speech" or "discourse." Those who pursued verbal controversy about matters of religious belief were known as mutakallimun (sing. *mutakallim*). The latter term applied not just to Muslim theologians but also to Christian, Jewish, and other religious intellectuals who entered into theological disputes with each other on behalf of their confessional communities.[13] Their disputations were about such matters as the nature of God and His attributes, scripture, prophets, good and evil, and the religious foundations of political authority and order. These topics framed discourses on doctrinal boundaries which separated the religious communities that existed within Islamicate society, and at the same time they bound them together in a common way of speaking about their relationship to each other. In contemporary parlance, kalam provided a rich discourse for the politics of religious identity in medieval Islamicate society. Terms like *mu'min* "believer," *kafir* "unbeliever," *murtadd* "denier of religion," and *ahl al-kitab* "People of the Book" were central to this discourse, in which boundaries between communities were carefully constructed and maintained along the lines of existing (and changing) conflicts.[14] Among Muslims themselves, sectarian disputes arose and divided opinions sharply. As these sectarian groups (*firaq*, sing. *firqa*) became normalized in early Islamicate society,[15] many of them were regarded as "schools" of doctrine (*madhahib*, sing.

madhhab). From the eighth to the eleventh centuries, the most prominent kalam madhhab, or cluster of madhhabs, was known as the Mu'tazila.[16]

Qadi 'Abd al-Jabbar was the last great mutakallim or theologian of the Mu'tazili school. His active life as Shaykh al-Mu'tazila occurred on the cusp of the school's decline, along with the disappearance of the more generous patrons of intellectual life, namely, some of the amirs and viziers of the Buyid dynasty in the late tenth century. Mu'tazili texts were copied and taught for the next thousand years, chiefly among Shi'i sectarians in Yemen and other places remote from the rival influences of still thriving schools of Ash'ari and Maturidi theology. The rediscovery in the twentieth century of many of the Qadi's works, including the one translated here (*Kitab al-usul al-khamsa*) and several volumes of his twenty-volume *summa theologica* (*Kitab al-mughni fi abwab al-tawhid wa l-'adl*) has deeply influenced the revival of interest in Islamic rationalism by thinkers like Harun Nasution. Indeed, as we have already indicated, in *The Mu'tazila and Rational Philosophy* translated below, Nasution several times cites a well-known eleventh-century commentary on 'Abd al-Jabbar's *Kitab al-usul al-khamsa*.

Thus, the two texts translated in this volume are expressions of what contemporary criticism might call a theological intertext. The texts contain traces of religious disputes that, with the continuing spread of Islam, were able to span a millennium and two very different languages and cultures – Middle Arabic as it was written and spoken in the conduct of state and religious affairs in the cultural pluralism of Buyid (Shi'i) Iran in the tenth/eleventh centuries, and Bahasa Indonesian in the most populous Sunni Muslim country in the contemporary world. Qadi 'Abd al-Jabbar begins his text with the first principle of religion according to the Mu'tazila, that God can and must be known rationally. Thus, in the context of classical Mu'tazili reflection, the first duty incumbent upon any Muslim was to know that God exists, on which acceptance of His commands and prohibitions was made to rest.

Harun Nasution begins his treatise with an equally important Mu'tazili claim, that Islamic politics and kalam arose out of a single troubling event in nascent Islam, the assassination of the third caliph or successor to Muhammad as head of the Muslim community, 'Uthman ibn 'Affan (d. 656). That the civil war (*fitna*) which soon followed had enormous implications for subsequent Islamic political and social history is not in dispute. The interpretation of that first fitna and the ones that followed, however, has been disputed throughout Islamic history. Nasution's text reminds us that the fitnas first occurred as political and social conflicts that generated theological discourses, and that also erupted in sectarian violence. Between the more extreme competing interpretations of Caliph

'Uthman's moral and religious standing, Nasution tells us that Mu'tazilism argued for a middle ground that sought to preserve human ethical responsibility as well as social cohesion.

The Mu'tazila

Western historians have characterized the Mu'tazila as rationalists and as heterodox theologians. Some Muslim historians and heresiographers have judged the Mu'tazili mutakallimun more harshly, however, finding unbelief (*kufr*) in their contention that the Qur'an was created (*khalq al-qur'an*) and that humans have free will and the power to act on it (*qadar*), to mention but two of the most controversial Mu'tazili doctrines. By the tenth century, two madhhabs rose in strong opposition to the Mu'tazila, the Ash'ariya (Ash'arites) and the Maturidiya (Maturidites). Each of these madhhabs was named after its founder, Abu l-Hasan al-Ash'ari (d. 935) and Abu Mansur al-Maturidi (d. 944), respectively. In the tenth and eleventh centuries, the Ash'ariya challenged Mu'tazili influence in the central Islamic lands of Iraq and Iran, while the Maturidiya thrived in Khurasan and Central Asia. Both schools put kalam in the service of defending what in hindsight we now characterize as "orthodox" or traditional Islamic theological doctrine.

Like the four acceptable madhhabs of Sunni jurisprudence – Hanafi, Shafi'i, Hanbali and Maliki – the Ash'ari and Maturidi kalam madhhabs are generally recognized today as acceptable alternative traditions of doctrinal discourse. The Mu'tazili madhhab is not so recognized among Sunnis, and hasn't been since the ninth century (although the Mu'tazila maintained public influence, chiefly among the Buyid Shi'i amirs in the tenth and eleventh centuries). In subsequent centuries, Mu'tazili kalam was conserved in the curriculum of the Zaydi (Fiver) and Imami (Twelver) Shi'a.[17] More recently, as we shall see in subsequent chapters, there is also growing interest among moderate and modernist Sunni Muslims in certain aspects of what we could call the "spirit of Mu'tazili discourse," especially its emphasis on reason, dialogue with others, and a rational basis of ethics.

Rationalism and Traditionalism

Readers will notice that "rationalism" has several different meanings in this study. It is the multivalent ambiguity of "rational" (*'aqli*) that made possible the disparate modernist appeals to rationalism, to which we shall refer in later chapters. The term "rationalism" as a label for thought systems normally refers to the seventeenth and eighteenth centuries in Western philosophy; thus it is both a modern and a Western concept, which must be applied cautiously to premodern, non-Western intellectual traditions. During the Enlightenment, philosophers such as Descartes, Spinoza, and Leibniz taught that reason alone, and not religious faith, was sufficient for knowing the nature of what exists in the world. The Mu'tazila would have agreed with some of the principles of Enlightenment rationalism. It was also characteristic of rationalist philosophies during the Enlightenment to hold that all of what humans can know is formed by a single, universal deductive system. The French philosopher Montesquieu (d. 1755) characterized the rational, but still remarkably theological, character of the universe as follows:

> Laws in their most general signification are the necessary relations arising from the nature of things. In this sense all beings have their laws: the Deity His laws, the material world its laws, the intelligences superior to man their laws, the beasts their laws, man his laws.[18]

In ¶ 28 of chapter 5 below, 'Abd al-Jabbar alludes to the Mu'tazili claim that God would never permit *istifsad al-adilla* "corruption of evidentiary proofs," that is, contravention of the customary pattern of the way things happen in the physical universe (nature). Thus, for the Mu'tazili mutakallimun, confidence in the rational and knowable nature of physical reality is based on theodicy: God would not deceive His creatures by creating an irrational universe (see ¶ 26 of the text in chapter 5 below). As with Montesquieu many centuries later, the early Mu'tazila also held that God operated according to rational laws. The Basra Mu'tazila argued, therefore, against those Shi'a Sufis (and even some of the Ash'ariya), who variously held that the Alid imams, Sufi saints, or righteous ancestors were also blessed with miracles and other extraordinary signs of their divine favor. For the Basra Mu'tazila, the only "irrational" occurrences thinkable in a divinely created rational universe would be a severely restricted number of miracles that vouchsafed the claims of prophets – mainly Moses, Jesus, and Muhammad – to be sent from God (see ¶ 43).

The Basra madhhab of the Mu'tazila, to which 'Abd al-Jabbar belonged, constructed a metaphysics of atomistic occasionalism. Similar to the Greek Atomists, the Basra Mu'tazila held that physical reality is composed of basic physical entities or atoms (sing. *jawhar*) and attributes (sing. *'arad*) that give beings their shape, color, and other distinguishing qualities. God creates the world in each instant by creating atoms and attributes that inhere in the physical substrates that atoms form; creation is thus a continual divine activity. Unlike the occasionalism of the French rationalist Malebranche, however, and in contrast to the atomistic occasionalism of the Ash'ariya, the Basra Mu'tazila did not make God the efficient cause of all that happens in the universe. They argued that humans are agents of their own acts and thus are morally responsible for them. The Mu'tazila further claimed that this constantly created reality behaves according to known patterns of events or "nature" (*'ada*) on which human reasoning about the world is based. In only one case, as just noted – the sending of prophets with miracles – does God permit the contravention of 'ada. Otherwise, God would be subverting the system of evidence on which human reason about this world and the next is based. Examples of what would constitute istifsad al-adilla occur in a commentary on another text by 'Abd al-Jabbar.[19]

In that passage, it is argued that God would not allow false prophets to perform real miracles, even if His purpose were later to reverse the event and expose the false prophet as a liar, for that would have the unfortunate side effect of sabotaging human rationality.[20]

Like many of the philosophers of the Enlightenment, the Mu'tazili mutakallimun were also men of religious faith, although their faith and status as good Muslims was constantly criticized by their opponents.[21] As Muslim rationalists, they held that reason can demonstrate the existence of God and the general ethical responsibility that is incumbent upon human beings in society. They also held that, in the act of revealing His divine will, God bestows a great benefit and advantage to those who accept Him and who learn from His revelation and His prophets the laws and rituals, the keeping of which will please Him on the Day of Judgment. Paragraph 12 in chapter 5 summarizes the Mu'tazili argument that the revelation is a divinely provided benefit and advantage above and beyond the human rational faculty, which can by itself know that God exists. This point is repeated and emphasized in Harun Nasution's text in chapter 9.

The greatest religious and political opposition to the Mu'tazila within the social fabric of Islamicate society in the ninth to eleventh centuries came not from Ash'ari and Maturidi mutakallimun, however, but rather from a loose grouping of pietists that has been broadly labeled "traditionalist." In this study we will use the term "traditionalist" to refer to reformist religious movements, primarily the Hanbaliya, the followers of Ahmad ibn Hanbal (d. 855). Thus, the "rationalist" Mu'tazila and the "traditionalist" Hanbaliya are schematized in this study as contrary and conflicting trends that formed on opposite edges of Islamicate society and sought to influence the religious, intellectual, and political center. In medieval Islamicate society, the broad center where power was concentrated in various groups of elites was characterized as the *khawass*, "people of distinction," whereas the commonality were characterized as the *'awamm*. Traditionalism, as it gained a foothold among the khawass by virtue of locating itself primarily among the ulama, nonetheless had much deeper roots among the 'awamm. On the other side, the majority of Mu'tazili (and Ash'ari) mutakallimun thought it dangerous to let common people debate kalam doctrine in public.

The primary purpose of the present study is not to write a "history" of the Mu'tazila or the Mu'tazili/Hanbali conflict. Such comprehensive histories would be desirable, and various studies of moments in this conflict, especially in the medieval period, inform the present work. Reference to these scholarly investigations, particularly the most accessible ones for Western readers, are made in the notes. What, then, is the primary purpose of this book if not to present a comprehensive history? To paraphrase the preface of a recent book on Muslim politics, this is a book about how to *think about* theological conflict in Islamic societies.[22] We are looking at old problems in the history of Islamic thought, with new questions. We are also looking over the shoulders of those who are deeply concerned about the "problem" of fundamentalism with a view toward problematizing their approaches.

One of the arguments of this book is that both trends, rationalist and traditionalist, continue to exist and define themselves, in part, in relation to each other. We will also argue in subsequent chapters that the two trends are not mutually exclusive. Modern Islamic thought, in the writings of theologians like Muhammad 'Abduh, has incorporated elements of both rationalism and traditionalism. Rather, we prefer to consider the ongoing conflict of rationalism and traditionalism in their various historical formations as a historically rooted discourse involving particular texts and contexts. The historian of religion must examine comparatively the texts and contexts of these conflicts in order to generalize about their significance.

In this study, for the sake of analysis, we are contrasting the rationalist and traditionalist trends with the orthodox center of Islam. The latter was led by the developing "Sunni" tradition of the religious notables known as the ulama. The orthodox center is variously referred to as "centrist," "traditional," or even "normative" Islam. All of these terms are useful, but misleading, because a great variety of schools of thought (madhahib) in law, theology, and other religious sciences formed the orthodox center of Islam. The Sunni formation and control of Islamicate society was catholic, but not monolithic or undifferentiated. The Islamic term that was generally applied to this cluster of traditional Muslim groups within Islamicate society during the first few centuries was *ahl al-sunna wa l- jama'a* "the People of the Sunna and the Community," from which the term "Sunni" is derived. Traditionalist (Hanbali) and rationalist (Mu'tazili) religious leaders also belonged to this broad and dynamic Sunni majority (though some Mu'tazili mutakallimun leaned toward Imami and Zaydi Shi'i political theologies), but both groups functioned as its critics – albeit from different points of view. Thus, "traditional" (as opposed to "traditionalist") Islam refers to the attempt of the ulama and the majority of Muslims who accepted their authority to preserve and conserve the status quo. "Traditionalist" Islam refers to the counter-tendency to renew and revitalize the status quo, usually from within, by criticizing present interpretations and practices with reference to an idealized past. "Rationalist" Islam refers to the historical impulse of the Mu'tazili mutakallimun in particular (but kalam more generally) to articulate the message of Islam within any given age's contemporary intellectual and social trends.

Both traditionalist and rationalist criticism, therefore, attacked directly or indirectly the authority of the ulama to interpret and implement the Qur'an and the Sunna in Islamicate society. For the traditionalists, the independent reasoning (*ijtihad*) of a faithful Sunni Muslim of sound mind, in interpreting the Shari'a, was more authoritative than blind acceptance (*taqlid*) of the teachings of the ulama. For the rationalists, speculative reason (*nazar*) was theoretically even prior to faith – a tool for bringing rational human beings to Islamic faith, from which they could discover the benefits of accepting God's revealed religious duties.

The term "traditionalist" sounds suspiciously like a modern, Western notion. As such, it too must be used advisedly, because in post-Enlightenment thought in the West, "tradition" is often contrasted with "modernity" and seen as its contrary. "Tradition" often connotes a static, irrational, and culturally monolithic past, while "modern" implies a dynamic, rational, and culturally pluralistic present. According to modernization theory at mid-century, the scientific worldviews associated with modernity are replacing the religious worldviews of tradition. Those dimininishing numbers of religious leaders and groups who opposed modernization were seen as resistant to change, and change (modernization) was considered to be necessary for political stability.[23] In this work we will argue that tradition in various senses plays an important role in modern Islamic thought and society, and that "dynamic," "rational," and "culturally plural" are ideas that apply equally well to premodern Islamicate societies.

The term "traditionalism" refers partly to the fact that many of the intellectual leaders of the Hanbali movement in early Islamicate society were *muhaddithun*, scholars who transmitted and studied the prophetic traditions. Their expertise formed the basis of the religious scholarship and juristic training of the ulama. More significantly, perhaps, they were known as *ahl al-hadith*, people committed to defending the authority of Hadith,[24] the reports circulating within the Muslim *umma* (community) about what the Prophet Muhammad had said, done, approved, or disapproved. The traditionalists valued the sayings of and about the Prophet Muhammad that had been transmitted by his Companions and the following two generations. The leading figures of the earliest generations, starting with the *sahaba* (Companions) were called the *salaf*, "forefathers" and *salihun*, "righteous ones." Their precedence as valid interpreters of the sacred texts and pious models to be emulated was central to the evolution of Sunni doctrine; it was to become reemphasized in the periodic reform movements that have characterized Islamic history, as we shall see.[25] The validity of Hadith as a source, along with the Qur'an, of divine legislation (Shari'a) was guaranteed by establishing a chain (*isnad*) of reliable transmitters, if possible several independent lines of transmission (*al-isnad al-mutawatir*). Among the epistemic certainties of the traditional ulama has been the claim that if uninterrupted and reliable transmission was confirmed, then the sayings attributed to the Prophet and his closest companions could be taken as authoritative. More information was not necessary to the normative Sunni project of interpretation, although disputes about interpretation (*ikhtilaf*) were not thereby obviated.

Mu'tazili mutakallimun also studied Hadith, but they held the rational sense of the content (*matn*) of these reports about the Prophet to be a more important test of their validity, along with analysis of the chain of transmitters (see ¶ 61 of chapter 5). The main issue between the traditionalists and the Mu'tazila was authority, the authority of two texts in particular: the divine word of God (Qur'an) and prophetic practice (Sunna) as remembered in reports or "Hadith" transmitted by the community (umma). To these two sacred texts of the Shari'a, most traditional Muslims add the fundamental principles of communal and scholarly consensus (*ijma'*) and reasoning by analogy (*qiyas*) from known commands and prohibitions in the Qur'an and Sunna to new and changing circumstances in which the Shari'a must be applied. The debate was over what constituted the hermeneutical warrants to interpret those texts, that is, to formulate and control the social and moral ethos of Islamicate society. The traditionalists claimed, in effect, that the texts themselves were their own expositors and sources of meaning. The Muslim umma, as represented by those it accepted as its religious leaders, the ulama, interpreted and applied the divine commands and prohibitions that all agreed (in principle) were contained in the texts. The Mu'tazila also accepted the authority of the two sacred texts, but made human reason (*'aql*) the warrant for determining what the text of the Qur'an and Hadith meant in particular circumstances.[26]

Reason, Revelation, and Doctrine

It is important to be clear that Hanbali traditionalists and contemporary Islamists do not deny that humans were created by God with intelligence, and they do not dispute that humans are expected to exercise their rational faculties. Nor do Mu'tazili rationalists and Islamic modernists deny the authority of Qur'an and Sunna. The problem has been that the starting point for Hanbali traditionalists, as for most Muslims, is revelation, and for the Mu'tazila it is reason. In this sense, the Mu'tazila were in the minority and thus they were more marginalized from the orthodox center than were the Hanbali traditionalists. This reason/revelation dilemma had been stated several centuries earlier by Plato in a dialogue between Socrates and Euthyphro. While waiting for his own trial, Socrates encountered Euthyphro, a pious young man who was bringing charges of manslaughter against his own father for having slain a servant (who was himself a murderer). Socrates asks: "In the name of Zeus, Euthyphro, do you think that your knowledge about divine laws and holiness and unholiness is so exact that, when the facts are as you say, you are not afraid of doing something unholy yourself in prosecuting your father for murder?"[27] Euthyphro replies that he is utterly certain about his own knowledge of the divine laws. This is based on his conviction that "what all the gods love is holy and, on the other hand, what they all hate is unholy."[28] Socrates challenges Euthyphro's claim to have a privileged knowledge of the minds of the gods – a knowledge that he cannot explain rationally to Socrates. We may reformulate the issue as it appears in Islam and other monotheistic traditions (Athens in Socrates' time was polytheistic) as follows: does God will to send down laws to humans because the laws are themselves good (holy), or are the laws good because He sent them down? In a poignant passage, Socrates asks Euthyphro:

> Is [our disagreement] not about right and wrong, and noble and disgraceful, and good and bad? And are not these the questions about which you and I and other people become enemies, when we do become enemies, because we differ about them and cannot reach any satisfactory agreement?[29]

The Hanbali traditionalists (as well as the Ash'ariya and other groups within the orthodox center) differed sharply with the Mu'tazila on whether the Law (Shari'a) that God revealed through His prophet Muhammad was good because God had revealed it, or whether God had revealed it because it was inherently good. Accordingly, they also differed on the question: wherein lay the authority to interpret the Shari'a, as revealed in the Qur'an and

16

exemplified in the Sunna (practice) of the Prophet? The traditionalists located the warrants in the plain sense of the texts (Qur'an and Hadith) and in the community that faithfully transmitted them. The Mu'tazila argued that reason ineluctably brings humans to a knowledge of God and thus to the knowledge that what God wills is necessary for salvation. Reason is the means for knowing that what Qur'an and Sunna require of humans (*taklif*) is good.

The modern study of theology recognizes that conflicting doctrinal positions do not, and never did, exist independently of historical context. As we shall see in chapter 2, social and political struggles within early Islamicate society motivated and helped frame the conflicting discourses of the Mu'tazila, traditionalists, the Shi'a, and other groups contending for power. The first point that Harun Nasution emphasizes in his defense of Mu'tazilism in chapter 9 below, as we have already remarked, is the association of doctrine and political struggle in the nascent Muslim umma. Thus doctrine also implies a community – an umma in the broadest sense of *dar al-islam*, "the Abode of Islam," and a madhhab in the more narrow sense of a theological school. Alister E. McGrath uses sociologist Robert Wuthnow's concept of "communities of discourse" in speaking about doctrinal communities. In McGrath's words:

> Doctrine entails a sense of commitment to a community, and a sense of obligation to speak on its behalf, where the corporate mind of the community exercises a restraint over the individual's perception of the truth. Doctrine is an *activity*, a process on the transmission of the collective wisdom of a community, rather than a passive set of deliverances.[30]

We may think, then, of the traditionalists and the Mu'tazili rationalists as among the several contending discourse communities within the social fabric of the Abbasid Age (750–1258). The social foundations of doctrine are again remarked by McGrath, who reminds us that "[t]here is an obvious need for a religious group to define itself in relation to other groups, and to the world in general." Citing the German sociologist of religion Niklas Luhmann, McGrath adds that

> doctrine arises in response to religious identity, which may be occasioned socially (through encounters with other religious systems) and temporally (through increasing chronological distance from its historical origins and sources of revelation) . . . Doctrine is thus linked with the affirmation of the need for certain identity-giving parameters for the community, providing ideological justification for its continued existence.[31]

The conflict between the Mu'tazili and traditionalist worldviews reached a dramatic and potentially explosive moment in the third decade of the ninth century. The caliph al-Ma'mun (*reg.* 813–833), himself a student of kalam, required his chief judges (qadis) in lands under Abbasid rule to accept publicly the Mu'tazili doctrine of the created Qur'an. We will explore this inquisition of traditionalist belief, known in Arabic as the *mihna*, in the context of the early history of kalam in chapter 2. Here we may note in passing that, among others, Ahmad ibn Hanbal (d. 855) refused to accede to the caliph's demand that all civil servants subscribe to Mu'tazili doctrine. Popular demonstrations outside the various prisons where Ibn Hanbal was successively incarcerated made it clear that the traditionalist worldview had broad support in Abbasid society, at least in Baghdad and in Iraq more generally. By mid-century, the caliph al-Mutawakkil reversed the mihna and released the aging but still popular Ibn Hanbal from prison.

With the loss of political support, the Mu'tazili madhhab began to lose its influence among the religious intelligentsia as well. Within the next century, the Ash'ari and Maturidi madhhabs rose in opposition to Mu'tazili doctrine. Adherence to the Mu'tazili madhhab fell back after the political ascendancy of the Seljuq dynasty in the middle of the eleventh century. Indeed, 'Abd al-Jabbar (d. 1024) was the last widely acclaimed teacher of the school in the Islamic Middle Ages, but he was not the last important Mu'tazili thinker. Although the Mu'tazili influence can be seen in a few later religious intellectuals, such as the Qur'an exegete al-Zamakhshari (d. 1144), it was the Zaydi (Fiver) and Imami (Twelver) Shi'a more often than the Sunnis who continued to discuss the early Mu'tazili writings. Among the Sunni theologians, the majority of whom identified with the Ash'ari madhhab after the eleventh century, Mu'tazili doctrine was the target of attack and derision; Mu'tazili masters were often condemned from pulpits during the Friday prayer service. So, too, traditionalist mutakallimun were unrelenting public critics of rationalist theologians, particularly the Mu'tazila.

Summary and Conclusion

If the Mu'tazili madhhab had well passed its prime by the end of the eleventh century, its rigorous devotion to a rational understanding of divine unity and justice has nonetheless not been forgotten, or universally deprecated. Indeed, something of the Mu'tazili spirit may be observed in modern Islam from Morocco to Indonesia. Harun Nasution's text translated in chapter 9 below is among the stronger contemporary expressions of Mu'tazilism. Some Muslim and non-Muslim historians refer to this movement as "neo-Mu'tazilism," although most of those who are associated with this trend are quite intellectually independent of each other (and often independent of the traditional religious establishment). That, however, was also true of Mu'tazili mutakallimun in the age of the Mu'tazila, the ninth to eleventh centuries.

Both rationalist and traditionalist intelligentsia in modern times have come to value the importance of ijtihad (independent reasoning) for Muslims as interpreters of their religion. Both the rationalist and the traditionalist interpretations of Islam have been critical of taqlid, "blindly following" the traditional teachings of the ulama.[32] Ironically, it was not neo-Mu'tazili or other rationalist thinkers who spearheaded late medieval and premodern reform movements in the Middle East, North Africa, South Asia and elsewhere in the Muslim world. Rather, it was the Hanbali scholar Ibn Taymiya (1263–1328) who challenged taqlid or "blind reliance" on the authority of the contemporary religious establishment (ulama). Ibn Taymiya argued against following tradition (another connotation of the term "taqlid") in favor of determining in each new context the teachings of "the righteous ancestors" (al-salaf al-salih) – the Companions of the Prophet Muhammad and their followers. It is not surprising, then, that the theology of Ibn Taymiya, based in part on Hanbali traditionalism, has fueled periodic movements of Islamic renewal (tajdid) since the fourteenth century.

Many contemporary Islamists (Islamiyun) give prominent place to the texts and teachings of Ibn Taymiya. The contemporary exponents of rationalism, on the other side, who are usually referred to as "Islamic modernists," often trace their theological agendum, at least in part, back to the Mu'tazila.

The nineteenth-century reformers Jamal al-Din al-Afghani and Muhammad 'Abduh were founders of an Islamic modernism which has called for greater rationalism in Islamic thought, while at the same time adopting Ibn Taymiya's discourse of ijtihad and tajdid, independent reasoning and renewal. We are getting ahead of our story, however. Chapter 2, the first chapter in the section of this book devoted to Qadi 'Abd al-Jabbar, takes up the narrative of the history of Mu'tazili kalam. Understanding this narrative will allow us then to situate the two texts that are featured in each of the next two sections, on 'Abd al-Jabbar and Harun Nasution, respectively.

Notes

1. The endowed madrasa or college for advanced training in the religious sciences, especially law, developed as a prevailing institution in the eleventh century, although recent research has located earlier precedents. See art. "Madrasa" by R.

19

Hillenbrand in *E.I.*² A good summary of scholarship on the history of the madrasas is Richard Bulliet, *The Patricians of Nishapur,* pp. 47–49, 249–255, et passim. The classic treatment of higher educational institutional learning in medieval Islam is Makdisi, *The Rise of Colleges.*

2. Malek, "Orientalism in Crisis."
3. Said, *Orientalism.*
4. Said, *Orientalism,* p. 239 (emphasis added).
5. Van der Veer, "The Foreign Hand," p. 40.
6. Sharpe, *Comparative Religion,* pp. 27–28.
7. *Fundamentalisms Observed,* ed. Martin E. Marty and R. Scott Appleby, The Fundamentalism Project 1.
8. Marty and Appleby, *Fundamentalisms Observed,* p. 817 (italics in original).
9. Lawrence, *Defenders of God,* p. 6.
10. Ibid., p. 2. Lawrence is referring to M. Hodgson's influential discussion of the Great Western Transmutation (G.W.T.), which we will consider in more detail in the last chapter.
11. Lawrence, *Defenders of God,* p. 83.
12. We use the term "Islamicate" in Marshall Hodgson's sense of society under Islamic rule, comprising several confessional communities that share the general culture generated by the Islamic lettered tradition. See Hodgson, *The Venture of Islam,* 1: 57–60.
13. The standard treatment of kalam among Muslims, Christians, and Jews in early Islamicate society is Wolfson, *The Philosophy of Kalam.* For a discussion of Jewish/Muslim communal and theological relations in early Islam, see Wasserstrom, *Between Muslim and Jew.* On Christian/Muslim kalam, see Griffith, "Comparative Religion."
14. Wasserstrom, *Between Muslim and Jew,* pp. 10–11 and chapter 4 generally addresses the terms of discourse that Muslims and Jews adopted for speaking about each other.
15. Islamic(ate) society refers, as we have indicated, to the composite polity of religious communities (Sunni, Shi'a, as well as various Christian, Jewish, and other protected [*dhimmi*] ummas) living under Islamic rule. The term "umma" in Islamic discourse, on the other side, refers specifically to a particular confessional community.
16. The feminine noun "Mu'tazila" refers to the group, while "Mu'tazili" is the adjectival/substantive form (Mu'tazili doctrine), the English equivalent of which is "Mu'tazilite."
17. On the comparison of Shi'i theology with the other trends mentioned thus far above, see Madelung, *Religious Trends in Early Islamic Iran.* See also Sachedina, *Islamic Messianism* for a history of Imami Shi'i doctrine and the dialogue with Mu'tazili mutakallimun. We shall discuss the influence of Mu'tazilism on Zaydi (Fiver) Shi'ism in chapter 2.
18. Montesquieu, *The Spirit of the Laws,* quoted in Jones, *A History of Western Philosophy,* 2: 806.

19. BMO 8613, fols. 3a: 19–3b: 15 *inter alia.*
20. This was an issue on which the Mu'tazili mutakallimun differed not only with the Shi'a and Sufis, but also among themselves. The Bahshamiya branch of the Basra Mu'tazila were the most strict in maintaining that in a rational universe only divinely sent prophets could actually perform miracles, and that with divine intervention.
21. Mu'tazilism as a form of Islamic religious piety rather than a consistent form of rationalism is discussed by A. Kevin Reinhart, *Before Revelation.*
22. Eickelman and Piscatori, *Muslim Politics,* p. ix.
23. For a discussion of tradition and modernization in Muslim societies, see Eickelman and Piscatori, *Muslim Politics,* pp. 22–30.
24. We will use the more common singular form "Hadith" for both singular and plural senses of the term.
25. See ¶ 25 of *Kitab al-usul al-khamsa* below. Mu'tazili discourse tended to stress the concept of "salihun" rather than "salafiya," that is, the virtue of the model to be emulated, and not just the members of the first three generations as such.
26. The Shi'a made yet another claim, that interpreting the meaning of the texts was the prerogative of the Imams, the limited number of designated descendants (five, seven, or twelve) of the Prophet through his cousin and son-in-law 'Ali. Curiously, despite the esoteric nature of Imami hermeneutics, both Zaydi (Fiver) and the main body of Shi'a (Twelver) became extremely rationalist after the occultation of the last Imam in the eighth and ninth centuries, adopting Mu'tazili kalam in large part. The Isma'ili (Sevener) Shi'a, by contrast, remained primarily oriented on expounding secret, interior meanings of the texts.
27. Plato, *The Euthyphro* (4 E), following the translation by Harold North Fowler in the Loeb Classical Library.
28. *Euthyphro* (9 E). That is, when we know that the gods hate murder, then it makes no difference who the murderer is or what the circumstances are.
29. *Euthyphro* (7 D).
30. McGrath, *The Genesis of Doctrine,* p. 11 (italics in the original).
31. Ibid., p. 38. His reference is to Niklas Luhmann, *Funktion der Religion* (Frankfurt: Suhr Kamp, 1982 [1977]), pp. 59–61.
32. The presumed opposite of ijtihad, taqlid, "unquestioning obedience," can be understood rather as the logical consequence of ijtihad. Taqlid as "strict obedience" is appropriate once one has established through the power of one's intellect (ijtihad) the proper interpretation and application of the Shari'a in a particular context. In this sense, ijtihad is the foundation of taqlid and implies it, and taqlid relies on the informative function of ijtihad.

I

‘Abd al–Jabbar *and* Classical Mu‘tazilism

two

The Rise *and* Fall *of the* Mu'tazila *in* Premodern Islam

The Beginnings of *Kalam*

I slamic tradition locates the beginnings of Mu'tazili *kalam* in the teaching circle of the ascetic and pious shaykh al-Hasan al-Basri (d. 728).[1] Hasan is perhaps best remembered in the history of Islamic thought for his forthright treatise (*risala*) in response to Caliph 'Abd al-Malik (*reg.* 685–705) on the question of human free will versus divine predestination. In his *Risala*, Hasan al-Basri used numerous Quranic *loci probantes* or "proof texts" to argue that human beings are created with freedom to commit, and thus they are shouldered with the moral responsibility for, their own acts.[2] Those who made the argument for the human capacity and free will to act were labeled the Qadariya (Qadarites), from *qadar*, which the Mu'tazila later defined as the power or capacity to perform an autonomous action. The Mu'tazila would also later defend and refine the doctrine of human freedom. Their opponents, who were labeled the Compulsionists (Jabriya or Mujbira), argued that all human agency is divinely derived and thus rooted in God's qadar alone. Nearly two centuries after al-Hasan al-Basri, the mainline Sunni school known as the Ash'ariya (Ash'arites) refined the position of the Mujbira. They sought a middle position by claiming that humans act autonomously (by their own will) but they acquire (*kasb*) the power to act from God at the moment the act occurs, thus preserving God's omnipotence.[3]

More divisive in early kalam disputations were issues that arose from the civil strife (*fitna*) that broke out following the murder of the third caliph,

25

'Uthman (*reg.* 644–656). As that contentious debate is remembered in Islamic tradition, 'Uthman's Meccan clansmen insisted that 'Ali ibn Abi Talib (*reg.* 656–661), the fourth caliph and the cousin and son-in-law of the Prophet Muhammad, should avenge 'Uthman's murder. Others argued to the contrary, that 'Uthman had not ruled according to Quranic and prophetic principle, and therefore he deserved punishment, even death.

'Ali's caliphate became hostage to this tragic fitna, which was exacerbated by an agreement between 'Ali and Mu'awiya to submit to arbitration the question of whether or not 'Ali should avenge 'Uthman's murder. Mu'awiya was a clansman of 'Uthman of the Meccan Umayyad family, and at the time of the arbitration he was governor of Damascus. The finding of the arbiters in Mu'awiya's favor, that 'Ali should have avenged 'Uthman's murder, put 'Ali and his partisans (*shi'a*) on the defensive. The members of 'Ali's party who faulted him for not defending those who had "justly" (in their view) murdered the third caliph seceded (*kharaju*) from 'Ali and his Shi'a, thus becoming known as the Khawarij or "Seceders" (Kharijites).

The Khawarij argued that faith (*iman*) is manifested in works, and that grave sin compromises one's status as a believer (*mu'min*) and thus one's membership in the Muslim *umma*. The fitna produced an opposite reaction on the part of many Muslims, who argued that only God can decide whether a *muslim* (one who submits to Allah) who sins is truly a mu'min (one who truly has the quality of iman); hence the umma must accept all who profess Islam (Muslims) as believers (*mu'minun*), and postpone (*irja'*) judgment about their status as believers or leave it in God's hands on the Final Day. This party became known as the Murji'a. Although these disputes were more than two centuries old by 'Abd al-Jabbar's time, they figure prominently in the text below (see chapter 5, ¶¶ 55–58).

The Early Mu'tazila

The foregoing issues were disputed in the circle of scholars who gathered around al-Hasan at Basra, Iraq, less than a century after the death of the Prophet Muhammad. Among those scholars who participated in these discussions were Wasil ibn 'Ata' (d. 748) and 'Amr ibn 'Ubayd (d. 762).[4] Tradition has it that once, when someone asked al-Hasan of Basra whether a grave sinner should be considered a believer or an unbeliever, al-Hasan hesitated, and Wasil ibn 'Ata' took the opportunity to assert that a grave sinner was neither, but rather in an "intermediate position" (*al-manzila bayn al-manzilatayn*), one of the five fundamentals of Mu'tazili kalam. Wasil is then said to have withdrawn (*i'tazala*) from Hasan's circle, followed by a number of Hasan's students, including 'Amr ibn 'Ubayd. To this "withdrawal" from the circle of al-Hasan of Basra the etymology of the Arabic term "Mu'tazila" is often traced.[5]

In the next generation after Wasil and 'Amr, which is to say, the beginning of the Abbasid Empire in Iraq, the Mu'tazili *madhhab* split into two main branches, the Basra and Baghdad madhhabs. The linking figure is Dirar ibn 'Amr (d. ca. 815), who flourished during the prosperous reign of the famed Abbasid caliph Harun al-Rashid, but who may have met and studied with Wasil ibn 'Ata' (although this is regarded by Watt as unlikely).[6] Dirar was an independent thinker who agreed, for example, with the Mujbira and argued against the Qadari/Mu'tazili position of human free will. This may be why Dirar receives little mention in later Mu'tazili biographical notices. He was also accused of *zandaqa* (irreligion) which was punishable by death, but the charges did not stick. In the continuing debate about 'Uthman's murder, which was now between Shi'i and Sunni (*ahl al-sunna wa l- jama'a*) parties, Dirar accepted the intermediate position of the Mu'tazila. Like the Mu'tazili *mutakallimun*, Dirar was a rationalist who gave reason (*'aql*) a role in understanding divine truth alongside revelation (*shar'*). Nonetheless, in Dirar's time the Mu'tazili madhhab had not formed into a definite school.

After Dirar the next major thinker was Abu l-Hudhayl, who in many ways was the founder of the Mu'tazili madhhab in its later, more formal existence in Basra.[7] Though only brief citations and quotes from Abu l-Hudhayl's works have survived in later works, from the titles attributed to him we can gather that he was an active polemicist with non-Muslims as well as Muslim sectarians of various sorts. Disputation, as we have already seen, was the chief modus operandi of the mutakallimun. Interesting for the purposes of this brief history of the early Mu'tazila is reference to a treatise on the five fundamentals (*al-usul al- khamsa*) of Mu'tazili kalam, attributed to Abu l-Hudhayl.[8] Titles of works on one or another of the five fundamentals (divine unity, theodicy, the intermediate position, etc.) were also attributed to Abu l-Hudhayl and other mutakallimun in the first half of the ninth century, as well as refutations of the Mujbira, Khawarij, Murji'a, and other theological opponents. Unfortunately, as we have just noted, very few texts from this early period have survived; only small fragments and quotations in later works exist to indicate what the early mutakallimun actually said.[9]

The Baghdad Branch and the Fall from Political Grace

As the Muʿtazila began to flourish in Basra during the lifetime of Abu l-Hudhayl, another branch found a home in Baghdad under the direction of Bishr ibn al-Muʿtamir.[10] Bishr was a noted poet as well as theologian and polemicist. He wrote refutations of the views of Abu l-Hudhayl and other Basra Muʿtazili mutakallimun. Bishr and several of the Muʿtazili scholars of Baghdad leaned toward ʿAli ibn Abi Talib in their political reflection on the conflict between ʿAli and Muʿawiya. The Basra madhhab, on the other side, held closer to Sunni political theology during this period. This was the issue of the imamate (*imamiya*) in kalam disputations, which ʿAbd al-Jabbar mentions briefly in ¶ 60 of the translation in chapter 5, where the Twelver Shiʿa are referred to by the derogatory nickname "turncoats" (*rafida*). Although the Muʿtazili madhhab in Basra was older and had greater prestige, Baghdad was the Abbasid capital, and the Muʿtazili scholars there were closer to leading figures in the Abbasid government, including the caliph, al-Maʾmun (*reg.* 813–833). As time went on, more and more scholars of the "Basra" madhhab found their way to Baghdad to dispute with the mutakallimun there, and even to teach.

The Baghdadi madhhab became directly embroiled in the political affair known as the "inquisition" (*mihna*) instituted by the caliph al-Maʾmun. From the beginning of his reign, al-Maʾmun sought to apply his theological views – some of them quite controversial – to matters of state. He began by appointing the eighth imam (Shiʿi leader and descendant of ʿAli ibn Abi Talib), ʿAli al-Rida, to be his heir to the caliphate. The latter's untimely death shortly after the appointment, as well as general resistance to the idea of giving power to the Shiʿa, thwarted al-Maʾmun's plans, which nonetheless had the support of Baghdad Muʿtazili teachers such as Bishr ibn al-Muʿtamir. A few months before his death in 833, the caliph instructed the governor in Baghdad to require the state-appointed judges, the qadis, to have their theological views submitted to examination (mihna). The qadis were forced to assent publicly to the Muʿtazili doctrine that God's speech, the Qurʾan, was created (*khalq al-qurʾan*). Only a few resisted, among them Ahmad ibn Hanbal (d. 855), the spiritual leader of the People of Hadith (*ahl al-hadith*) and spokesman for the popular view that the Qurʾan was uncreated.[11]

With the reversal of the mihna during the reign of al-Mutawakkil around the year 850, the Baghdad Muʿtazila in particular, and the older branch of the school in Basra as well, fell into political disfavor and became the subject of popular resentment and mistrust. Ahmad ibn Hanbal and the traditionalist People of Hadith seem in historical hindsight to have been more representative of the religious views of Islamic society as a whole, at least in Iraq in the vicinity of Baghdad, than were the mutakallimun. In Basra the great Arabic littérateur and proponent of Mu'tazili kalam known as al-Jahiz,[11] "the Bug-Eyed" (d. 868–869), composed a treatise, now lost, titled *Fadilat al- mu'tazila* (The excellence of the Mu'tazila) to restore the fallen image of the mutakallimun.[12] The work was refuted by a free-thinking mutakallim critic of the Mu'tazila, Ibn al-Rawandi (d. 910), in a work also now lost, titled *Fadihat al-Mu'tazila* (The ignominy of the Mu'tazila). Indeed, Ibn al-Rawandi and others like him were accused of atheism (*ilhad*) for their attacks on the Qur'an and all scriptures, prophets, and revealed religion generally.[13] Many topics in kalam are linked to the critiques of Ibn al-Rawandi and his ilk. Paragraphs 32–44 in the translation in chapter 5 reflect the Mu'tazili response to issues raised by free-thinkers and atheists (*mulhida*) in the tenth century.

The Classical Age of *Kalam*

By the end of the ninth century, the Mu'tazili mutakallimun reacted to attacks from the right (the traditionalists) and from the left (the Mulhida, philosophers, and non-Muslim intellectuals) by answering their critics more systematically. For the Baghdad branch of the Mu'tazila, the most important thinker of the Classical Age was Abu l-Qasim al-Balkhi (d. 929).[14] He gained a reputation in Baghdad as a theologian, but his greatest influence was in Khurasan and Transoxiana, on the northeastern frontier of Islamic rule, where he taught during the latter part of his life and trained many mutakallimun in the Baghdad madhhab. In the first few paragraphs of 'Abd al-Jabbar's *Kitab al-usul al-khamsa*, the position taken on intuitive versus empirical knowledge was an issue on which al-Balkhi apparently had much to say and on which there was some dispute between the two branches. The question disputed among Mu'tazili mutakallimun was: how much of religious knowledge (*'ilm shar'i*) is unmediated, intuitive, and therefore necessary knowledge, and how much of it is known by rational inference, drawn from what we know empirically about the world?

The classical period of the Basra madhhab was established by the father and son team known as the "Two Masters" (*al-shaykhan*), Abu 'Ali al-Jubba'i (d. 915) and Abu Hashim ibn al-Jubba'i (d. 933).[15] In the longer treatises of 'Abd al-Jabbar and other later teachers in the Basra Mu'tazili madhhab, the Two Masters are routinely cited first, often followed by an account of the minor differences that occurred between them, reflecting the growing independence of Abu Hashim after he left his father's circle (or, more likely, after the latter's death). In the published commentary on 'Abd al-Jabbar's *Kitab al-usul al-khamsa* (see chapter 3), many of the topics and positions in the earlier, briefer text are identified with one or both of the Jubba'is. Abu Hashim's sister and his son Ahmad also studied kalam and became teachers of minor recognition.[16]

It was Abu Hashim, however, who was to have the greatest influence on later scholars in the Basra Mu'tazili madhhab, among whom the most illustrious was Qadi 'Abd al-Jabbar. Those who followed the teachings of Abu Hashim in particular were called the Bahshamiya (a contraction of his name). A conflict developed between the Abu Hashim and the loyal followers of his father Abu 'Ali, led by a mutakallim named al-Saymari (d. 927).[17] The latter had studied with Abu 'Ali and also with the Mu'tazila of Baghdad. The conflict became so heated that al-Saymari accused Abu Hashim of unbelief (*kufr*). More serious conflict erupted between Abu Hashim and Ibn al-Ikhshidh (d. 932), who had studied with al-Saymari in Baghdad.[18]

With the Two Masters we are still dealing with Mu'tazili mutakallimun whose teachings are known to us primarily only in later texts that cite or quote earlier sources. Their work is otherwise lost.[19] So, too, for the next generation, the pupils of Abu Hashim who became the mentors of 'Abd al-Jabbar. The most important was Abu 'Abdallah al-Basri (d. 977).[20] Like most of the Mu'tazila, Abu 'Abdallah subscribed to the Hanafi madhhab in *fiqh* (religious jurisprudence), in which he achieved some status as a jurist. Also, like many of the Mu'tazila of Baghdad (where Abu 'Abdallah eventually moved), he held positions on the imamate that were close to milder forms of Shi'i doctrine, such as those of the Zaydi Shi'a. It is important to note that Abu 'Abdallah and his successors for the next century lived under the Shi'i political influence of the Buyid princes and viziers; more on this will be said below. In this respect, Abu 'Abdallah departed from the more narrow Sunni interpretation of the imamate that was characteristic of Abu Hashim and many mutakallimun associated with the Bahshamiya.

Abu 'Abdallah al-Basri flourished in the period when the Sunni Abbasid caliphate in Baghdad was rivaled by the Shi'i Fatimid caliphate, first in North Africa (from 909), and then in Egypt (from 969). Even in Iraq and Iran, the caliphate lost control of most lands (except those surrounding Baghdad) to a family of Shi'i warlords known as the Buyids (Buwayhids), who held the caliphate captive from 945 to 1055. Of this period, one historian has stated: "The Caliphs were allowed to continue in nominal authority; indeed, the 'Abbasid dynasty lasted until 1258, but they no longer ruled; the 'Abbasid empire had ceased to exist."[21] Official patronage of the ulama, including the mutakallimun, came increasingly from Buyid sultans and viziers in Iran and Khurasan. Thus, despite political turmoil (or perhaps because of it) the cities of Iran and Khurasan in the tenth and eleventh centuries were vital centers of kalam disputation.

Moreover, the last Imam of the Ithna 'Ashari (Twelver) Shi'a was believed to have gone into complete occultation in 941, thus leaving the Shi'a of Iraq and Iran to struggle to develop Shi'i doctrine for an extended period without the direct guidance of an Imam about to return. Shi'i rituals and shrines were sponsored and built by Buyid princes and patrons. Many Ithna 'Ashari Shi'i mutakallimun found greater intellectual kinship with Mu'tazili thinkers such as Abu 'Abdallah al-Basri than with the traditionalists and other urban ulama.

Abu 'Abdallah al-Basri, then, was the most renowned Mu'tazili mutakallim of the generation before Qadi 'Abd al-Jabbar. Before turning to the Qadi's life and works, it is necessary to say something about the Ash'ari madhhab of kalam which, after 'Abd al-Jabbar, became the dominant madhhab of kalam throughout much of the Islamic east.

The Ash'ari *Madhhab*

Abu 'Ali al-Jubba'i had two pupils of consequence for the later history of kalam. We have already discussed his son Abu Hashim and the Bahshamiya sub-branch of the Basra Mu'tazila. 'Abd al-Jabbar became the most celebrated proponent of that sub-branch of the Mu'tazila, and indeed, of all the Mu'tazila, in the late tenth and early eleventh centuries. Al-Jubba'i's other famous pupil was Abu l-Hasan al-Ash'ari (d. 935), who left the circle of his mentor to found a rival kalam madhhab, the Ash'ariya.[22]

Al-Ash'ari studied kalam as a pupil of Abu 'Ali al-Jubba'i in Basra and remained within his circle of senior pupils until well into mature adulthood. As such, he was a product of the same intellectual environment as Abu Hashim and other influential Mu'tazili mutakallimun. For reasons that are now buried in incongruous legends, al-Ash'ari left Abu 'Ali's circle to found his own theological school, which thereafter took his name, the Ash'ariya. A popular version has it that al-Ash'ari was a zealous advocate of al-Jubba'i's rationalist approach to kalam until one day the two men differed on the Mu'tazili doctrine of human free will; after a heated dispute al-Ash'ari exercised independence of mind and left his mentor. A more recent refinement of the break is that al-Ash'ari eventually concluded that

Mu'tazili doctrine more broadly (including such issues as the created Qur'an) was contrary to Islam as interpreted by Hadith scholars such as Ahmad ibn Hanbal. Indeed, al-Ash'ari's thought has close affinities with traditionalist Sunni Islam. The major difference is that al-Ash'ari and his followers sought to put the rational methods of kalam argumentation to the service of defending popular Sunni notions of the eternal, uncreated Qur'an, God's absolute omnipotence over His creatures, and the severe limits of human reason to understand the divine will.

Al-Ash'ari wrote numerous works, according to one source some three hundred. His biographer, Ibn 'Asakir, attributes ninety-nine titles to al-Ash'ari. Of the very few that have survived, the most important for the history of kalam is a heresiography of Muslim and non-Muslim sects and groups titled *Maqalat al-islamiyin* (Islamic teachings).[23] Three other texts by al-Ash'ari from the post-Mu'tazili period have been edited and translated into English.[24] While the majority of Mu'tazili mutakallimun subscribed to the Hanafi madhhab in law, al-Ash'ari and many who followed him associated with the Shafi'i madhhab.

These Mu'tazili/Hanafi and Ash'ari/Shafi'i associations were not rigid. 'Abd al-Jabbar, for example, who was, as we have seen, a Mu'tazili, was a Shafi'i jurist of some note.[25] Nonetheless, the kalam/fiqh associations and conflicts were of some consequence for the social history of Khurasan and Iran in the time of 'Abd al-Jabbar. The jurists of the Hanafi madhhab gave greater weight to the personal judgment (*ra'y*) of the individual jurisconsult in preparing legal opinions, while the Shafi'i madhhab placed greater emphasis, in justifying legal judgments, on Hadith, and sought to restrict the use of individual reasoning. In the mid-eleventh century, a fitna broke out in Nishapur between Hanafi/Mu'tazili and Shafi'i/Ash'ari elites and their families. This Mu'tazili persecution of the Ash'ariya, led and sanctioned by a Seljuq vizier, coincided with the years when the Buyid Shi'i dynasty was losing its political grip on the Abbasid caliphate to the Seljuqs, a rising Turkish Sunni dynasty.[26] The days when social and political elites affiliated with the Mu'tazili and Hanafi madhhabs could oppress Ash'ari intellectuals and their families were coming to an end.

The Hanafi jurists in Khurasan and Central Asia were not all sympathetic to Mu'tazili kalam. Many Hanafi jurists followed the teachings of the Maturidi madhhab, which is usually regarded as the second kalam madhhab in medieval Islam to defend the beliefs of Sunni Muslims. As mentioned previously, it was founded by a contemporary of al-Ash'ari, Abu Mansur al-Maturidi (d. 944).[27] The Maturidi school had influence primarily on the northeastern borders of Islam, in Transoxiana (Central Asia). Today, the Maturidi madhhab is still influential among Muslims in Southeast Asia.

Of the several Ash'ari theologians contemporary with 'Abd al-Jabbar, the best known was al-Baqillani (d. 1013).[28] Unlike most Ash'ari theologians, Baqillani studied law in the Maliki madhhab (which had become more influential in Spain and North Africa), and he served as a qadi in a small jurisdiction in Iraq near Baghdad for a while. In 981 he made a trip to Byzantium as the ambassador of a Buyid prince. One version of the story has it that in the presence of the Byzantine emperor al-Baqillani debated and defeated a Christian theologian on points at issue between the two religions. Stories like this reflect the cultural rules of engagement between and among rival religious communities in Islamicate society during the Abbasid Age. Like 'Abd al-Jabbar, al-Baqillani composed systematic treatises on kalam, one of which has survived and has been published.[29] A portion of his treatise on the miracle of the Qur'an (*i'jaz al-qur'an*) has been translated into English.[30] That al-Baqillani and 'Abd al-Jabbar met, as some have speculated, perhaps in Baghdad, is not unlikely. It was the custom in medieval Islamicate society for distinguished visiting scholars to pay calls on their intellectual peers, even (and especially) those belonging to contending madhhabs.

With this background, we turn now to the author of the *Kitab al-usul al-khamsa*.

Qadi 'Abd al-Jabbar

His full name was Abu l-Hasan 'Abd al-Jabbar ibn Ahmad ibn Khalil ibn 'Abdallah al-Hamadhani al-Asadabadi (d. 1024), called Qadi al-Qudat ("chief magistrate" of Iran).[31] He was born of peasant Persian parentage sometime around 932 or 937 in Asadabad (a village southwest of Hamadhan in western Iran). His early training was in Hadith and Shafi'i fiqh (legal theory) in or near his natal village. He performed the pilgrimage (hajj) to Mecca in 951 and again in 952. Thereafter he continued Hadith studies in Hamadhan, and then in Basra in 957. It was in Basra with Abu Ishaq ibn 'Ayyash that he most likely began the study of Mu'tazili kalam.[32] Later, he moved to Baghdad to study with the renowned pupil of Abu Hashim mentioned on p.30, Abu 'Abdallah al-Basri. He apparently studied with al-Basri in Baghdad for some time before leaving his circle to dictate works on kalam and fiqh on his own authority.

We next find 'Abd al-Jabbar among Mu'tazili colleagues in the Gulf city of Ramahurmuz in the year 970, when he began to dictate his monumental systematic work on kalam, *Kitab al-mughni* (The book that makes sufficient), as well as other works on kalam and fiqh. From Ramahurmuz, he was invited to the Persian city of Rayy (near modern Tehran) by al-Sahib ibn 'Abbad, a literary and theological connoisseur and advisor to the Buyid prince Mu'ayyid al-Dawla. In 977 Ibn 'Abbad was appointed vizier to Mu'ayyid al-Dawla, and Ibn 'Abbad in turn appointed 'Abd al-Jabbar to the post of Qadi al-Qudat of the region surrounding Rayy; later, 'Abd al-Jabbar's jurisdiction was extended to other provinces to the east. Al-Sahib ibn 'Abbad, a learned and rather earthy but apparently not particularly religious man, was famous for his gatherings of poets and intellectuals. These were occasions when more secular-minded scholars, as well as eminent Shi'i and Sunni, Ash'ari, and Mu'tazili personalities of the day, including 'Abd al-Jabbar and his leading students, would gather for an evening of artistic and intellectual riposte. It was not uncommon even for non-Muslim intellectuals to take part in these debates.[33]

The Qadi's official stature and protection disappeared when Ibn 'Abbad died in 995. It is said that 'Abd al-Jabbar not only lost his post as qadi, but that his books were confiscated, perhaps owing to his refusal to pray over the remains of the rather worldly and often impious vizier, Ibn 'Abbad. But he stayed on to teach in Rayy for the rest of his life. He made a trip through Baghdad on his way to Mecca for the hajj in 999, after which he returned to the Abbasid capital to transmit Hadith. He is reported to have left Rayy once more to lecture in Qazwin in 1018. He died in Rayy in 1024. This was just thirty years before Seljuq Turkish sultans defeated the Buyid princes and restored Sunni rule to lands beyond Baghdad. Indeed, the city of Rayy was wrested from Buyid control in 1029 by Mahmud of Ghazna, who had Mu'tazili books and property burned and confiscated, although Mu'tazili teachings and influence continued on in Rayy and elsewhere among Zaydi Shi'a mutakallimun.[34]

Although the widespread influence of the Mu'tazila was coming to a close by the time 'Abd al-Jabbar died, he had several students of note, some of whose works have survived. We will consider some of them and their followers below, after assessing the decline of the Mu'tazila in the eleventh century.

As indicated above, the last decades of Qadi 'Abd al-Jabbar's life were tumultuous politically in Rayy, in Iran and Khurasan more broadly, and indeed in the Abbasid capital in Iraq, Baghdad. The eleventh century marked a period of transition when Islamic civilization as we understand it today developed its most lasting institutions and ideas. It was in this period when, through continued conversion, Muslims became the most populous religious community (umma) in Islamicate society. Four Sunni madhhabs – the Hanafi, Shafi'i, Hanbali, and Maliki – became institutionalized through endowed law colleges (madrasas), and the Imami, Zaydi, and Isma'ili Shi'a formed durable communities around the cultivated memories of their Imams and leaders. Sufi orders (*tariqas*) formed religious and social organizations that would weather the political vicissitudes of the later Middle Ages. A century after 'Abd al-Jabbar, the greatest Sunni theologian, Abu Hamid al-Ghazali (d. 1111), lived and wrote texts that have been dictated, copied, studied (and now printed and reprinted) continually in all parts of the Islamic world.[35]

'Abd al-Jabbar was the last great thinker of a school of thought that was already on the wane during the last years of his life. There were many reasons why Hanbali traditionalists, Ash'ari mutakallimun, and others had been able to displace the Mu'tazila from the prominence the school had enjoyed in the ninth and tenth centuries. Surely one reason was political. The permanent withdrawal of caliphal support for the Mu'tazila after the theological inquisition (mihna) instituted by Caliph al-Ma'mun in 833 was less consequential at the time than historians often conclude. Not long after the caliph al-Mutawakkil reversed al-Ma'mun's inquisition in 848, the Mu'tazila entered what many historians regard as their classical age with the Two Jubba'i Masters in Basra and Abu l-Qasim al-Balki, whose influence spread from Baghdad to Khurasan and Transoxiana.

During the mid-tenth century, under Buyid patronage, Mu'tazili scholars such as Abu 'Abdallah al-Basri and 'Abd al-Jabbar enjoyed considerable official support and public influence. Nonetheless, during the latter part of the tenth century when the Buyid princes and their viziers struggled among themselves for power, their retainers among the intelligentsia, including Mu'tazili and Shi'i mutakallimun, often lost their books and property, if not their lives. 'Abd al-Jabbar lost his public office and his personal property in 995, as we have seen, when the vizier who had appointed him chief magistrate died. Then, four years after the Qadi himself died, Mahmud of Ghazna laid siege to Rayy (1029), and ousted the Shi'a and Mu'tazila, confiscating their books and property. Later the Seljuq Turkish conqueror Tughril-beg defeated the Ghaznavids, taking Rayy in 1042. Control of the Abbasid caliphate and the remaining lands formerly under Buyid rule fell completely to the Sunni Seljuq Turks in 1055.

The Mu'tazila nonetheless had stimulated a sizable number of Muslim intellectuals to rationalize their religion by constructing arguments that could stand up to the philosophers, Christians, Jews, and atheists, and to opponents among the Muslims themselves. Although by Qadi 'Abd al-Jabbar's time theological discourse had been co-opted by traditional thinkers, chiefly the Ash'ariya and Maturidiya, the methods pursued and

35

questions disputed were characteristically Mu'tazili. That is probably why the traditionalists, mainly the Hanbaliya, remained the sharpest opponents, not only of Mu'tazili doctrine, but also of the kalam method, even as practiced by Sunni Ash'ari and Maturidi mutakallimun.

Greatness in Decline: 'Abd al-Jabbar's Pupils

Mu'tazilism did not altogether disappear from Islamic intellectual life when the Qadi died in 1024. Indeed, the Qadi had trained many students in kalam, both Sunni and Shi'a, some of whom enjoyed considerable local reputations for the next few centuries. Among 'Abd al-Jabbar's more senior students and colleagues was Abu Rashid al-Nisaburi (d. after 1024).[36] Abu Rashid was already a mutakallim of some substance in the Baghdadi Mu'tazili madhhab in Nishapur when he went to Rayy to study with 'Abd al-Jabbar, henceforth associating himself with the Basra madhhab. Al-Hakim al-Jushami adds that 'Abd al-Jabbar addressed Abu Rashid and no one else as "Shaykh," meaning he regarded Abu Rashid as a colleague as well as a student. When he was busy with other writing projects, he asked Abu Rashid to write a work titled *Kitab diwan al-usul*, a book of theological opinions which was to be read and interpreted in the manner of legal opinions, as in fiqh.[37]

Although he apparently wrote extensively otherwise, just a few titles by Abu Rashid are known, and only one work has survived. It is a comparative study of the theological differences between the Basra and Baghdad madhhabs in the classical age of the Two Masters (Abu 'Ali al-Jubba'i and Abu Hashim) on one side and Abu l-Qasim al-Balkhi on the other.[38] Another work, a commentary titled *Ziyadat al-sharh* (Addition to the commentary), on the fundamentals of Mu'tazili kalam as construed by the Two Masters, is largely reproduced in a later supercommentary on Abu Rashid's *Ziyadat*.[39] We know little about Abu Rashid after the Qadi died. Al-Hakim al-Jushami recorded that he succeeded 'Abd al-Jabbar as head of the Mu'tazila at Rayy after the latter died.[40] On that occasion, 'Abd al-Jabbar's most trusted students, such as Abu Rashid, were relegated places behind the first row of mourners, which was taken by Shi'i dignitaries.[41] No date of death for Abu Rashid is given in the scant biographical notices.

A student of Abu Rashid, Abu Muhammad al-Hasan ibn Mattawayh (d. ca. 1076), is also said to have studied with 'Abd al-Jabbar in Rayy before the latter died, and he wrote commentaries on the Qadi's works.[42] One was a four-volume commentary on 'Abd al-Jabbar's *al-Muhit bi l-taklif* (The encompassing [treatment of that which God] makes incumbent).[43] Ibn

Mattawayh wrote another work on kalam that has been published in a critical Arabic edition.[44] Ibn Mattawayh is listed second to last among the Qadi's students, which suggests that he was among the youngest and perhaps among the last to study with him.[45] Ibn Mattawayh was also among the few students of 'Abd al-Jabbar who did not subscribe to Imami or Zaydi Shi'i doctrines of the imamate.

Another of the Qadi's students of some fame was Abu l-Husayn al-Basri (d. 1044),[46] who studied with 'Abd al-Jabbar in Rayy, then went to Baghdad where he studied philosophy. Indeed, his philosophical approach to kalam and fiqh (Hanafi) led to some criticism of him by the Bahshamiya. Nonetheless, Abu l-Husayn had several students who preferred his more philosophical methods. A work on legal theory by Abu l-Husayn has been edited and published.[47]

Among the Qadi's more distinguished pupils was the Imami (Ithna Ash'ari or "Twelver") Shi'i spiritual leader (*naqib*) in Baghdad, al- Sharif al-Murtada (d. 1044).[48] The two men met in Baghdad when the Qadi stopped there on the way to perform the hajj in 999, and perhaps again during the Qadi's stay in Baghdad on his way back. That was probably before al-Sharif al-Murtada became naqib of the Imami Shi'a, because his mentor and predecessor al-Shaykh al-Mufid (d. 1022) was, at the time, the Imami naqib. Al-Murtada wrote a kalam work in defense of the Imami Shi'a doctrine of the imamate which the Qadi refuted in the twentieth volume of his magnum opus, *al-Mughni*.[49]

Al-Murtada was also an Arabist and littérateur of considerable reputation. Another issue on which he and the Qadi differed was on the nature of the miracle of the Qur'an. Tradition holds that none of the Arabs could imitate the lofty pure Arabic speech of the Qur'an when the Prophet Muhammad had challenged them to do so. Al-Murtada argued that when the Arabs were so challenged to try to imitate the speech of the Qur'an recited by Muhammad,[50] they were deflected (*sarfa*) by God from being able to respond. The doctrine of sarfa had first been advanced in the ninth century by Ibrahim al-Nazzam, a Mu'tazili contemporary of Abu l-Hudhayl, and was revived in the tenth century by Imami Shi'i mutakallimun and perhaps by Bagdhadi Mu'tazili mutakallimun. 'Abd al-Jabbar, the Bahshamiya, the Ash'ariya, and Sunni Islam generally held that Quranic speech itself was intrinsically inimitable. The inimitability of the Qur'an (*i'jaz al-qur'an*) is discussed without reference to the doctrine of sarfa in ¶ 43 of the translation in chapter 5.[51] It is quite possible that the Qadi did not feel the need to defeat the theory of sarfa until after he met and and debated with al-Sharif al-Murtada in Baghdad.

Another Shi'i theologian who studied Basra Mu'tazilite kalam, first with Abu 'Abdallah al-Basri, then with the Qadi, was the Zaydi Imam al-Mu'ayyad Billah (d. 1020).[52] The association with the Qadi was in Rayy, where al-Mu'ayyad Billah also frequented the literary circle of the vizier al-Sahib ibn 'Abbad. The "al-Mu'ayyadiya" became one of the two most influential madhhabs in Zaydi fiqh over the rest of Zaydi history in the Caspian enclaves at Daylam, Gilan, and Tabaristian, and in San'a in Yemen.

The most important Zaydi Shi'i follower of 'Abd al-Jabbar for the purposes of our story was al-Sharif Abu l-Husayn al-Qazwini, known as Manekdim (d. 1034).[53] Manekdim studied Zaydi/Mu'tazili kalam with al-Mu'ayyad Billah. Whether or not Manekdim actually studied with the Qadi is not known, although he was a mature Mu'tazili scholar living in Rayy during the last years of the Qadi's life (ca. 1020–1024). Manekdim was also among the Zaydi mourners in the first row at 'Abd al-Jabbar's funeral, ahead of Abu Rashid and other non-Shi'i pupils (mentioned above). Manekdim is an important figure in the generation following 'Abd al-Jabbar because he wrote a supercommentary (*ta'liq*) on the text of 'Abd al-Jabbar's *Sharh al-usul al-khamsa*. This latter *sharh* (commentary) was written by the Qadi as a gloss on his own *Kitab al-usul al-khamsa,* the text translated in chapter 5 of this volume. More will be said about Manekdim's supercommentary in chapter 3.

The Limited Survival of Mu'tazilism in the Central and Eastern Lands

After the eleventh century, Sunni Mu'tazili mutakallimun continued to dictate and comment on the classical kalam works of the two Jubba'is, Abu l-Qasim al-Balkhi, 'Abd al-Jabbar, and his pupils for at least two centuries, until the end of the Abbasid Age. Shi'i Mu'tazila, especially among the Zaydi mutakallimun, continued to study and teach Mu'tazilism even longer – in the Caspian region until the rise of the Safavi empire in the sixteenth century, and in northern Yemen until the past century. Zaydi Mu'tazilism in particular, however, had little appeal beyond the Imams and ulama of the Zaydi Shi'a. Mu'tazili mutakallimun were no longer defining the issues for intellectuals in *dar al-islam* to debate. Nonetheless, in the narrow Mu'tazili scholasticism of fourteenth-century Yemen much of the earlier Mu'tazili textual tradition was copied and preserved for the rationalist enlightenment that took place in the twentieth century. The rest of this chapter surveys the final decline of Mu'tazilism before its hibernation in manuscript collections.

After 'Abd al-Jabbar, the Mu'tazili intellectual most remembered in

Islamic intellectual history is the Quranic exegete Jar Allah Mahmud ibn 'Umar al-Zamakhshari (d. 1144).[54] Along with the Sunni *tafsirs* (commentaries) of Fakhr al-Din al-Razi (d. 1209) and al-Baydawi (d. 1286), his Qur'an commentary, titled *al- Khashshaf 'an haqa'iq al-tanzil* (Explorations of the truths of the [revelation] sent down),[55] ranks among the classic Qur'an commentaries of medieval Islam. In assessing al-Zamakhshari's thought, Wilferd Madelung focuses on the province of Khwarazm in northern Iran as an important venue for Mu'tazili kalam. In the latter half of the twelfth century, the Sunni polemicist Fakhr al-Din al-Razi reports that Mu'tazili disputants eventually forced him to leave Khwarazm.[56] Al-Razi also reports that by the late twelfth century, the Mu'tazila existed in two contending madhhabs, Bahshamiya (the followers of Abu Hashim of whom 'Abd al-Jabbar was a staunch later representative) and the followers of Abu l-Husayn al-Basri (d. 1044).[57] We know very little about the followers of the Baghdad madhhab of the Mu'tazila in the eleventh century and after, except that the works of Abu l-Qasim al-Balkhi continued to be dictated and studied.

The teachings of the Bahshamiya madhhab had been dictated and discussed among the Sunni Mu'tazilia who were 'Abd al-Jabbar's pupils, the most important of whom were Abu Rashid al-Nisaburi and Muhammad ibn Mattawayh, mentioned above. A later scholar and biographer of the Mu'tazila, al-Hakim al-Jushami (d. 1101) may have spread the teachings of the Bahshamiya Mu'tazila in Khwarazm.[58] The influence of the other branch mentioned by al-Razi, the followers of Abu l-Husayn al-Basri, is hard to trace. Perhaps because he was deeply entrenched in the Bahshamiya, al-Hakim al-Jushami accuses Abu l-Husayn and his followers of being excessively concerned with *falsafa*, "philosophy," and thus of being overly critical of some Basra Mu'tazili doctrines.[59]

Abu l-Husayn's most important disciple, Mahmud al-Malahimi, instructed al-Zamakhshari in kalam. In his analysis of al-Zamakhshari's brief treatise, *Kitab al-minhaj fi usul al-din* (Book of methods in the fundamentals of religion), Madelung concludes that al-Zamakhshari was primarily a Qur'an exegete whose theological views included teachings from both the Bahshamiya and the followers of Abu l-Husayn al-Basri. Madelung refers to this convergence of madhhab differences among the Mu'tazila as a "broadly based, catholic Mu'tazilism."[60] "Catholic" here does not imply universally established. Rather, as in the case of the modern revival of interest in Mu'tazilism, which we will begin to consider in Part II, al-Zamakhshari constructed his own theological rationalism out of various conflicting possibilities offered by the two competing Mu'tazili madhhabs, without feeling bound to uphold one madhhab over another. The Mu'tazilism of al-Zamakhshari, too, represented, as Mu'tazilism has in modern times, the position of a tiny minority among religious intellectuals. We hear very little about Mu'tazilism in Sunni Islam after al-Zamakhshari – only that in Khwarazm the school thrived for at least three more centuries, receiving little mention elsewhere in the Islamic world (except Yemen) until modern times.[61]

Apart from Khwarazm, Yemen was the other main venue for the survival of Mu'tazilism, in large part as a result of the benefaction of the Zaydi Imams at San'a. Zaydi tradition holds that Zayd ibn 'Ali (d. 740), the brother of the fifth Imam (Muhammad al-Baqir) of the Twelver Shi'a, studied Mu'tazili kalam with Wasil ibn 'Ata'.[62] Zayd led a revolt in Kufa against the Umayyads. His following spread beyond lower Iraq in the following generations. Zayd's followers, the Zaydiya (also called the Fivers), were politically more radical but theologically more moderate than the Imami or Ithna 'Ashari (Twelver) Shi'a from whom they separated. Like the Khawarij, they actively led rebellions against what they perceived to be unjust (Sunni) rulers. Yet the Zaydis were willing to acknowledge the partial legitimacy of the caliphs who led Islam before 'Ali ibn Abi Talib. In kalam, they eventually accepted the teachings of the Mu'tazila, especially the Bahshamiya, except on the question of the imamate where, as just indicated, they held a position between Sunni and Imami Shi'i theologians.

A little over a century after Zayd ibn 'Ali, a Zaydi Imam named al-Qasim ibn Ibrahim al-Rassi (d. 860) became well known for his teachings in fiqh and kalam.[63] From Kufa (and Jabal al-Rass near Medina, where al-Qasim taught), Zaydi teaching spread to Iran and established stronghold communities, especially in the more remote regions around the Caspian Sea. One of al-Qasim ibn Ibrahim's grandsons, the Imam al-Hadi ila l-Haqq Yahya ibn al-Husayn, brought the Zaydi *da'wa* (teaching) to Yemen in 898. For the next two centuries, the teachings of al-Hadi dominated Zaydi circles.

An extremely conservative and reactionary focus on the teachings of al-Hadi was established by Mutarrif al-Shihabi. The Mutarrifiya became vigorous opponents of Mu'tazili kalam within the Zaydiya. In one incident in particular, a famous public dispute took place in 1004 in San'a between Mutarrif and a certain Mu'tazili (Zaydi) mutakallim named 'Ali ibn Shahr. At issue was the Mu'tazili teaching of *creatio ex nihilo* (Ar. *ikhtira'*). The Mutarrifa followed a deistic doctrine that God created the four elements then did not intervene in the world except in the case of miracles.[64] Most of the Mu'tazila, as we have seen earlier in this chapter, held to a doctrine of atomistic occasionalism: God creates all particles and attributes that comprise existence in all instances. The opponents of the Mutarrifa on this issue were called the Mukhtari'a, the followers of the doctrine of ikhtira', although in reality it was the new Mu'tazili influence from Iran and Iraq that fueled this dispute in Yemen.[65]

Mu'tazili influence reached its zenith in Yemen nearly a century after Qadi 'Abd al-Jabbar during the da'wa of Ahmad ibn Sulayman, who proclaimed himself Imam al-Mutawakkil 'ala llah in 1137 (he died in 1160). Al-Mutawakkil was himself an active scholar and teacher as well as an able administrator. Among his teachers in Mu'tazili kalam were two scholars of note. One was a Mu'tazili scholar from Iraq, Zayd ibn 'Ali al-Bayhaqi. His influence in Yemen was so considerable that he won over a Mutarrifi, Abu Yahya Ja'far, to the Mu'tazili cause. Sometime around 1150 the Qadi Abu Yahya Ja'far set out with Zayd ibn 'Ali al-Bayhaqi for Iraq, to learn more about Mu'tazilism and to bring back books to Yemen. Ayman Fu'ad Sayyid believes this was the moment when Mu'tazili and other books found their way in large numbers to the great Mutawakkiliya library in Yemen and were copied for posterity.[66] As it turned out, al-Bayhaqi died on the trip to Iraq. Abu Yahya studied the Mu'tazili kalam of the Bahshamiya in Iraq and Iran and returned with many books to San'a in 1159. Another scholar, 'Abdallah al-'Absi (or al-'Ansi), is said to have brought books to Yemen from Iraq, including the works of the Zaydi Imam and pupil of 'Abd al-Jabbar, al-Mu'ayyad bi llah. The Qadi Abu Yahya, appointed by the Imam al-Mutawakkil, headed a massive project to refute the theologians of the Mutarrifa and their books. The middle of the twelfth century was also a period of increased migration of Zaydi Shi'a from the Caspian and elsewhere to Yemen.[67]

A history of Mu'tazili influence in Yemen after the imamate of al-Mutawakkil in the twelfth century has yet to be written. With the concerted and successful effort to defeat the older conservatism of the Mutarrifa under al-Mutawakkil's leadership, Mu'tazili kalam had one less enemy, at least for a while. Isma'ili, Shafi'i, and Ithna 'Ashari madhhabs continued to challenge the Zaydi/Mu'tazili rapprochement that had fructified in the tenth century, especially in the circle of Qadi 'Abd al-Jabbar in Rayy, Iran. For our purposes it is enough to know that Mu'tazilism, by the end of the Abbasid Age in the thirteenth century, was no longer an intellectual force in Dar al-Islam. It existed only in small, remote outposts in the Caspian region and in the madrasas and libraries of Zaydi northern Yemen. The spirit of Mu'tazili rationalism was hibernating, but it was not dead, as we shall see in Parts II and III below. Mu'tazili texts would be read again centuries later by those seeking to find Islamic answers to the problems posed by modernity and change.

Notes

1. Abu Sa'id al-Hasan b. Abi I-Hasan Yasur al-Basri. See *GAL,* SI: 102–103; *GAS,* I: 591–594; *EI²,* s.v., "Hasan al-Basri"; *Theologie,* 2: 41–118.

2. For a discussion of al-Hasan al-Basri's *Risala* to 'Abd al-Malik (and other theological positions), see *Formative Period,* pp. 100–102, et passim.

3. *Formative Period,* pp. 118, 193–194, et passim. George F. Hourani, *Islamic Rationalism* discusses these doctrines in relation to the kalam works of 'Abd al-Jabbar, esp. pp. 39–43 and 97.

4. Abu Hudhayfa Wasil b. 'Ata' al-Ghazzal, born in Medina in 699 where he became a *mawla* (client) of an Arab tribe and thus Muslim. He migrated to Basra where he met al-Hasan. See *GAL,* SI: 103; *GAS,* I: 593; *SEI,* s.v. "Wasil b. 'Ata'"; *Tabaqat,* pp. 28–31; and *Theologie,* 2: 234–280. Abu 'Uthman 'Amr b. 'Ubayd was also a mawla, although less biographical information is available on him than on Wasil. See *GAL,* SI: 338; *GAS,* I: 594; *EI²,* s.v. "'Amr b. 'Ubayd"; *Tabaqat,* pp. 35–36; and *Theologie,* 2: 280–310.

5. There are many variations of this story, some of them conflicting on certain points with others. Watt (and others) believe the derivation of the mu'tazila/i'tizal from remarks made by al-Hasan al-Basri is fictional. Watt also thinks 'Amr was better known than Wasil. For a review of the debate on how the Mu'tazili madhhab got its name, see *Formative Period,* pp. 209–217; and *Theologie,* 2: 335–342.

6. Abu 'Amr Dirar b. Amr al-Ghatafani al-Kufi. See *GAS,* I: 614; *EI²,* s.v. "Dirar b. 'Amr"; *Formative Period,* pp.189–199; and *Theologie,* 3: 32–63.

7. Abu I-Hudhayl Muhammad b. Abi I-Hudhayl al-'Allaf al-'Abdi, a mawla of the tribe of 'Abd al-Qays. See *GAL,* SI: 338; *GAS,* I: 617–618; *EI²,* s.v. "Abu I-Hudhayl"; *Fihrist,* I: 386–389; *Tabaqat,* pp. 44–49; *Formative Period,* p. 219 et passim; *Theologie,* 3: 209–296.

8. Cited by Josef van Ess, *ER,* s.v. "Mu'tazilah," 10: 220–229.

9. Josef van Ess has collected, situated, and interpreted fragments of kalam texts from the early centuries of Islam in *Theologie und Gesellschaft im 2. Und 3. Jahrhundert Hidschra: Eine Geschichte des religiosen Denkens im frühen Islam,* cited simply as *Theologie* throughout this book.

10. Abu Sahl Bishr b. al-Mu'tamir al-Hilali, born in Kufa. See *GAL,* SI: 338; *GAS,* I: 615; *EI²,* s.v. "Bishr b. al- Mu'tamir"; *Fihrist,* 2: 390–391; *Tabaqat,* pp. 52–54; *Formative Period,* p. 222 et passim; and *Theologie,* 3: 107–130.

11. On the mihna and al-Ma'mun's meddling in theology, see *Formative Period,* pp. 177–179 and index, and *EI²* , s.v. "Mihna," and "Ma'mun . . . b. Harun al-Rashid."

12. Abu 'Uthman 'Amr b. Bahr al-Kinani al-Fuqaymi al-Basri. On his life and works, see *EI²* s.v. "Djahiz," and Pellat, *The Life and Works of Jahiz.*

13. On Ibn al-Rawandi, see *GAL,* SI: 340; *GAS,* I: 620–621; *EI²,* s.v. "Mulhid" and "Ibn al-Rawandi"; *Formative Period,* index; and *Theologie,* 4: ¶ 8.22 (forthcoming).

14. Abu I-Qasim 'Abdallah b. Ahmad al-Balkhi al-Ka'bi. See *GAL,* SI: 343; *GAS,* I: 622–623; *EI²,* s.v. "al-Balkhi, Abu I-Kasim." For a brief English summary of al-Balkhi's thought see the article by Josef van Ess, *EIr,* s.v. "Abu I-Qasem al-Balkhi al- Ka'bi."

Though only a few fragments of his theological writings have been preserved in later texts by his Basra Mu'tazili opponents, much of his system can be reconstructed on this basis. See al-Nisaburi, *al-Masa'il fi l-khilaf.*

15. For Abu 'Ali Muhammad b. 'Abd al-Wahhab. Salam al- Jubba'i, see *GAL,* SI: 342; *GAS,* I: 621–622; *EI²,* s.v. "Djubba'i"; *Tabaqat,* pp. 80–85; *Formative Period,* index. For Abu Hashim 'Abd al-Salam b. Abi 'Ali b. Muhammad . . . al-Jubba'i, see *GAL,* SI: 342; *GAS,* I: 623–624; *EI²,* s.v. "Djubba'i"; *Tabaqat,* pp. 94–96; *Formative Period,* index.

16. *Tabaqat,* 109: 5–10.

17. Abu 'Abd Allah Muhammad b. 'Umar al-Saymari. See *Tabaqat,* 96: 15–18; *Fadl,* 308: 15–309: 8.

18. Abu Bakr Ahmad Ibn 'Ali Ma'jur al-Ikhshidh, known as Ibn Ikhshidh. See *Tabaqat,* 100: 1–13.

19. For a discussion of the works by the Two Masters, see Gimaret, "Matériaux pour une bibliographie des Ğubba'i," pp. 277–332; and idem, "Matériaux pour une bibliographie des Jubba'i: Note complémentaire," pp. 31–38.

20. Abu 'Abdallah al-Husayn b. 'Ali al-Basri. See *EI²,* s.v. "Abu 'Abd Allah al-Basri"; *Tabaqat,* pp. 105–107.

21. Lapidus, *Islamic Societies,* pp. 132–133.

22. Abu l-Hasan 'Ali b. Isma'il b. Ishaq al-Ash'ari. See *GAL,* SI: 345; *GAS,* I: 602–604; *EI²,* s.v. "al-Ash'ari, Abu l- Hasan"; and *Formative Period,* index.

23. Abu l-Hasan 'Ali b. Isma'il al-Ash'ari, *Kitab maqalat al-islamiyin,* ed. H. Ritter, 2nd ed. (Wiesbaden: Franz Steiner, 1963), referred to throughout simply as *Maqalat.*

24. The *Kitab al-luma'* and *Risala fi istihsan al-khawd fi l-kalam* were published and translated, with an excellent introduction by Richard J. McCarthy, *The Theology of al-Ash'ari* (Beirut: Imprimatur Catholique, 1953). *Al-Ibana 'an usul al- diyana* was translated by Walter C. Klein, *The Elucidation of Islam's Foundation* (New Haven, Conn.: American Oriental Society, 1940).

25. When he became a student of Mu'tazili kalam, 'Abd al-Jabbar asked his mentor, Abu 'Abdallah al-Basri, whether or not he ('Abd al-Jabbar) should become a Hanafi in fiqh (law) – the madhhab of most Mu'taziliti mutakallimun. Abu 'Abdallah advised him not to bother changing madhhabs. Nonetheless, conflicts between the Mu'tazila and the Ash'ariya in Khurasan were often also conflicts between the Hanafi and Shafi'i madhhabs in fiqh.

26. For a history and analysis of this conflict, see Bulliet, *The Patricians of Nishapur,* pp. 28–46.

27. Abu Mansur Muhammad b. Muhammad b. Mahmud al-Maturidi al-Samarqandi. See *GAL,* SI: 195; *GAS,* I: 604–606; *EI²,* s.v. "Maturidi."

28. Abu Bakr Muhammad b. al-Tayyib b. Muhammad b. Ja'far b. al-Qasim al-Baqillani. See *GAL,* SI: 197; *GAS,* I: 608–610; *EI²,* s.v. "Baqillani."

29. Al-Baqillani, *Kitab al-tamhid,* ed. Richard J. McCarthy (Beirut: al-Maktabat al-Sharqiya, 1957).

30. Von Grunebaum, *A Tenth-Century Document of Arabic Literary Theory and Criticism.*

31. See *GAL,* SI: 343; *GAS,* I: 624–626; *EI²,* s.v. "'Abd al-Djabbar"; *Tabaqat,* pp. 112–113;

Sharh al-uyun, pp. 365–371; Peters, *God's Created Speech,* pp. 6–38. What is known from medieval sources about the life of 'Abd al-Jabbar has been summarized by Wilferd Madelung, art. "'Abd al-Jabbar . . . al-Asadabadi," *Elr.* The following account of the Qadi's life is drawn primarily from Madelung.

32. Madelung regards as unlikely the claim of some biographers that 'Abd al-Jabbar first studied Ash'ari kalam before becoming a Mu'tazili; it is more likely that this was assumed by later biographers because the Qadi studied and practiced Shafi'i fiqh, which had a strong association with Ash'ari kalam.

33. On the the cultural and literary ethos of tenth-century eastern Islam, including some discussion of Ibn 'Abbad and 'Abd al-Jabbar and their contemporaries, see Kramer, *Humanism in the Renaissance of Islam.* On Ibn 'Abbad's literary and more prurient interests, see Bosworth, *The Mediaeval Islamic Underworld,* esp. vol. I.

34. Scholarship on the later Mu'tazila in Iran has been done by Wilferd Madelung. See his *Religious Trends in Early Islamic Iran,* p. 44; and *Der Imam al-Qasim ibn Ibrahim,* pp. 153–222.

35. Lapidus, *Islamic Societies,* pp. 225–237 provides a good summary of what was taking shape during this transitional period from the eleventh to thirteenth centuries.

36. Abu Rashid Sa'id b. Muhammad b. Sa'id b. Hasan b. Hatim al-Nisaburi: *GAS,* I: 626; *Tabaqat,* p. 116; *Elr,* s.v. "Abu Rashid Nisaburi"; *EI²,* s.v. "Abu Rashid al-Nisaburi."

37. *Tabaqat,* p. 116.

38. Al-Nisaburi, *al-Masa'il fi l-khilaf.*

39. This is a partial fragment (BMO 8613) of some 144 folios, from what must have been a much larger original work. A critical Arabic edition and English translation is under preparation by Richard C. Martin and Adel S. Gamal.

40. *Tabaqat,* p. 116.

41. Madelung, *Der Imam al-Qasim ibn Ibrahim,* p. 182.

42. Abu Muhammad al-Hasan b. Ahmad b. Mattawayh: *Sharh al-uyun,* p. 389; *Tabaqat,* p. 119.

43. Ibn Mattawayh, *Kitab al-majmu' fi l-muhit bi l-taklif.* Volume I was edited by J. J. Houben (Beirut, 1965) and by 'Uthman al-Sayyid 'Azmi (Cairo, 1965). Volume 2 was begun by Houben but revised and finished by D. Gimaret (Beirut, 1981). Volume 3 has been under preparation by J. Peters and M. Bernand (the latter, unfortunately, is now deceased).

44. Ibn Mattawayh, *al-Tadhkira fi ahkam al-jawahir wa l- a'rad,* ed. S. N. Lutf and F. B. 'Awn (Cairo, 1975).

45. *Tabaqat,* 119: 17.

46. Abu l-Husayn Muhammad b. 'Ali b. al-Tayyib al-Basri: *Tabaqat,* pp. 118–119.

47. Abu l-Husayn al-Basri, *Kitab al-mu'tamad fi usul al- fiqh.* One of the editors, H[asan] Hanafi, is among the Islamic modernists discussed in chapter 10 below.

48. Abu l-Qasim 'Ali b. al-Husayn al-Murtada 'Alam al-Huda: *Sharh al-'uyun,* p. 383. See Madelung, "Imamism and Mu'tazilite Theology," pp. 13–29.

49. Al-Sharif al-Murtada, *al-Shafi fi l-imama,* refuted by Qadi 'Abd al-Jabbar in volume 20 of *al-Mughni.* See Sachedina, *Islamic Messianism,* p. 80 and index.

50. See Qur'an 52:33–34, 11:13, 10:38, and 17:88.

51. Al-Murtada is named and the doctrine of sarfa is refuted by 'Abd al-Jabbar (or Abu Rashid; the interlocutor is not named in the text) in the commentary on Abu Rashid's *Ziyadat al-sharh* (BMO 8613, fols. 17b–28a).

52. Abu l-Husayn Ahmad b. al-Husayn al-Mu'ayyad bi-llah: *Sharh al-'uyun*, p. 376. See Madelung, *Der Imam al-Qasim ibn Ibrahim*, pp. 177–178.

53. Abu l-Husayn Ahmad b. Abi Hashim Muhammad al-Husayni al-Qazwini, surnamed Shashdiw and referred to in most sources as Manekdim (Mankdim). See Gimaret, "Les Usul al-hamsa du Qadi 'Abd al-Jabbar et leurs commentaires," pp. 57–60, and Madelung, *Der Imam al-Qasim ibn Ibrahim*, pp. 181–183.

54. The history of the Mu'tazila for the next century after 'Abd al-Jabbar has been usefully summarized by Wilferd Madelung, "The Theology of al-Zamakhshari," pp. 485–495. The following paragraphs rely on this text unless otherwise indicated.

55. Published frequently; we have referred to the four-volume Beirut: Dar al-Ma'rifa, 1947, edition.

56. Madelung, "The Theology of al-Zamakhshari," p. 485; referring to a remark made by al-Razi, *I'tiqadat firaq al-muslimin wa l-mushrikin*, ed. A. S. Nashshar (Cairo, 1938), p. 45.

57. Madelung and al-Razi, ibid.

58. An alternate view, also discussed by Madelung ("The Theology of al-Zamakhshari," p. 486), is that Abu Mudar al-Isfahani (d. 1114) was the link from 'Abd al-Jabbar's circle of pupils in Rayy and central Iran to al-Zamakhshari in Khwarazm.

59. *Fadl*, p. 387; *Tabaqat*, 119: 3–5. Madelung discusses the conflict between these two branches in "The Theology of al-Zamakhshari," pp. 491–492.

60. Madelung, "The Theology of al-Zamakhshari," pp. 492–493.

61. Ibid, p. 485, and idem, "The Spread of Maturidism and the Turks," pp. 115–117.

62. Sayyid, *Ta'rikh al-madhahib* p. 254. We have relied on this text as a major source for information about the Mu'tazili Zaydiya in Yemen.

63. The definitive study on al-Qasim is Madelung, *Der imam al-Qasim ibn Ibrahim* esp. pp. 86–152.

64. Madelung, *Der Imam al-Qasim ibn Ibrahim*, p. 202.

65. On the doctrines of the Mutarrifa, see Madelung, "A Mutarrifi Manuscript," pp. 75–90.

66. Sayyid, *Ta'rikh al-madhahib*, p. 259.

67. A good source of information about the Zaydi imamate in Yemen is Gochenour, "The Penetration of Zaydi Islam into Early Medieval Yemen." We have consulted especially pp. 150–186.

three

The Life *and* Works *of* Qadi 'Abd al-Jabbar

Qadi 'Abd al-Jabbar (d. 1024) was the last great *mutakallim* (theologian) of the *madhhab* (school) known as the Mu'tazila.[1] His biographer, al-Hakim al-Jushami (d. 1101), says that the Qadi's fame in the discipline of theology (*'ilm al-kalam*) was spread from east to west, and that "the length of his life was devoted to teaching and dictating until [at the end] the earth was covered with his books and students."[2] In the view of a modern interpreter of 'Abd al-Jabbar's teachings, the Qadi was not so much an original thinker as "a true and good Mu'tazili":

> he knew the history of his school and its ideas and became the great "compiler" of the Mu'tazili ideas as developed in former centuries by his great predecessors. But he did more than that: he built a comprehensive, coherent, and closed system of theological thinking on the foundations laid for him by the older generations of Mu'tazila. He himself considers his greatest merit to be the making of a systematic approach to theological questions and the elaboration of argumentation in general.[3]

The purpose of this chapter is to introduce the reader to the life and works of Qadi 'Abd al-Jabbar in the context of Mu'tazili *kalam* in the tenth and eleventh centuries. In particular, we will identify the compendium of Mu'tazili kalam, titled *Kitab al-usul al-khamsa*, which is translated in chapter 5. To do this, it will be useful to review the bibliography of works by 'Abd al-Jabbar and to discuss problems of identification and dating. First, however, we shall briefly describe the cultural context in which kalam texts were produced and transmitted and then discuss the modern discovery of a cache of Mu'tazili works.

The Cultural Context of Mu'tazili *Kalam*

In traditional Islamic societies, the transmission of knowledge from teacher to pupil combined oral and written means. Teachers dictated to their students the works that their teachers had dictated to them. To become authorized to transmit his own copy of a book, a student was required to read the text back to his teacher, making those corrections the teacher called for. The student was then given a certificate known as an *ijazat al-tadris*, which entitled him to teach the text on his own authority, that is, to dictate it to his students. In this way, important texts, such as al-Bukhari's collection of Hadith and al-Shafi'i's treatise (*al-Risala*) on jurisprudence, as well as lesser-known texts, were transmitted from one generation to the next. Handwritten copies of such texts came to abound in private libraries in Islamic lands, and consequently these texts were widely read. Nonetheless, the authority to transmit a text was restricted (until quite recently) to the teacher/pupil relationship and the ijazat al-tadris.[4]

The literary mode of most of the kalam works from the Islamic Middle Ages is that of the point/counterpoint debate (*munazara, jadal*). The same is true for works in the other religious sciences in which scholars engaged in disputations, such as in *usul al-fiqh* (legal theory). Thus, in the Qadi's *Kitab al-usul al-khamsa*, some sixty-seven points and subpoints are introduced by the locution: "If it is said [or asked] (*in qila*)." The author's response, sometimes lengthy and itself subdivided, is signaled by the phrase: "It should be said to him (*qila lahu*)." This dialogic literary mode reflected the cultural context of disputation, munazara, in which doctrinal issues were debated among sectarian groups (*firaq*, sing. *firqa*) and madhhabs, as well as among confessional communities (*umam*, sing. *umma*), including Christians and Jews. Mosques, public squares, private homes, and the audience halls of caliphs, viziers, and princes were the venues of disputation among the leading mutakallimun of Islamic society.[5]

A compendium or handbook of kalam like *Kitab al-usul al-khamsa* was normally meant to be memorized by students of kalam who studied with the Qadi or with one of his pupils to whom he dictated the work. In this way a student was in mental possession of a basic text of kalam, which was to be further interpreted by his chosen madhhab and mentor. As we saw previously, Qadi 'Abd al-Jabbar dictated a commentary (*sharh*) on *al-Usul al-khamsa*, and in the next generation after him a Zaydi-Mu'tazili pupil known as Manekdim wrote a supercommentary (*ta'liq*) on the Qadi's commentary. Thus, a text like the one translated here often became embedded in larger and larger texts of multiple authorship and commentary, as time went on.[6] Such works functioned as school texts, reflecting the theological issues on which the mutakallimun trained their students to dispute with opponents.

The Mu'tazili madhhab had existed for two centuries when Qadi 'Abd al-Jabbar became its last great teacher. His texts on kalam reflect the achievement of the Bahshamiya at the end of this period. Before describing what we know of the life of 'Abd al-Jabbar and mentioning his better-known texts, we shall discuss the modern rediscovery of his works, an essential element of this introduction to the translation of *Kitab al-usul al-khamsa*.

A Modern Discovery of Mu'tazili Manuscripts

Several Mu'tazili writings, including works by 'Abd al-Jabbar, were discovered in Yemen by a team of Egyptian scholars in 1950.[7] The team had been sent by the famous Egyptian literary figure and intellectual Taha Husayn (d. 1973), then Minister of Education. It had been known among European Orientalists at least since the late nineteenth century that collections of old religious manuscripts existed in private homes and in mosques in San'a. Some had already been purchased or otherwise removed and cataloged in European collections by the time the Egyptians made their discovery.[8] Leading the Egyptians in 1950 was the director of the Egyptian National Archives, Dar al-Kutub al-Misriya, Dr. Fu'ad Sayyid, who was among several Egyptian scholars who subsequently published a report on the Arabic manuscripts found during the first trip to the Yemen.[9]

The Egyptians microfilmed as many of the manuscripts as possible and put the films on deposit at Dar al-Kutub in Cairo. The original manuscripts remained in Yemen. In Cairo the microfilmed texts were identified and cataloged. As we mentioned in the previous chapter, a part of the Zaydi community – including Mu'tazili mutakallimun – migrated to Yemen at the end of the Buyid Age (mid-eleventh century). Thus, many of the texts filmed by the Egyptians turned out to be Mu'tazili kalam texts. The most significant find was six of the twenty volumes of the *Kitab al-mughni* by 'Abd al-Jabbar. Subsequently some of the other volumes were found and added to the collection in Cairo. These discoveries stimulated further searches among manuscripts already on deposit in Dar al-Kutub, which led to further discoveries of Mu'tazili kalam texts. Taha Husayn appointed a team of Egyptian scholars to edit the extant volumes of *al-Mughni* under his general direction. Publication by the Egyptian Ministry of Culture began in 1960 and was completed in 1969.[10] These include volumes 4–7, 9, 11–17, and 20.

It is impossible to overstress the importance of the discovery and publication of 'Abd al-Jabbar's *al-Mughni*. First, as indicated above, it encouraged more searches through Egyptian manuscript collections, and other collections in Europe as well, for the additional volumes of *al-Mughni* and for other kalam works (some were found right in the Dar al-Kutub in Egypt). Second, these discoveries stimulated new scholarship on kalam and the Mu'tazila in particular.[11] Third, this has led to a fuller appreciation of Islamic intellectual history during the Abbasid Age. We will evaluate the impact of the twentieth-century recovery of Mu'tazili manuscripts in a subsequent chapter.

Other works by 'Abd al-Jabbar were discovered and some of these have been published, including the *Sharh al-usul al-khamsa*, first published in 1965 as 'Abd al-Jabbar's work, identified by Gimaret in 1979 as Manekdim's supercommentary on (*ta'liq 'ala*) the Qadi's commentary on his own work (although never republished as such). Before coming to a brief description of the known works of 'Abd al-Jabbar, it is important to mention what is known of his life from various sources.

The Biography of 'Abd al-Jabbar

'Abd al-Jabbar's full name was Abu al-Hasan 'Abd al-Jabbar ibn Ahmad ibn Khalil ibn 'Abdallah al-Hamadhani al-Asadabadi, known honorifically as 'Imad al-Din, "upholder of religion," and also by his professional title, Qadi "judge," and more fully, Qadi al-Qudat, "Chief Magistrate." In these pages, we have been following the practice of referring to him more briefly by his given name, 'Abd al-Jabbar, sometimes preceded by his title, Qadi. He was born probably around 935 of peasant Iranian stock in Asadabad, a town southwest of the Iranian city of Hamadhan.[12] In Asadabad he would have begun his education at about seven years of age, learning to recite the Qur'an from a teacher at a school known in Arabic as a *kuttab*, or perhaps from his father. Following the common educational trajectory, according to biographical notices, he "heard" (took in dictation) Hadith from a well-known Asadabadi transmitter (*muhaddith*) known as Zubayr ibn 'Abd al-Wahid (d. 958) and others. Indeed, for the next several years as he moved about for religious and educational purposes, 'Abd al-Jabbar "heard" Hadith from a number of muhaddithun. Thus, despite his later reputation as a Mu'tazili opponent of traditionalist worldviews, he was well grounded in the religious training required of Muslim intellectuals of his day.

We are told that the Qadi first made the hajj or pilgrimage to Mecca as a young man in 951, after which he continued his studies in Hadith in

Hamadhan and perhaps Isfahan. Soon thereafter he is reported to have studied Hadith in Basra, still a center of Mu'tazili teaching. By this time, the Buyid princes had seized virtual control of lands under Abbasid suzerainty, especially in Iran. One result of Buyid management of Abbasid tax lands east of Baghdad was the beginning of Shi'i influence in the Buyid courts in such cities as Hamadhan and Rayy. Shi'i amirs and viziers supported the spread of Shi'i educational institutions and the display of Shi'i piety in such public rituals as the *ta'ziya*, the festival that commemorated the Passion of Husayn, and *ghadir khumm*, the anniversary of the occasion on which Shi'a believe the Prophet Muhammad designated 'Ali as the one to lead the Muslim umma after him. The year 941 (when 'Abd al-Jabbar perhaps would have been a young boy reciting Qur'an in a kuttab) was determined by the Shi'i Ithna 'Ashari (Twelver) leadership (*niyaba*) as the beginning of the Greater Occultation of the twelfth Imam. Thus, the Shi'i intelligentsia began to turn from immediate messianic expectations to the theological task of guiding the Ithna 'Ashari community in the world. Many Ithna 'Ashari and Zaydi Shi'i mutakallimun studied kalam with Mu'tazili shaykhs during the tenth century. The Zaydi Shi'a in particular were among the Qadi's most influential students in the first half of the eleventh century.

Al-Jushami (d. 1101) says that 'Abd al-Jabbar first studied Ash'ari kalam, then saw the light and became a student of Mu'tazili shaykhs.[13] Madelung advises us to regard this in the light of the concomitant statement that the Qadi studied Shafi'i *fiqh* (whereas most Mu'tazili mutakallimun studied Hanafi law). The association of Shafi'i fiqh with Ash'ari kalam increasingly became a dominant expression of Sunni orthodoxy in the tenth and elventh centuries. Perhaps al-Jushami had assumed that a pupil of the madhhab of Muhammad al-Shafi'i (d. 820) would necessarily have studied Ash'ari kalam. Another point to consider is that conversion from an opponent madhhab to one's own madhhab formed part of the school rhetoric against the former. The famous story of al-Ash'ari's conversion, told in the last chapter, is a case in point. Whatever the truth of 'Abd al-Jabbar's youthful association with the Ash'ariya may have been, the sources are unanimous that he studied for many years under the leading Mu'tazili shaykhs of the day.

At Basra 'Abd al-Jabbar studied Mu'tazili kalam first with Abu Ishaq ibn 'Ayyash, a pious and ascetic scholar who had studied with Abu 'Ali ibn Khallad, who was himself a pupil of the famed Abu Hashim ibn al-Jubba'i. Madelung reports that the Qadi early on also studied with a mutakallim who was fanatically opposed to Abu Hashim, Abu Ahmad ibn Abi 'Allan (d. 1018) but soon left his circle, indicating his growing commitment to the

Bahshamiya (followers of Abu Hashim).[14] Indeed, because of his opposition to the Baghdad branch of the Mu'tazila and his departures from the teachings of his father, Abu 'Ali al-Jubba'i, Abu Hashim drew sharp and sometimes personal attacks from other Mu'tazili mutakallimun. This antagonism toward the Bahshamiya remained very much alive in the next generation when 'Abd al-Jabbar studied kalam.[15] Soon the Qadi became the pupil of the leading Mu'tazili mutakallim of the day, Abu 'Abdallah al-Basri (d. 977). Abu 'Abdallah in turn had been the leading pupil of Abu Hashim.

'Abd al-Jabbar studied for many years with Abu 'Abdallah in Baghdad. Under the latter's tutelage he eventually began to dictate his own work. Indeed, we learn from one biographer that the Qadi worried about his Shafi'i affiliation in fiqh and thus wanted to study Hanafi fiqh, the preferred madhhab among Mu'tazili mutakallimun. His mentor, Abu 'Abdallah, who was also a distinguished Hanafi jurisconsult, advised the Qadi to remain a scholar of the Shafi'i madhhab, and that both the Hanafi and Shafi'i schools were valid. As we know already, 'Abd al-Jabbar was later entrusted with the office of Chief Magistrate of Iran. Perhaps it was in part because of his Shafi'i affiliation that his reputation survived for several generations among leading jurists.[16]

The Qadi was already a Mu'tazili teacher and author of some stature when he left the circle of Abu 'Abdallah to dictate and teach on his own. The biographical sources next catch up with him in the Persian Gulf city of Ramahurmuz. A former prize pupil of al-Jubba'i, Abu Muhammad 'Abdallah ibn al-'Abbas al-Ramahurmuzi, had established a well-known Mu'tazili circle of scholars at a mosque compound in the city whose name he bore.[17] There, in 970, the Qadi began dictating his magnum opus, the twenty-volume *Kitab al-mughni,* which we shall describe further in the next section. Despite his reputation as a champion of the Bahshamiya branch of the Basra Mu'tazila, 'Abd al-Jabbar was well acquainted with the theological differences between the Two Masters, al-Jubba'i and his son Abu Hashim. His knowledge of al-Jubba'i's work may have increased during as a result of his association with 'Abdallah al-Ramahurmuzi.

Apparently 'Abd al-Jabbar's reputation as a teacher and author by this point had begun to spread, especially in the Iranian cities under Buyid control, where Mu'tazili kalam was still influential. We next learn that al-Sahib ibn 'Abbad, a Mu'tazili intellectual in the entourage of the Buyid amir Mu'ayyid al-Dawla, invited the Qadi to join him at Mu'ayyid's court at Rayy. After Ibn 'Abbad succeeded to the office of vizier, he appointed 'Abd al-Jabbar Qadi al-Qudat (Chief Magistrate) as mentioned above. That was in 977. Rayy in the last decades of the tenth century was a heady atmosphere in which to teach and adjudicate. Al-Sahib ibn 'Abbad's evening gatherings of poets and philosophers, as well as theologians representing Muslim and non-Muslim communities, were reputed to be raucous occasions of free debate and secular enjoyments. In addition to his judicial appointment, 'Abd al-Jabbar established a circle of students of Mu'tazili doctrine at Rayy. Students and their professors traveled from far and wide to receive his lectures in dictation; mutakallimun sent him questions (*masa'il*) on points of kalam in dispute in other locales.

As previously noted, when the vizier al-Sahib ibn 'Abbad died in 995, the Qadi lost his judicial position and his possessions were confiscated. Exactly why his fortunes fell so precipitously is not clear.

The Works of 'Abd al-Jabbar

Al-Hakim al-Jushami tells us that the Qadi wrote or dictated some four hundred thousand folios (*waraqa*) during his lifetime. He then mentions some twenty-seven titles, presumably the best known when al-Jushami was writing his biographical dictionary of the Mu'tazila at the end of the eleventh century.[18] The Qadi himself names several of these at the end of part two of volume 20 of *al-Mughni*, and as we mentioned in this regard above, this allows us to reconstruct a rough chronology of his known writings.[19]

Works Written or Dictated Prior to *al-Mughni*

'Abd al-Jabbar began dictating the work for which he is most remembered, *Kitab al-mughni,* in 970, while he was visiting the Mu'tazili enclave at Ramahurmuz in the Persian Gulf. There he was hosted by the local shaykh and pupil of Abu 'Ali al-Jubba'i, Abu Muhammad 'Abd Allah ibn al-'Abbas al-Ramahurmuzi.[20] At the end of *al-Mughni*, the Qadi mentions several titles of works he dictated previously while still in the company of his mentor, Abu 'Abdallah al-Basri (20/2, 358: 12–14): (1) *Naqd al-luma'* (a refutation apparently of al-Ash'ari's *Kitab al-luma'*;[21] (2) *Kitab al-'umad* (on usul al-fiqh);[22] (3) *Taqrib al-usul* (not mentioned elsewhere); (4)*Tahdhib al-sharh* (a revision of a commentary); (5) *Kitab al-mabsut*;[23] (6) *Sharh al-fami' al-saghir* (a commentary on Abu Hashim's *Jami' al-saghi*r);[24] (7) *Kitab al-nihaya* (a work on jurisprudence).[25] After the last title, the Qadi adds: "and others dictated in [Abu 'Abdallah's] presence."

Works Written or Dictated During *al-Mughni's* Dictation

The Qadi also mentions at the end of *al-Mughni* (20/2, 258: 4–7) several other titles he dictated during the period he had dictated *al-Mughni* (970–990). Foremost among these, of course, was the *al-Mughni* itself, whose full title was (8) *Kitab al-mughni fi abwab al-tawhid wa l-'adl* (Book of the plenitude on the topics concerning unity and justice). It was a twenty-volume systematic work of the magnitude, in the history of theology, of St. Thomas Aquinas's *Summa Theologica* and *Summa Contra Gentiles*. Having begun dictating the *al-Mughni* in the Persian Gulf city of Ramahurmuz in the year 970, the Qadi completed dictation twenty years later in Rayy while he was serving as Chief Magistrate under the vizier, al-Sahib ibn 'Abbad. He adds that it took so much time because he was busy with "teaching (*tadris*) and other things," presumably his duties as Chief Magistrate. He also notes that at the beginning of the period, when he mentioned his mentor Abu 'Abdallah al-Basri, he gave the appropriate blessing for one who still lives, but that in later volumes the blessing for the deceased appears, indicating that his mentor had died in the meantime. The extant volumes of the *al-Mughni* were edited, as indicated above, by individual scholars under the general editorial supervision of Taha Husayn, and published between 1960 and 1969 by the Ministry of Culture in Egypt.

Also mentioned as belonging to this period are: (9) *Sharh al-maqalat* (a commentary on a biographical dictionary of the Mu'tazila by Abu l-Qasim al-Balkhi, who was mentioned in chapter 2 above); (10) *Bayan al-mutashabih [fi] l-qur'an* (a book of theological exegesis that has been edited and published);[26] (11) *Kitab al-i'timad*;[27] (12) *Sharh al-jawami'*;[28] (13) *Kitab al- tajrid*;[29] (14) *Sharh kashf al-a'rad*;[30] (15) a part of *Sharh adab al-jadal* (concerning a genre of texts on how to conduct disputations);[31] (16) *Sharh al-usul al-khams[a]* (a commentary by the Qadi on the *Kitab al-usul al-khamsa*, one of the two texts translated in this volume (see chapter 5).[32]

Other Works by 'Abd al-Jabbar that have been Edited and Published

Mention of several other works by 'Abd al-Jabbar is found in the biographical dictionaries and in texts such as *al-Mughni* and Manekdim's *Ta'liq 'ala sharh al-usul al-khamsa*. A comprehensive discussion of the Qadi's works is given by his modern biographer, 'Abd al-Karim 'Uthman.[33] In the remainder of this section, books by the Qadi that have been published or are known to exist will be described briefly.

Al-Sahib ibn 'Abbad, who died five years after 'Abd al-Jabbar completed his dictation of *al-Mughni*, asked the Qadi to compose a compendium of kalam for more popular usage. This work was titled (17) *al-Mukhtasar fi usul al-din* and has been published.[34] It is a compendium of Mu'tazili kalam that covers much the same topics as the *Kitab al-usul al-khamsa*, but it is a longer text, more detailed in the presentation of its arguments. Another work of considerable interest that has been edited and published is (18) *Tathbit dala'il al-nubuwwa* (Establishing the evidences of prophethood). In the text of the *Tathbit* (168: 10–11), the Qadi mentions that he composed the book in 995 (the year in which the vizier Ibn 'Abbad died, as a result of which the Qadi had his property confiscated).[35]

Of considerable importance for the history of the Mu'tazila is the work frequently cited here as *Sharh al-'uyun*, but whose published title is (19) *Fadl al-i'tizal wa tabaqat al-mu'tazila*. This work was edited by the curator of Dar al-Kutub in Egypt, the man who led the delegation to film the manuscripts in Yemen, Fu'ad Sayyid.[36]

Another systematic treatment of kalam by the Qadi is (20) *al-Muhit bi l-taklif*.[37] When it was composed is not known. Like the *Sharh al-usul al-khamsa*, we have *al-Muhit* only in the paraphrased form in which it appears in a commentary by one of his pupils, in this case Abu Muhammad ibn Mattawayh (d. 1076).[38] The history of the publication of the four volumes of this work (not yet completed) is briefly described by Daniel Gimaret in his introduction to volume 2.[39] Thus far two volumes have been published and the latter two are under preparation.

It is clear from this brief description of twenty works by 'Abd al-Jabbar, some of them quite long and well attested in later literature, that he was a prolific writer as well as a dedicated teacher and jurist. Among the other writings mentioned in the biographical dictionaries are answering treatises (*jawabat*), written in response to questions (*masa'il*) from individual mutakallimun and from groups of mutakallimun from different locales, such as *al-Raziyat* (answers to questions from Rayy) and *al-Nisaburiyat* (. . . from Nisabur).[40] These, too, show the importance of the Qadi in his own lifetime; his influence extended to many circles of Mu'tazilite learning in Iraq, Iran, and Khurasan.

The *Kitab al-usul al-khamsa* and its Commentaries

In brief, the text translated in chapter 5 is (1) a short compendium of Mu'tazili kalam titled *Kitab al-usul al-khamsa*. The Qadi then wrote (2) a commentary on it, now lost, titled *Sharh al-usul al-khamsa*. In the next generation, a Zaydi Mu'tazili mutakallim wrote (3) a supercommentary on the Qadi's commentary, which exists and has been published, titled *Ta'liq 'ala sharh al-usul al-khamsa*.[41] In addition, two other supercommentaries (ta'liqs) were written on Manekdim's supercommentary. One was by the Zaydi Mu'tazili al-Farrazadhi (d. late eleventh century).[42] According to the manuscript, the Mu'tazili *usul* were dictated to al-Farrazadhi by Ibn Mattawayh, from Abu Rashid al-Nisaburi, from Qadi 'Abd al-Jabbar, from Abu 'Abd Allah al-Basri, from Abu Hashim, from al-Jubba'i (and so on, to) from Muhammad ibn al-Hanafiya, from 'Ali ibn Abi Talib.[43] The other extant ta'liq on Manekdim's text was by a certain al-Muhalli, who died probably in the latter part of the thirteenth century.[44]

In the Mu'tazili bio-bibliographical works cited in the previous section of this chapter, no mention is made of the *Kitab al-usul al-khamsa*. As we have already seen, the lists of titles given in these works are presented by their authors as being selective, and not comprehensive. We can only speculate, then, that it was an earlier work, because the Qadi's commentary on it was among those books written between 970 and 990, while he was dictating *al-Mughni*. The *Kitab al-usul al-khamsa* might have been written before the Qadi went to Ramahurmuz and began dictating *al-Mughni* in 970. Moreover, the brevity of the work as a whole, as well as the succinctness of the discussion of many of the topics, distinguishes this work from the larger, more detailed discussions of these works found in his extant works. More important, however, is the fact that 'Abd al-Jabbar's *Sharh al-usul al-khamsa* was to become an important school text for the Mu'tazila. It may simply be that the text translated in this study no longer had to be mentioned once the Qadi's own commentary had been written and circulated among students.

The text of 'Abd al-Jabbar's *Kitab al-usul al-khamsa* was discovered by Daniel Gimaret in a collection of manuscripts at the Vatican.[45] He subsequently published an edition of the text along with his identification of it as the work on which the Qadi's *Sharh al-usul al-khamsa* was based, and later, Manekdim's *Ta'liq 'ala sharh al-usul al-khamsa*. Gimaret further showed that the text edited and published by 'Abd al-Karim 'Uthman in 1965 as the *Sharh al-usul al-khamsa* by 'Abd al-Jabbar was in fact the *Ta'liq 'ala sharh al-usul al-khamsa* by Manekdim.[46] Following Gimaret's arguments, the original text and the supercommentary by Manekdim exist, but still missing is 'Abd al-Jabbar's commentary – the middle text that stands between the other two. Moreover, Manekdim's *Ta'liq* presents only a paraphrase of the Qadi's *Sharh al-usul al-khamsa*. Therefore, it is difficult to estimate how long that latter text was.

Gimaret made the comparison of the two texts easier by placing at frequent intervals in the margins of his edition of *Kitab al-usul al-khamsa* the page and line numbers of corresponding passages in Manekdim's *Ta'liq 'ala sharh al-usul al-khamsa.* By comparing the two texts it is easy to confirm Gimaret's finding that virtually the same order of topics is followed in each text. Gimaret has also shown that it is easy to distinguish some of the passages of comment in Manekdim's *Ta'liq* from the commentary by the Qadi. Such formulaic phrases as *thumma qala rahimahu llah* "then he said, may God have mercy on him" indicate the voice of Manekdim introducing the words of 'Abd al-Jabbar, who by that time was deceased and required the benediction.

Still, between the known base text, the *Kitab al-usul al-khamsa*, and passages in the *Ta'liq 'ala sharh al-usul al-khamsa* directly attributable to Manekdim, there remains considerable text that could either be that of 'Abd al-Jabbar's *Sharh al-usul al-khamsa* or perhaps unmarked commentary by Manekdim. It is to be hoped that someday the *Sharh al-usul al-khamsa* will be found. This would enable scholars to analyze more precisely how 'Abd al-Jabbar, for example, worked the *Kitab al-usul al-khamsa* into the text of his commentary. Did he use direct quotations or did he paraphrase himself, as Manekdim later paraphrased him? Similarly, by comparing the Qadi's *Sharh* with Manekdim's *Ta'liq*, scholars could learn more about how selective later commentators were, what important passages they might have left out, and so on. In short, we still have much to learn about the interpretive devices of textual commentary.

We turn now from situating the text in its intellectual environment in the tenth and eleventh centuries to a discussion of Mu'tazili doctrine. In so doing, our intention is to map out for readers not only the structure of kalam doctrine and how it is understood by scholars, but also other layers of significance in the dialectical passages of the text of *Kitab al-usul al-khamsa*.

Notes

1. Qadi al-Qudat Abu l-Hasan-'Abd al-Jabbar ibn Ahmad al-Hamadhani. See *GAL*, SI: 343; *GAS*, 624–626.
2. *Tabaqat*, p. 112. Al-Hakim al-Jushami cites a certain Abu Sa'd al-Samman as saying, "I never went anywhere or entered a country in which I did not find someone who had studied with the Qadi and had been his student" (*Sharh al-'uyun*, p. 382).
3. Peters, *God's Created Speech*, pp. 14–15. Peters cites 'Abd al-Jabbar, *al-Mughni*, 20/2: 255–257 in support of his report on 'Abd al-Jabbar's self-understanding.
4. On the transmission of texts in Khurasan and Iran in the period when 'Abd al-Jabbar flourished, see Bulliet, *Islam* pp. 13–22 et passim.
5. The practice of disputation among the mutakallimun is described by van Ess, "Disputationspraxis in der islamischen Theologie," pp. 23–60. The literary development of cultural rules of behavior (*adab*) for theological and legal disputation is discussed by Miller, "Islamic Disputation Theory."

6. On this process of text formation and commentary, see Messick, *The Calligraphic State*, chapter 1, "Genealogies of the Text," pp. 15–36.

7. The discovery is described by Peters, *God's Created Speech*, pp. 25–27.

8. Purchases by the German E. Glaser and the Italian G. Capriotti are described by Caspar, "Un aspect de la pensée musulmane moderne," pp. 141–201.

9. For this and other published reports in Arabic, see Peters, *God's Created Speech*, p. 26, n. 112.

10. Volumes 6 and 20 consist in two parts each, which were substantial enough to have been published as separate books.

11. Much of the work on Mu'tazili kalam cited in this work is a product, directly or indirectly, of the discovery, editing, and publication of *al-Mughni*.

12. Unless otherwise indicated, we have relied on Wilferd Madelung's informative article on "'Abd al-Jabbar1", in *EIr* for biographical information about the Qadi.

13. *Sharh al-'uyun*, p. 366.

14. See *Sharh al-'uyun*, p. 378 and n. 78 for more on Abu Ahmad ibn Abi-Allan.

15. This intra-Mu'tazili antagonism, described briefly in the previous chapter, is mentioned in several sources and discussed by Kraemer, *Humanism in the Renaissance of Islam*, pp. 73, 179.

16. See Kraemer, *Humanism in the Renaissance of Islam*, pp. 178–191 for more information about Abu 'Abdallah al-Basri and his school in Buyid Baghdad.

17. *Tabaqat*, pp. 98–99.

18. See *Tabaqat*, p. 113.

19. For the following section on the Qadi's writings, we have relied upon lists composed by 'Abd al-Jabbar himself and by other sources indicated below. We have also consulted the recently published dissertation by Heemskerk, *Pain and Compensation in Mu'tazilite Doctrine*, esp. pp. 49–69.

20. Al-Ramahurmuzi's biography is given in *Tabaqat*, 98: 6–99: 10, including reference to the Qadi's visits to the Shaykh's mosque and beginning the dictation of *al-Mughni* there. See also *al-Mughni*, 20/2: 258: 8–14.

21. *Tabaqat*, 113: 11, and *Sharh al-'uyun*, 368: 8.

22. A work now lost but widely cited in later texts., e.g. in the *Kitab al-mu'tamad fi usul al-fiqh* (see vol. 2, p. 18 of French introduction), by the Qadi's pupil, Abu 'Abdallah al-Basri (see pp. 30–31 above). See also *Tabaqat*, 113: 11.

23. Mentioned in *Tabaqat*, 113: 8, and *Sharh al-'uyun*, 368: 1.

24. *Tabaqat*, 113: 9 and *Sharh al-'uyun*, 368: 3 mention a *Sharh al-jami'ayn*, a dual subject, which may refer to Abu Hashim's *al-Jami' al-saghir* and *al-jami' al-kabir*. Daniel Gimaret concludes that both of Abu Hashim's texts were collections of theological discussions, and he translates known passages from both works in "Matériaux pour une bibliographie des Gubba'i," pp. 313–317.

25. See *Tabaqat*, 113: 10, and *Sharh al-'uyun*, 368: 6.

26. 'Abd al-Jabbar, *Bayan mutashabih al-qur'an*. The work is described by Peters, *God's Created Speech*, pp. 11–12.

27. See *Muqulut*, 113. 6, and *Sharh al 'uyun*, 368: 17.

28. The "collections" (*jawami'*) may include Abu Hashim's *al-Jami' al-kabir*. See title number 6 in text and n. 24.
29. *Sharh al-'uyun*, 369: 3.
30. Perhaps the same as *Sharh al-a'rad* in *Tabaqat*, 113: 10 and *Sharh al-'uyun*, 368: 3.
31. *Sharh al-'uyun*, 369: 4 mentions a work titled simply *Jadal* (Disputation). On the literary history of the *adab al-jadal* genre, see Miller, "Islamic Disputation Theory."
32. *Tabaqat*, 113: 12, and *Sharh al-'uyun*, 368: 2. The work has yet to be found, except in paraphrase in Manekdim's supercommentary on it. The relationship of 'Abd al-Jabbar's text to his commentary and to Manekdim's supercommentary has been essayed by Gimaret, whose findings will be discussed in more detail below.
33. 'Uthman, *Qadi al-Qudat 'Abd al-Jabbar b. Ahmad al-Hamadhani'*.
34. In 'Amara, *Rasalil al-'adl wa l-tawhid*, pp. 189–342.
35. 'Abd al-Jabbar, *Tathbit dala'il al-nubuwwa*. Peters, *God's Created Speech*, pp. 12–13. *Tabaqat* does not mention the work at all; *Sharh al-'uyun* mentions the title *al-Adilla*, which may be a shortened form of the title.
36. 'Abd al-Jabbar's work, *Fadl al-i'tizal wa tabaqat al-mu'tazila wa mubayanatuhum li-sa'ir al-mukhalifin*, is edited and published in a single volume, along with the section on the Mu'tazila from Abu l-Qasim al-Balkhi, *Maqalat al-islamiyin*, and on the eleventh and twelfth generations of Mu'tazili teachers, those of 'Abd al-Jabbar and his pupils, from al-Hakim al-Jushami, *Kitab sharh al-'uyun*.
37. See *Tabaqat*, 113: 8 and *Sharh al-'uyun*, 368: 1. Mention of *al-Muhit* is also made by Manekdim, *Ta'liq*, 98: 7.
38. Ibn Mattawayh is discussed in chapter 2 above.
39. Ibn Mattawayh, *Kitab al-majmu' fi l-muhit bi l-taklif*, pp. 19–32.
40. See *Tabaqat*, 113: 12–13.
41. The editor of the edition, 'Abd al-Karim 'Uthman, thought it was in fact the Qadi's *Sharh al-usul al-khamsa*, 'Abd al-Jabbar's own commentary on his *Kitab al-usul al-khamsa*. See Gimaret, "Les usul al-Hamsa," and p. 53 above.
42. Abu Muhammad Isma'il b. 'Ali al-Farrazadhi. A unique Arabic MS exists, San'a Kalam 73 (Dar al-Kutub microfilm B 27800). On his identity, see Gimaret, "Les *usul al-Hamsa*," pp. 60–62.
43. The mutakallimun in this chain of transmission were identified in chapter 2 above. See Gimaret, "Les *usul al-Hamsa*," pp. 60–61 and 'Abd al-Karim 'Uthman's introduction to 'Abd al-Jabbar, *Sharh al-usul al-khamsa*, p. 24, n. 1.
44. Al-Qasim b. Ahmad b. Humayd al-Muhalli al-Wadi'i al-San'ani. The manuscript is Milan, Ambrosiana, F 192. On his identity see Gimaret, "Les *usul al-Hamsa*," pp. 60, 64–66.
45. The copyist's signature is 'Ali 'Abd Allah al-'Anari, dated Shawwal 3, A.H. 1108 /1696 C.E.
46. Gimaret, "Les *usul al-Hamsa*," pp. 47–78. The Arabic text is found on pp. 79–96. Gimaret's edition is based on Vatican Arab 989.

four

A "Thick Description" of the Five *Usul* [1]

An outline of the contents of *Kitab al-usul al-khamsa* appears below. The same outline appears as headings and subheadings of the translation in chapter 5. In the latter they appear in square brackets, indicating that these headings and subheadings do not appear in the original text. Why are such elaborate measures taken to package and present 'Abd al-Jabbar's discussion of the characteristic doctrines of the Mu'tazila?

Resisting the Text

Readers who are unfamiliar with the manner and style of *kalam* will no doubt find it difficult to follow. One reason is that *Kitab al-usul al-khamsa* is an extremely brief and succinct discussion of a broad range of doctrines defended by Mu'tazili *mutakallimun*, with no one point receiving much elaboration. It reads like a shorthand for very complicated theological disputes. In order to describe what is going on at the surface of the text, it is necessary to illumine the history of its *pre*-texts as well as its interpretation in later scholarship. In chapter 3 we pointed out that the Qadi himself had written a *sharh* or "commentary" on the original work, now lost, and that later, Manekdim wrote a *ta'liq* or "supercommentary," which in published form comes to nearly eight hundred pages. The original text that follows, then, lacks virtually all reference to the opponents to whom the Qadi alludes, who are marked in the text uniformly by the Arabic locution: *fa in qila* "then if he says (or asks)."

In the greatly more expansive supercommentary by Manekdim (hereafter, *Ta'liq*), a theological opponent, Muslim or non-Muslim, was occasionally introduced by the copyist or one dictating the text with a phrase such as *al-kalam 'ala l-ashab al-ma'arif wa Abi l-Qasim al-Balkhi*, "a discourse against those who maintain that all knowledge is necessary knowledge, namely, [the Baghdadi mutakallim] Abu l-Qasim al-Balkhi" (*Ta'liq*, p. 55) or *fasl fi l-kalam 'ala l-nasara*, "a section of discourse against the Christians" (*Ta'liq*, p. 291). Often in larger texts, such as 'Abd al-Jabbar's *Kitab al-mughni* or commentaries like Manekdim's *Ta'liq*, an opponent or an authoritative shaykh of the Mu'tazila would be mentioned at the end of the argument with a locution like: "this was the view held by the Determinists (al-Mujbira)." 'Abd al-Jabbar's *Kitab al-usul al-khamsa* gives the reader very little help in locating the text in the rich and vibrant history of theological issues debated among Muslim intellectuals in the eighth to eleventh centuries. In fleshing out traces of that larger history of the text in the rest of this chapter, we shall refer to information added in Manekdim's commentary as well as to research in more recent scholarship on kalam texts.

Another matter of style that may frustrate the modern reader is what appears to be the truncated nature of argumentation. Neither the voice of the fictional opponent, the interlocutor, nor the rejoinder by 'Abd al-Jabbar gets very far before the see-saw of "thus if he says . . . then say to him . . . " interrupts the point being made with a new point or objection. The whole argument is seldom developed beyond a few lines, especially in compendia of kalam like the *Kitab al-usul a-khamsa*. Thus, we have in the next chapter not a text that explains and situates theological arguments, as Harun Nasution's modern text does in chapter 9 below, but rather one that trains students to memorize positions held by the Bahshamiya *madhhab* of the Mu'tazila in 'Abd al-Jabbar's time. Like the modern reader, the medieval Muslim mutakallim had to clothe the fundamental text with commentary. This came from years of taking texts in dictation from various teachers, from practicing with fellow students of one's madhhab in mock debates implicit in the "if he says . . . then say to him . . . " structure, and from participating with real opponents in front of critical audiences of mutakallimun and other intellectuals. By then, much was at stake as one sought to confuse an opponent with a telling question, or trump his point with a heavy-handed rejoinder. At the level of intellectual culture in Abbasid society, the process of kalam and other religious sciences was formal in its oral-performative and written forms. And it was entertaining. As noted in chapter 3, men of power like the vizier al-Sahib ibn 'Abbad, who had appointed 'Abd al-Jabbar Chief Magistrate of Iran, invited scholars from various confessional communities and intellectual interests around themselves evenings to debate theological and other matters. Few, if any, conversions resulted from these publicly rehearsed culture wars, but positions were gained and reputations were made (and lost) under the critical scrutiny of connoisseurs. What is missing for the modern reader in our text, then, is not only information about the opponents of 'Abd al-Jabbar, which we will supply as best we can in this chapter and in notes in the next, but the cultural ethos of kalam disputation. This we ask the reader to try to imagine, on the basis of what we have been able to provide above and in chapter 2, as he or she works through *Kitab al-usul al-khamsa*.

A cross-cultural problem also arose in preparing the translation. A Muslim reading through this text will find it awkward at first because of the absence of the obligatory formulaic phrases following mention of the names of God, the prophets, and 'Ali and his family (the later commentators and copyists were Shi'a). The phrases do occur in the original Arabic. We consulted several Muslim and non-Muslim colleagues on whether or not to translate the pious phrases – which sometimes occurred twice or more in a single sentence. Interestingly, some Muslims recommended not translating the phrases – so that non-Muslims would not be distracted by them, and some non-Muslims thought we should – because they are a genuine aspect of what is said in the original text. The majority of those whom we consulted, and we ourselves, came to the considered conclusion that it were best not to translate *ta'alla, salla llah 'alayhi,* and so on, every time they occurred. We hope that our Muslim and non-Muslim colleagues who advised us to do otherwise will recognize that we have opted to follow a precedent in Western scholarship on Islam that makes some sense, especially in a book intended for readers who may not be acquainted with Islamic religious literary style.

Finally, in translating the Qur'an, we have usually consulted Marmaduke Pickthall's *The Meaning of the Glorious Koran*. In some cases, especially when Qadi 'Abd al-Jabbar was laboring to derive a more theological etymology, we have rendered the text in such a way as to allow the nonspecialist to see his point. We have also generally not followed the archaisms of Pickthall's scriptural expressions.

Outline of Text

The following outline of *Kitab al-usul al-khamsa* was constructed by the authors as a map of the arguments and doctrines in the text.

I. *First Principles*
    A.   Knowledge of God (¶¶ 1–9)
    B.   The Fundamentals of Religion (¶¶ 10–15)

II. *Divine Unicity, al-tawhid*
    A.   Inferring God's Existence from Physical Bodies (¶¶ 16–17)
    B.   Inferring God's Attributes (¶¶ 18–27)

III. *Theodicy, al-'adl* (¶¶ 28–44)

IV. *Eschatology, al-wa'd wa l-wa'id* (¶¶ 45–54)

V. *The Intermediate Position, al-manzila bayn al-manzilatayn* (¶¶ 55–58)

VI. *Commanding the Good and Prohibiting Evil, al-amr bi l-ma'ruf wa l-nahy 'an al-munkar* (¶¶ 59–67)
    A.   Political Theology: the Imamate (¶ 60)
    B.   The Validity of Tradition (¶ 61)
    C.   God's Decree (¶ 62)
    D.   Repentance and Faith (¶¶ 63–67)

Summary of Text

I. First Principles

A. Knowledge of God (¶¶ 1–9)

We have already had much to say about the Mu'tazili first principle, which holds that it is incumbent on all human beings to exercise speculative reason in order to know God. From the certainty of the rational knowledge that God exists follows access to the content of revelation, such as the commands and prohibitions, the religious duties contained in the Five Pillars, and so on. 'Abd al-Jabbar and the Mu'tazila generally contend that it all hangs on speculative reason (*al-nazar*), which is a duty that God imposes on humankind. In another commentary by a later Mu'tazili mutakallim on a work by 'Abd al-Jabbar, al-nazar is defined as "the way (or the method) to knowledge (*al-'ilm*) by virtue of that which is signified (*al-madlul*) in the sense that [the signified] necessitates and generates [the knowledge]."[2]

Paragraph 2 presents the religious motive for this argument, the fear that if one does not come to know God through reason one might inadvertently disobey Him and thus "perish" in Hellfire. The Mu'tazila held strictly, as we have seen, to the doctrine of *al-wa'd wa l-wa'id* "the promise and the threat," which meant that humans will be held accountable for what God imposes (*taklif*) on them in the way of revealed stipulations (*shara'i'*) and religious duties (*'ibadat*). In a later work, the Qadi demonstrates the importance of speculative reasoning in a discussion of how rational beings know that some pain may be ethically good because it may prevent an even greater harm. After giving several examples he goes on to argue: "In this way do we construct the discourse on the necessity of reasoning speculatively (*al-nazar*) about the method of knowing God, for by this knowledge one is liberated from the great fear which the mind presents."³ What does it mean to say that speculative reasoning is a duty, an obligation? In his commentary on the text, Manekdim says (citing, it would seem, the Qadi's own commentary [sharh] on the *Kitab al-usul al-khamsa*, now lost): "Obligatory is that which, if it is not done by one who is capable of it, deserves blame in some respects."⁴ Moreover, as the Qadi says in ¶ 3 of our text, the rest of what we need to know about religion can't be known until we first know (rationally) that there is a God. In chapter 9, Harun Nasution draws this argument out more fully (III, L and M). 'Abd al-Jabbar uses the term "grace" for God's creation of reason in humans and His giving them the power and moral duty to act for the good; indeed, it is the primary grace (¶ 4). He then moves in the next few paragraphs to identify that on which speculative reasoning is based, that is, the kinds of evidence (*dalil*, pl. *adilla*) on which knowledge of God is drawn.

The Qadi names four kinds of evidence on which al-nazar is appropriately based: rational argument (*hujjat al-'aql*), the Book or scripture (*al-kitab*), the paradigmatic practice of the Prophet Muhammad (*Sunna*), and the consensus of the community (*ijma'*). Rational argument is primary because, as we have already pointed out, the validity of scripture, Sunna and communal consensus all rest on knowing that God is and that He is truthful and would not deceive His creatures. The four kinds of evidence given in ¶ 6 are like the four fundamentals of Islamic jurisprudence (*usul al-fiqh*) with the exception that rational argument has been added as the first and foremost, and the more orthodox interpretive form of reasoning by analogy (*al-qiyas*) has been deleted. The Qadi's list of acceptable modes of proof must have raised some questions among opponents, for example, among the scholar-jurists (*fuqaha'*). Thus, we find in Manekdim's supercommentary the explanation that such additional intellectual tools as analogical reasoning and relying on single reports are established implicitly in scripture, Sunna, and communal consensus (*Ta'liq*, p. 88).⁵

The primacy, among the four kinds of evidence, of rational argument that leads to knowledge of God rests on an argument from contingency.

The Qadi reasons that bodies (indeed his own body) are contingent and not eternal. Therefore there must be another, noncontingent being who is the designer and creator of contingent beings. This process of reasoning from the contingency of created bodies to the necessary conclusion that there must be an eternal creator appears in greater length in Manekdim's commentary (*Ta'liq*, pp. 87–120). There Manekdim specifies particular opponents of the argument from contingency, for example, astrologers, who also appear to be rationalists, but who assert that the stars influence the behavior of sublunar beings. This is irrational, Manekdim points out, in drawing out 'Abd al-Jabbar's commentary, because stars do not have the attribute of living, much less that of power; and a freely choosing agent (*al-fa'il al-mukhtar*) who acts effectively upon others must be living and possess power (*Ta'liq*, pp.120–122).

B. *The Fundamentals of Religion* (¶¶ 10–15)

In the previous chapter, we presented some evidence to suggest that *Kitab al-usul al-khamsa* may have been among the earliest writings by 'Abd al-Jabbar. It belongs to a kalam genre of works on the *usul al-din*, the fundamentals of religion. The early Mu'tazila identified five basic doctrines, or clusters of doctrine, that marked their madhhab off from others. These five doctrines are given in ¶ 10 of the translation as: (1) divine unity (*al-tawhid*); (2) divine justice or theodicy (*al-'adl*); (3) the promise and the threat (of reward or punishment in the hereafter, *al-wa'd wa l-wa'id*); (4) the "intermediate position" on the matter of who is a true Muslim (*al-manzila bayn al-manzilatayn*); and (5) commanding the good and prohibiting evil (*al-amr bi l-ma'ruf wa l-nahy 'an al-munkar*). They are also discussed in Harun Nasution's text, translated in chapter 9 below, in III, P. Elsewhere, 'Abd al-Jabbar reduced to two the five main points of doctrine, unity and justice (*al-tawhid wa l-'adl*), with the latter three points of doctrine subsumed under the second, al-'adl. Accordingly, the later Mu'tazili mutakallimun are often referred to as the People of Unity and Justice (*ahl al-tawhid wa l-'adl*).

In his commentary on ¶ 10, Manekdim says that in a later work, *al-Mughni*, the Qadi set the number of fundamentals of religion at two: unity and justice. The full title of that work, *Kitab al-mughni fi l-tawhid wa l-'adl* bears out his remark, as do the extant portions of the text. Manekdim goes on to say:

[the Qadi] mentioned in *al-Mukhtasar al-Husna*[6] that the usul al-din are four: unity, justice, prophethood (*al-nubuwwat*) and divine legislation (*al-shara'i*); and ['Abd al-Jabbar] made the promise and the threat, the names and rules [i.e., the intermediate position], and commanding the good and prohibiting evil subdivisions of divine legislation. And he mentioned in the *Kitab* [*al-usul al-khamsa* (¶ 10 in the next chapter)] that the five are unity, justice, the promise and the threat, the intermediate position, and commanding the good and prohibiting evil, in order to show the differences among people concerning each of these usul. Best is what he mentioned in *al-Mughni*, that prophethood and divine legislation are included under [the *asl* of] justice.[7]

Nonetheless, it is the five fundamental doctrines given above that, in 'Abd al-Jabbar's time, structured the main contents of many kalam treatises and which are given as defining characteristics of the Mu'tazila by Harun Nasution.

In his still highly regarded article on the Mu'tazila for the first edition of *The Encyclopaedia of Islam*, H. S. Nyberg had suggested that the five fundamentals, *al-usul al-khamsa*, formed the main points of Mu'tazili propaganda in the earliest period, and only later served more structurally as "a kind of framework of speculative dogmatics."[8] In Nyberg's view, all five principles – unity, justice, promise and threat, intermediate position, and commanding the good – could be traced to the circle of al-Hasan al-Basri from which Wasil ibn 'Ata' and 'Ubayd ibn 'Amr emerged as the first Mu'tazili mutakallimun.

In his discussion of the historical development of the five principles, Wilferd Madelung argues that even though absolute divine unity (al-tawhid) was logically prior, the principle of justice (al-'adl) was more urgently debated in the beginning. Caliph 'Abd al-Malik (*reg.* 685–705) and his immediate successors had condemned the doctrine of *al-kalam fi l-qadar*, the discourse of the Qadariya, which held that evil and ethically bad things exist in the world not through divine agency but through human agency and other causes. For the Qadariya, God is removed from doing ethically bad and evil acts. Caliphs like 'Abd al-Malik rightly understood *al-kalam fi l-qadar* as a theological critique of Umayyad rule. In his famous exchange of letters with Caliph 'Abd al-Malik, al-Hasan al-Basri develops an argument based on numerous proof texts from the Qur'an, for example Sura 4:123 which says: "he who does evil will gain his reward for it." Unethical state practices that transpired under the aegis of Umayyad rule, al-Hasan al-Basri was saying, were to be attributed to the Umayyad rulers, not to God. This was, as one analyst of the text has noted, a clear case of political theology.[9] Similarly, *al-wa'd wa l-wa'id*, "the promise and the threat," and *al-manzila bayn al-manzilatayn*, "the intermediate position," can also be traced to the circle of al-Hasan al-Basri. Recall from chapter 2 that the early Mu'tazili position on the promise and the threat was a critique of the Murji'i teaching that the grave sinner was to be held by other Muslims to be just as much a believer as Muslims without grave sin. The Mu'tazila sought to refute both the the Khariji and the Murji'i positions.[10]

Madelung argues that the first Mu'tazili principle we find in texts like 'Abd al-Jabbar's *Kitab al-usul al-khamsa*, unity (al-tawhid), was historically the last to emerge. It played no role in the recorded teachings of al-Hasan al-Basri. It first appears in doctrines attributed to al-Wasil ibn 'Ata' and to al-Jahm ibn Safwan (d. 745), an uncompromising monotheist (*al-muwahhid*) who used the doctrine of tawhid as a polemical weapon against Buddhist monks (known in kalam as the *sumaniya*) and others.[11]

In his supercommentary, Manekdim does not add much to the Qadi's basic text, except to identify some of the opponents of the five fundamentals of Mu'tazili kalam. Those who would deny God's unity are labeled unbeliever (*kafir*), which bore serious consequences in Islamic law and society (*Ta'liq*, p. 125).[12] Elsewhere, idol worship, star worship, the Sabeans of ancient Harran, the dualism of Zoroastrians, and the tritheism of Christians are refuted at greater length under the doctrine of tawhid.[13] Those who deny that God is just, the second fundamental of Mu'tazili kalam, maintain that God is capable of all manner of evil because He is omnipotent and thus what He is capable of doing cannot be limited. It follows from their position that God would be capable of iniquity and lying, of manifesting miracles through liars, and of punishing the children of polytheists for their parents' sins. All this, in the Mu'tazili view, is also unbelief (*Ta'liq*, p. 125).

Those who oppose the fundamental Mu'tazili doctrine of the promise and the threat, by saying that God does not promise eschatological reward for obedience in this life or threaten punishment for those who are disobedient (the Murji'a are meant but not named) are also regarded as kafirs. They deny the religion of the Prophet. The Murji'a and others might claim that it would be noble on God's part to rescind the punishment He threatens; or that *sub specie aeternitatis* God knows of conditions or exceptions regarding human obedience and sin that are unknown to humans. The first argument Manekdim calls unbelief; the second he terms the cause of error (*mukhti'*, ibid.), which in Islamic law is less consequential than unbelief (*kufr*).

In his *Ta'liq* (p. 126), Manekdim comments that among those who oppose the Mu'tazili doctrine of the intermediate position are those who say that grave sinners are, under the Shari'a, the same as dualists, Magians, and others, namely, they are kafirs. Others say, Manekdim tells us, that grave sinners have the Shari'a status of believers. Again, the Khawarij and Murji'a, respectively, are meant. Manekdim also mentions those who say a grave sinner is neither a believer nor an unbeliever, but they are nonetheless to be called believers; those he regards as being in error. The fifth Mu'tazili fundamental of commanding the good and prohibiting evil, *al-amr bi l-ma'ruf wa l-nahy 'an al-munkar*, finds opponents among those who deny that God imposed this on human beings. They are unbelievers, Manekdim reasons, because in effect they are denying what follows necessarily from the religion of the Prophet Muhammad. The phrase *al-amr bi l-ma'ruf wa l-nahy 'an al-munkar* itself occurs several times in the Qur'an. Manekdim, himself a Zaydi Shi'i mutakallim, mentions that, on the other side, they are in error who allow that commanding the good and prohibiting evil is an obligatory principle, but only under the existence of an Imam (*Ta'liq*, p. 126). He is referring to the Imami or Twelver Shi'a. At issue in this case is the Shi'i doctrine of dissimulation (*taqiya*) in which Shi'ites under persecution may disclaim their religious views publicly (but not privately, before God). The Zaydi Shi'a did not follow the Imami and Isma'ili Shi'a in allowing taqiya and Manekdim calls it error to do so, but not unbelief.

II.   Divine Unicity (¶¶ 16–27)

Our text returns in the sixteenth paragraph to the general problem of divine unity and the theological basis for holding that God's being is different from that of His creatures, as well as the assertion that God is one, not more.[14] This was the sometimes hotly disputed problem of divine attributes (*sifat allah*), to which Harun Nasution also gives considerable space for discussion. Why was this so? By the time 'Abd al-Jabbar was writing in the latter part of the tenth century, Islam was finally the faith of the majority of people living within lands under Islamic rule. The earlier socio-political function of the Mu'tazili mutakallimun of spreading the faith (commanding the good and prohibiting evil) and disputing with Christians, Jews, polytheists, Zoroastrians, and others was no longer as urgent as it once had been. The doctrine of God's unity, specifically the controversial matter of what could be attributed to God, was now a matter of sharp theological conflict among theologians within Islam vying for political favor with the new amirs and sultans who were challenging Abbasid rule. The most pronounced differences among Muslims themselves by the tenth century was between what we have identified in this study as the rationalist and the traditionalist theological positions. Specifically, the Mu'tazila were in sharp disagreement over many issues with the Hanbaliya, the Ash'ariya, and in some of the eastern regions, the Maturidiya.

Given the early and persistent struggle of Islam with polytheism, various forms of dualism, Christian tritheism, and philosophical atheism (*ilhad*), the paramount question posed by Mu'tazili mutakallimun was: what, if anything, can be said about, that is, attributed to, God's being? The Mu'tazila were described by their opponents as having advanced a *theologia via negativa*, that is, refraining from attributing any thing or quality to God, preferring instead to state what God is not. Al-Ash'ari, the early tenth-century Mu'tazilite who left Mu'tazili circles to establish a kalam madhhab in the traditionalist mode, characterized the Mu'tazili concept of God as follows:

> The Mu'tazila agree that God is one; there is no thing like him; he is hearing, seeing; he is not a body (*jism*), not a form, not flesh and blood, not an individual, not substance nor attribute . . . not begetting nor begotten; magnitudes do not comprehend him nor veils cover him; the senses do not attain him; he is not comparable with men and does not resemble creatures in any respect . . . he is ceaselessly first, precedent, going before originated things, existent before created things; he is ceaselessly knowing, powerful, living . . . not as [men are] knowing, powerful, living . . . he may not experience benefit or harm, joy or gladness, hurt or pain . . . he is too holy to be touched by women or to have a consort and children.[15]

Mu'tazili mutakallimun not only proactively challenged various non-Muslim doctrines of God circulating in *dar al-islam* during the early centuries – conceptions that contradicted their own concept of divine unicity, tawhid. From the beginning, proto-Mu'tazila like Wasil ibn 'Ata' reacted sharply to a popular view of God among traditionalist Muslims, who took Quranic statements about God literally. For example, there is the revealed statement (Q. 38:75) "O Iblis! What prevents you from prostrating yourself before that which I created with my two hands?" The Qur'an also describes God as seated on a throne, having a face, seeing with His eyes; therefore God must have a body. Given the enormous piety that surrounded the text of the Qur'an, it was perhaps inevitable that many Muslims would take all references to God within the text literally. Those who held such a view of God – and many of the *ahl al-Hadith* and other traditionalists did – were labeled by the mutakallimun as the Mushabbiha, the purveyors of anthropomorphism (*tashbih*) and as the Mujassima, those who embodied God (*tajsim*).

As the passage from al-Ash'ari above shows, the Mu'tazila denied the attribution of any human qualities to God. Elsewhere in the same source,

al-Ash'ari discloses that the Mu'tazila interpreted such reference in the
Qur'an to God's body metaphorically (*ta'wil*), thus taking, for example,
reference to God's eye to mean His knowledge,[16] or to God's face to mean
His essence. A later Ash'ari heresiographer, al-Shahrastani, said that as early
as Wasil ibn 'Ata' (d. 748 in Basra at the end of the Umayyad Kingdom) a
technical discourse against anthropomorphism was forming in proto-
Mu'tazili circles. According to al-Shahrastani, Wasil said: "whoever asserts
that an accident (*ma'na*) [or] attribute (*sifa*) is eternal asserts two
divinities."[17] That is, if one asserts that God has an attribute which is other
than Himself or His essence (power, knowledge, speech, etc.) and if such
attributes eternally characterized the eternal God, then there would have to
be more than one Eternal Being, and this would be absurd and anathema to
the absolute concept of tawhid, divine unicity.

Who were the opponents, then, presumed in 'Abd al-Jabbar's succinct
statement of the manner in which God possessed such characteristics as
power, knowledge, living, etc., ¶¶ 18–27 in the *Kitab al-usul al-khamsa*? *Inter
alia*, it was the Ash'ariya and al-Ash'ari's precursors among the
traditionalists. For example, 'Abdallah ibn Kullab (d. 854), a mutakallim
who lived during the Abbasid inquisition (*mihna*) of Ahmad ibn Hanbal and
who was to influence the development of Ash'ari doctrine in the next
generation, taught the doctrine that God's names (i.e., His ninety-nine
Beautiful Names) were His attributes. In a section on Ibn Kullab's teaching
"concerning the names and the attributes," al-Ash'ari reports that Ibn
Kullab held God's names and attributes to be eternal, and that to say that
God is powerful (*qadir*) means He has the attribute of power (*qudra*), and so
on through the list of attributes. Recognizing the logical problem with which
he would be charged by the Mu'tazila, Ibn Kullab said that God's "names
and essential attributes are not God and not other than He, but they inhere
in God, for attributes cannot inhere in [other] attributes."[18]

The Mu'tazila tackled the problem raised when one asserted the
existence of divine attributes in an interesting way. Prior to Ibn Kullab, his
older Mu'tazili contemporary Abu l-Hudhayl had said that God "is knowing
by virtue of a knowledge which is He, and He is powerful by virtue of a
power which is He . . . and so on for His other essential attributes   (*sa'ir
sifatihi li dhatihi*)."[19] This led later Mu'tazili mutakallimun like Abu 'Ali al-
Jubba'i to distinguish between God's essential attributes (the attributes that
inhere in His essence, *sifatuhu li dhatihi*) and His active attributes (*sifat al-
af'al*), which are associated with God's acting in the world, His *operatio ad
extra*. Neither is separate from God and thus they cannot be coeternal with
Him. However, as Watt points out:

[t]he general effect of this account is the negative one of shutting man off from any real knowledge of God. Though the human mind takes each attribute or name as different from the others, it does not follow that there is any difference in God; and therefore all the names tell us is that God is.[20]

In other words, unlike the supple and heady conflicts with Christians, polytheists, dualists, and others, who were seen by the Mu'tazila to have compromised God's oneness and unity, the dispute among the mutakallimun within Islam was more narrowly about language, not about God per se.

It was al-Jubba'i's son and contemporary of al-Ash'ari, Abu Hashim ibn al-Jubba'i (d. 933), who constructed the solution to the problem of divine attributes that was to be followed by later teachers of the Bahshamiya branch of the Mu'tazila, such as 'Abd al-Jabbar. Again turning to language analysis, Abu Hashim proposes that in a common Arabic locution such as "Zayd came riding" (*ja'a zaydun rakiban*), the accusative adverbial "riding(ly)" (*rakiban*) expresses a state or mode (*hal*, pl. *ahwal*). Watt explains how this was applied to the problem of attributes. The hal expresses, he says,

> the state or condition or circumstances of the subject (or object) of the act while the act was taking place. In Abu-Hashim's theory, when we say "God is knowing", "knowing" expresses the *hal* or "state" of God's essence distinct from that essence . . . [W]e cannot say "knowing" is existent or non-existent apart from God. In other words the theory is avoiding the suggestion of the word *sifa* and of nouns such as "knowledge" (*'ilm*) that these have a quasi and substantive and partly independent existence within the being or essence of God.[21]

Watt goes on to point out that Abu Hashim's theory of hal was modified and adopted by Ash'ari theologians in the following century. Thus, a problem that was largely linguistic found a solution in language itself. That does not mean that disputes about the appropriate language for divine attributes were bloodless and devoid of passion. As Harun Nasution's rather lengthy discussion of the problem shows, it remained a matter in which the mutakallimun continued to have a large stake.

In *Kitab al-usul al-khamsa*, 'Abd al-Jabbar's language presumes Abu Hashim's theory of "states." His succinct language is focused on the problem that if God does not have independent attributes, how do we know that He is omnipotent, knowing, living, hearing, existent, eternal, and self-sufficient? The Qadi adduces various evidentiary proofs (*adilla*) that demonstrate that it is valid to assert that God is powerful, knowing, etc. He then follows with the *theologia via negativa* to which we referred above, adducing proofs that God cannot have a physical body and that He is unseen. On this basis he concludes in the last paragraph in this section that God must be one, and that there cannot be besides Him a second (or third, or fourth, etc.) who is eternal in Himself. At the end of the paragraph he specifically names the dualists and Christians as his opponents in this discussion.

III. Theodicy (¶¶ 28–44)

The Qadi's text next turns to another extremely important cluster of problems for the early mutakallimun, the claim that God cannot act in an evil or unethical manner, the doctrine of al-'adl. Associated with this is Mu'tazili doctrine that humans are morally answerable to God for their actions. This was the old contest between the asserters of free will (Qadariya) and the Compulsionists (Mujbira, to which the Qadi returns at the end of the text) and later the Mu'tazila and the traditionalists, including the Ash'ariya, respectively. As we showed in chapter 1, citing Plato's *Euthyphro*, it was a larger problem for any society in whose worldview an omnipotent deity and universal justice are linked and in logical tension.

Madelung has parsed the problem of divine justice (al-'adl) into two theses: (1) God wants good for humans; He does not will or create evil and lying, etc. God offers guidance (*huda*) in the right path, but does not force humans to go astray (*dalal*). (2) It follows from this that acts and deeds, and thus punishable immoral acts, are not forced on creatures by their creator. God would be unjust if He punished His creatures for acts that He created in them.[22] We have discussed the Mu'tazili doctrine of al-'adl already at some length. Here, we may make just a few additional points to place it in theological context.

Within the kalam, Mu'tazili discourse in particular, theodicy was framed by the notion of taklif; God as *al-mukallif* imposes duties on human beings. Humans, then, are often referred to by the plural form of the passive participle, *mukallafun*. We are thus far dealing with a verbal noun, an active participle, and a passive participle that surround the notion of "the obligating," God the "obligator," and humankind the "obligated." A key issue is the one the Qadi mentions in ¶ 30:

> If it is asked: What is the proof that the power (*qudra*) precedes the act?
> Say to him: Because if it were simultaneous with the act then necessarily
> the unbeliever would not have had the capacity [power] to have faith.
> And if he did not have the power for it, it would not be good for God to
> command it, because God does not impose on human beings what they

do not have the power to do, according to His saying: "On no one does Allah place a burden greater than he can bear" (Q. 65:7).

Therefore, as Watt points out, paraphrasing a passage in the Qur'an " '*taklif* implies *qudra*', 'imposition of duty implies power'."[23] The Ash'ariya and other traditionalists held that the qudra or power that is the efficient cause of an act is created by God at the time of the act and was a power for that act alone, not the power to act in general.

It was one of the earliest Mu'tazili mutakallimun, Dirar ibn 'Amr (d. ca. 815) who, in differing from most of his colleagues on this particular point, established a way for the Ash'ariya later to contend that power (*istata'a*, the term preferred by the Ash'ariya over qudra) does not precede the act, but is created at the moment of the act by God in conjunction with the human will to act. Al-Ash'ari said of Dirar:

> That which separated Dirar ibn 'Amr from the Mu'tazila was his statement that human acts are created (*makhluqa*) and that an act has two agents, one of whom created it (*khalaqahu*), namely God, and the other acquired it (*iktasabahu*), namely the human being; [he also said] God is the agent of human acts in reality, and [humans] are the agents of their acts in reality. And he used to claim that power [exists] prior to the act and is coterminous with it.[24]

This move on Dirar's part became refined later and was known among the Ash'arites by the term *kasb*, the root of the Arabic verb used above, *iktasaba*. Watt speculates that the Ash'ariya (and perhaps Dirar and his followers) preferred the term "istata'a" over "qudra" for "power" because the former was derived from the root *ta'a*, meaning "obedience."[25] Be that as it may, it is important to note Richard Frank's translation of "qudra" specifically as "the power of autonomous action."[26] Dirar, and later the Ash'ariya, denied (or seriously qualified) the notion that human beings had the power to act independently of God's creative power.

The position taken by the Mu'tazila left them open to the question that appears in ¶ 31 of *Kitab al-usul al-khamsa*, namely, why do they "deny that everything that happens in the world is by the will and wish of God?" This question arose as a consequence of the extreme sovereignty and omnipotence of God in the traditionalist worldview. In his answer, the Qadi argues that bad things do happen in the world, but to attribute them to God would be like saying that a wise man would "command something he loathed" and prohibit "something he wanted." Here, divine commanding and prohibiting seem to be equated with God willing and exercising His total power over and within His creation. The Qadi then asserts, in so many words: if it is possible, in the Ash'ari worldview, for God to will (command) that which He hates and is detestable, He would in effect be willing to curse and condemn Himself, since the Ash'ariya remove from humans the power to act autonomously.

Where the argument became heated was over specific cases of divine willing of punishments that seemed, *prima facie*, to be patently unjust. An interlocutor is made to ask in the Qadi's text (¶ 34): "What do you say about the affliction of the children of polytheists, do you allow that God would do it? Say to him: may God protect me from permitting that of Him, for it would be an injustice and an [act of] insolence." He cites a few Qur'an verses and a well-attested Hadith in support of his claim, which otherwise is supported by the argument: "punishment is morally good only for one who has committed a sin . . . Now, a child is without sin, so, how can it be said that God would punish him?" Manekdim's distaste for the Ash'ari position is manifest in his supercommentary: "[Qadi 'Abd al-Jabbar] entered into this entire preceding discussion [of theodicy] without making specific mention [of his opponents]; however, some of the Mujbira (Compulsionists, i.e., Ash'ariya) contradicted [our position] and attached weak-minded counter-arguments, which we shall mention later, God willing."[27]

With ¶ 40, the Qadi begins a discussion of revelation as divine favor. An implication of the Mu'tazili theodicy is that if God is just He must make His truth (*al-haqq*) available to all humans. Here the text makes a transition that links theodicy to the revelation, which introduces another problematic in kalam. The interlocutor asks: "Has God indicated the truth to everyone He has created, and has He guided them to religion?" In his supercommentary, Manekdim expands on 'Abd al-Jabbar's example of food being offered to starving persons; these examples perfectly express the Mu'tazili theodicy and the role of revelation in the Mu'tazili cosmology:

> [God's making His truth available to all humans] is like someone who casts down his rope to two drowning persons so that they can cling to it. One of them clings to it and thereby is saved; the other does not cling to it and thereby perishes. And it is like someone offering food to two people overcome by hunger and on the point of dying because of it. Then one of them takes some of the food and does not die; the other does not and thus dies and is destroyed. Just as the one who offered the food and threw out the rope was benevolent toward both of them equally [in each case], and just as it could not be said that he was benevolent only toward the one who received [the food or the rope] and not toward the one who did not, so in this case [of God making the truth available to everyone].[28]

Manekdim's extended discussion of this point makes clear what the issue is. Is a kafir, a nonbeliever, really like a starving person who turns down food, thus starving himself? For the believer (*al-mu'min*) chooses faith (*al-iman*), but the unbeliever doesn't always have that opportunity. Moreover, a cynical disputant might claim that an omnipotent donor presumably would know which starving person will accept the food and give the food to that person. This is the position taken by the Ash'ariya and other traditionalists, and 'Abd al-Jabbar and Manekdim reject it out of hand.

Manekdim's supercommentary argues, contrary to the Ash'ari interlocutor, that it would be ethically wrong for God to impose the Shari'a (taklif) on the unbeliever if He knew in advance that that person would act to become a kafir, just as it would be wrong not to offer food to a starving person if one knew that person would not accept it. Again, we see in this exchange between 'Abd al-Jabbar/Manekdim and Ash'ari opponents the choice between rational intuitionism and theistic subjectivism, the terms used by George F. Hourani in his excellent study of the ethics of 'Abd al-Jabbar. It had been posed by Socrates, as we have shown, in the *Euthyphro*: does God will to send down laws to humans because the laws are themselves good (holy), or are the laws good because He sent them down? (See chapter 1.) The former position was taken by the Mu'tazila, the latter by the Ash'ariya. George F. Hourani distinguished between these two positions in Islam in a passage worth quoting:

> Now the Ash'ariyya (Ash'arites), maintaining as they did that values in action are determined exclusively by the will of God, known to man through revelation and certain legitimate extensions, had little to say on a general theory of ethics beyond criticism of their opponents. The logical consequence of their position was just the theory of an all-embracing divine law, which had indeed been worked out by jurists prior to Ash'ari. It was their opponents, the Mu'tazila, who had the strongest stimulus to develop a system of ethics in the sense understood today. For, since they asserted the efficacy of natural reason as a source of ethical knowledge, they were inevitably challenged in the course of the controversy to show how it was possible for man by his unaided reason to know the right and the good, and if possible to define what these were in their reality, independent of the divine will.[29]

How does 'Abd al-Jabbar, Manekdim, or indeed Harun Nasution know that it is good to offer food to a starving man, and bad not to, even if one knows the starving man won't accept it? How, the Ash'ariya and the traditionalists ask, can one know the good without revelation? The Mu'tazila maintained that we know intuitively that injustice, iniquity, murder, theft, etc., are ethically wrong. They offered reasons, but they started with propositions about what is ethical and what is not that they believed all rational people could agree upon. This was the basis on which they determined God's *sifat al-af'al*, His *operatio ad extra*, His characteristic acts outside Himself upon His creation. Revelation was situated within this cosmology as a blessing, a grace from a God whose ethical and just workings could first be established by reason. In chapter 9 we notice that Nasution is at pains to stress the importance of knowing, after reason does its work, what the revelation can teach humans, such as the religious duties ('ibadat), etc.

Inevitably the question had to be asked: if humans can know the good and the bad by reason, then can one be saved from the punishment of Hellfire without revelation? Abu 'Ali al-Jubba'i, al-Ash'ari's mentor for many years before the latter converted to a more traditionalist theology, apparently argued that one could. A person living outside Dar al-Islam who had never heard of the Quranic revelation and had never received the invitation (*da'wa*) to Islamic faith was not automatically destined to eternal punishment. Through the exercise of reason such a person, Abu 'Ali argued, could determine the ethical content contained in the revelation, live by it, and thus be saved. It is not clear just how widely his position was accepted among the Bahshamiya in the tenth and eleventh centuries. Traditionalist Muslims, in the past and in the present, have strenuously rejected the troubling implication of rationalism that the revelation is ultimately unnecessary. Ibn al-Rawandi, the late ninth-century renegade *mutakallim* who critiqued the Mu'tazila precisely on this point, put in the mouths of the Hindu Brahmins the following logical dilemma: either the content of revelation is logical, in which case it should be followed, or it is absurd, in which case it would be irrational to follow it.[30]

Neither 'Abd al-Jabbar nor Harun Nasution is willing to go as far as Abu 'Ali al-Jubba'i in limiting the significance of divine revelation. This becomes clear in ¶¶ 42 and 43, where the divine goodness in revealing the Qur'an and in sending the Prophet Muhammad is extolled in language that is far more religious than much of the rest of the text. Buried within the Qadi's response to question 42 is the hint of a Mu'tazili doctrine that was controversial in the extreme: the claim that the Qur'an was created, not eternal with God. This was the issue that so sharply provoked Ahmad ibn Hanbal and other traditionalists during Caliph al-Ma'mun's reign and led to the inquisition (*mihna*) that both imprisoned Ibn Hanbal and also popularized his traditionalist stance. What we notice, both in this text and in Nasution's, is that the doctrine of *khalq al-qur'an*, the creation of the

Qur'an, is hardly mentioned. In Nasution's case it is probably because the doctrine is still extremely controversial among Islamists and traditionalists, and Nasution did not find it necessary to risk discussing such a controversial Mu'tazili view of the Qur'an in order to make his case for Mu'tazili rationalism in Indonesia today.

We learn from 'Abd al-Jabbar's *Kitab al-usul al-khamsa* that this infamous ninth-century clash of religion and politics, in which the Mu'tazili doctrine of the created Qur'an was enforced by the state but resisted by the population at large, fitted into the Bahshamiya system of kalam under theodicy. After defending the revelation as one of God's favors, he goes on in ¶ 42 to say that just as God created His creatures, and hence His doing good is a created thing, so His speech, the Qur'an, is one of His favors and it is a created thing. He offers several Quranic verses to provide linguistic evidence that the revelation views itself as created (like all that is not God) in a specific time and place. The Qadi's line of argument attempts to demonstrate that the Qur'an is a part of creation. Nevertheless, because He created it, humans marvel at it and no one else can produce the like of it. 'Abd al-Jabbar quotes a passage about the wonder of the Quranic text, well known to Muslims. God says to the Prophet: "Say, if the whole of humankind and the jinns were to gather together to produce the like of this Qur'an, they could not produce the like thereof, even if they backed up each other with help and support" (Q. 17:88).

Manekdim's supercommentary again identifies the Ash'ariya (al-Mujbira) as the opponents on this issue. This controversy was much older than al-Ash'ari and rise of the Ash'ari madhhab in the tenth century, however. Already in the ninth century, the creation of the Qur'an was a doctrine taught by the Mu'tazila, as we know from the mihna (833–848). In an important article on the history of this controversial doctrine, Madelung analyzes the charge that the doctrine can be traced to two unpopular figures during the period of Abbasid rebellion against the Umayyads, Ja'd ibn Dirham, who was executed in 743, and Jahm ibn Safwan, who died in the rebellion of Harith ibn Surayj in 745. This would locate the origins of the controversy as at least contemporaneous with the circle of al-Hasan al-Basri, Wasil ibn 'Ata' and Dirar ibn 'Amr. Citing Ahmad ibn Hanbal's surviving refutation of Jahm and his followers, Madelung identifies Jahm's motive: in saying that "God has never spoken and does not speak" Jahm was attacking anthropomorphism (which we have discussed above).[31]

It was not until Ahmad ibn Hanbal (d. 855) and 'Abdallah ibn Kullab (d. 854) that the traditionalist counter-doctrine of the eternal Qur'an was formulated, later to be adopted and refined by the Ash'ariya and the

Maturidiya. Madelung further suggests that it was the mihna that forced the formation of the dispute precisely over the creation versus the eternity of the Qur'an. He cites Ibn Taymiya (d. 1328), the Hanbali traditionalist reformer whom we shall discuss at greater length in chapter 6, as not entirely agreeing with the Ash'ari position. Ibn Taymiya said that the Prophet's Companions and their followers among the Salaf – venerable early generations of Muslims – held only that the Qur'an was the word of God. In response to Ja'd and Jahm's assertion that the Qur'an was created, traditionalists counter-asserted that it was not created. Ibn Taymiya believed, then, that the Salaf did not, in denying that the Qur'an was created, intend to affirm that it was eternal. Ibn Taymiya held that it was Ibn Kullab who constructed the doctrinal language asserting the eternity of the Qur'an. Madelung believes it was in fact Ibn Hanbal who did so, and that it was in response to the mihna. He adduces this from a preserved letter from Ibn Hanbal to Caliph al-Ma'mun. Madelung concludes, "it was no doubt more due to the authority of Ibn Hanbal than to Ibn Kullab that the eternity of the Koran henceforth became a dogma for the great majority of the Sunnite Muslims." [32]

What makes this particular Mu'tazili point of doctrine, the creation of the Qur'an, interesting for our study is that several modernists, beginning with Muhammad 'Abduh, have advocated the Mu'tazili position on the temporal nature of revelation. As we will see in chapter 10, this is no less controversial than it was in ninth-century Baghdad. Structurally, the issue is not unlike the Christological debates of early Christianity – the struggle to locate the revelation (Christ) primarily in the nature of his humanity, on the one side, or in the nature of his divinity, on the other.

In ¶ 43 of this section on revelation as divine favor, another central topic of kalam is introduced by the Qadi, the miraculous inimitability of the Qur'an (*i'jaz al- qur'an*). By the ninth century, the mutakallimun had advanced an argument for the authority of the Prophet Muhammad that was based on the divine production of a miracle in the hands of the Prophet, just as Moses had parted the Red Sea and Jesus had raised the dead. Construction of the argument along these lines shows that opponents in this case included non-Muslim scriptuaries living within Dar al-Islam, particularly Christians and Jews. By 'Abd al-Jabbar's time, the doctrine of i'jaz al-qur'an had been adopted by the Ash'ariya with little modification. The term for miracle used by the Mu'tazila, and then later orthodox Islam more generally, is *mu'jiz*, which means the rendering of someone or something powerless or incapable of something. Nonetheless, "mu'jiz" (and *mu'jiza*) meant prophetic miracles generally. As a technical term for the Quranic miracle, there is little textual evidence for its use prior to the late ninth century.[33] Al-Jahiz (d. 869), the littérateur and defender of the Mu'tazila during the intense period of post-mihna attacks, may have been the first to use mu'jiz in its more general sense of referring to any miracle the Prophet is reported to have performed. In ¶ 43, after mentioning the Quranic miracle, 'Abd al-Jabbar mentions several others that are frequently reported in medieval discussions of Muhammad's miracles, such as the tree that bent over to offer shade to the Prophet when he preached. In its more technical sense, the phrase in the verbal noun form of i'jaz (al-qur'an) seems to have emerged in the circle of al-Jubba'i. It appears in the title of one of al-Jubba'i's students, Abu 'Abdallah Muhammad al-Wasiti (d. 919), an older contemporary of Abu Hashim and al-Ash'ari.[34] In the next two centuries, the Bahshamiya became the most avid defenders of the doctrine of i'jaz al-qur'an.

The main points of the argument are touched upon by 'Abd al-Jabbar. At the end of ¶ 42, he quotes the "challenge" (*tahaddi*) that appears in Qur'an 17:88 and in four other verses: God orders Muhammad to challenge the Arabs of Muhammad's time, who were regarded by later generations of Muslims as the most gifted orators and poets of all time, to produce ten suras, even one sura, like that of the Qur'an. Among the Bedouin, cultural conflict was often managed ritually in front of critical tribesmen by tribal poets, who challenged the poets of other tribes to match a line of poetry. This was known as the contest, the *mu'arada*, a term that came into the kalam to describe the cultural context that surrounded this miracle in particular. The Qur'an does not report that any Arab took up the challenge. The Bahshamiya argue that since the Arabs hated Muhammad and his mission, they surely would have accepted the challenge in order to shatter his miracle and expose him as not being a prophet. Something as important as defeating the Prophet, so the argument goes, would surely have been reported, but it wasn't. The violent conflict between the Meccans and the Prophet and his followers in Medina are brought in as evidence that the Arabs could not imitate the Qur'an so they had to resort to force to resist his mission.[35]

The reason the Arabs could not imitate Quranic speech lay in the linguistic purity (*fasaha*) of the text of the Qur'an itself, according to 'Abd al-Jabbar and the Bahshamiya. What the Qadi leaves out of his brief reference to this doctrine is the philosophical explanation of the miracle. Like Moses' parting of the Red Sea and Jesus' raising of the dead, Muhammad's recitation of the Qur'an, the like of which no one could produce when challenged to do so, violated (*naqd*) the natural course of events (*al-'ada*) in the phenomenal world. *Naqd al-'ada* was established by most of the Mu'tazila and the Ash'ariya as the metaphysical basis of the miracle. The issue that was still open to dispute was to establish just why the Arabs did not or could not answer Muhammad's challenge.

Interestingly, the chief opponents of the Bahshamiya were not the Ash'ariya who, as we have pointed out, also defended the popular notion that the Qur'an was a miracle and sign of Muhammad's prophethood. Rather, it was the Mu'tazili mutakallim Ibrahim al-Nazzam (d. 845) who was among the first to offer a challenge to the notion that the language of the Qur'an was implicitly miraculous and inimitable. Al-Nazzam was a nephew of Abu l-Hudhayl and was for a while the latter's pupil in Basra. From the very few fragments of his work that have survived in later Mu'tazili and Ash'ari writings, he emerges as a very independent thinker, interested both in science and poetry, as well as kalam. In a kalam commentary by 'Abd al-Jabbar that was itself subject to considerable commentary by his students and later disciples, the Qadi (or one of his commentators) says the following about al-Nazzam's theory of the nature of the Quranic miracle:

> Know that al-Nazzam took the position that the Qur'an is a miracle only under the aspect of *sarfa* [the act of deflecting]. The meaning of sarfa is that the Arabs were able to utter speech like that of the Qur'an with respect to linguistic purity and eloquence until the Prophet was sent. When the Prophet was sent, this [characteristic] eloquence was taken away from them and they were unable to produce speech like the Qur'an.[36]

In other words, al-Nazzam did not deny that the event of the Qur'an was a miracle. Rather, he denied that the miracle was specifically the linguistic quality of the text of the Qur'an per se. Elsewhere, al-Nazzam was reported to have said that any speaker of Arabic, native or not, was capable of producing the eloquence of Quranic order and composition.[37] He also asserted that the Qur'an contained information about things unseen in the phenomenal world and about events to come that the Prophet could not have known about by ordinary means. Mention of these other forms of miracle gained a more or less uncontroversial place in the discussion of Muhammad's prophethood. Four are mentioned in the latter part of ¶ 43. The historian of comparative religion will take interest in all of them, for example, the feeding of the multitudes from a small portion of food. Far more controversial among Muslim intellectuals was the Mu'tazili/Ash'ari claim that the linguistic quality of the Qur'an as such was the real miracle.

The sarfa doctrine gained some support in the next two centuries after al-Nazzam, especially among the mutakallimun of the Baghdad branch of the

Mu'tazila and some of the Imami (Twelver) Shi'a.[38] Later in the text just quoted, we are told that the doctrine of sarfa was defended by the head of the Imami Shi'a in Baghdad, al-Sayyid al-Murtada (d. 1044), a younger contemporary and a one-time kalam student of 'Abd al-Jabbar. Indeed, this same text devotes a lengthy chapter to refuting al-Murtada's theory of sarfa.[39]

Manekdim's ta'liq on this passage from 'Abd al-Jabbar's *Kitab al-usul* does not treat of the doctrine of sarfa. The Qadi and his predecessors may not have attached much importance to the doctrine of sarfa until it was defended by al-Sayyid al-Murtada toward the end of the tenth century, perhaps at the time the two men met and discussed theology during the Qadi's visit to Baghdad (see chapter 3 above). What Manekdim does stress in his supercommentary are the "challenge" verses and the reason why Muslims after the time of the Prophet can safely conclude that no Arab ever accepted Muhammad's challenge to produce a sura like those of the Qur'an.

In the last paragraph of this section (44), the Qadi deals with the objection that the Qur'an contains verses that are in disagreement (*ayat mukhtalifat*), that is, verses that appear to contradict each other. Manekdim mentions these but also refers to the specious counter-arguments (*shubah*) of the "Mulhida," the generic term for atheists and deniers of religion (*Ta'liq*, pp. 598ff.). Again, the figure of Ibn al-Rawandi emerges in the historical and textual background of this dispute (see p. 29). Ibn al-Rawandi was roughly contemporary with Abu 'Ali al-Jubba'i. The former had learned kalam as a Mu'tazili mutakallim, but subsequently mounted virulent pointed, often scoffing, criticism of monotheism in general, and the Qur'an and Muhammad's prophethood in particular.[40] In his supercommentary on Qur'an passages that are alleged to be contradictory (*tanaqud*) in meaning, Manekdim argues they are not. Statements must be contradictory in more than just expression, but also in meaning. "Zayd is in the house" and "Zayd is not in the house" are contradictory in expression (*al-'ibara*) but not in meaning (al-ma'na) if in one case "Zayd son of 'Abdallah" is meant and in another "Zayd son of Khalid" is meant (*Ta'liq*, 599: 1–4).

Out of these early controversies about the consistency of the text grew the orthodox Sunni doctrine that the Qur'an contains both those verses whose meanings are plain or "univocal" (*muhkam*) and those whose meanings are obscure or "equivocal" (*mutashabiha*). The Qadi cites Qur'an 3:7, the chief proof text for this doctrine.[41] Manekdim goes on in his supercommentary to mention the Imami (Twelver) Shi'a as among those who dispute the orthodox doctrine of the Qur'an, for they allow that there can be verses added or subtracted from the text of the Qur'an that had been collected under the direction of the third caliph, 'Uthman. Against this view, Manekdim argues that if that were the case, then the Qur'an would no longer be a miracle, in the sense described above, and it would follow that one could not trust any of the revealed laws and religious duties stipulated in the Qur'an (*Ta'liq*, 601: 5–18). Others with whom the Mu'tazila were in dispute, according to Manekdim, were the Murji'a (*Ta'liq*, 604: 15–606: 7).

IV. Eschatology (¶¶ 45–54)

In the next several paragraphs, Qadi 'Abd al-Jabbar discusses the question of the social as well as the eschatological consequences of sin, the threat and the promise (*al-wa'd wa l-wa'id*). This was the issue that divided the Khawarij and Murji'a in the first decades after Muhammad's death when events had required the Muslim *umma* to establish a consensus on how the umma should be governed. The theological issue was not over minor deviations from the straight path, but rather grave sin (*fisq, kabir*), such as murder, fornication, or denying religion. In the Mu'tazili cosmology, as we have seen, an ethical God must punish the grave sinner with eternal Hellfire. *Loci probantes* from the Qur'an, Hadith, and poetry are adduced in ¶¶ 45–50 in support of the Mu'tazili position.

With ¶ 50 begins a discussion of intercession. Could the Prophet Muhammad, or indeed saints and holy men, intercede with God on behalf of sinners? To this, 'Abd al-Jabbar replies yes, God responds to intercession for believers, except in the case of grave sinners (*fasiqun*). The chief opponents, Manekdim tells us (*Ta'liq*, 688: 3) are the Murji'a, who hold that grave sinners among the "people of prayer" have access to intercession: "Where there is iman [faith] sin does no harm."[42] A somewhat softer position was attributed to Abu Hanifa, the jurist, who also rejected the view of the Khawarij that the grave sinner was destined to be eternally in Hellfire.

The Qadi, because of the firm position taken by the Mu'tazila regarding the promise and the threat, held that there could be no intercession for grave sinners but there could be for persons with lesser sins. The Bahshamiya were not in total agreement on this. Abu Hashim was apparently more lenient in allowing prophetic intercession for sinners (*Ta'liq*, 689: 1–3). The Murji'i position was based on the Hadith: "My intercession is for the people of grave sin in my umma [community]" (*Ta'liq*, 690: 14–15).[43] To this, Manekdim replies, in defense of the Qadi's position, that it is a weak Hadith, not reported multilaterally by several transmitters. More tellingly, Manekdim asserts that the Qadi's position had been arrived at more knowledgeably (*bi-tariq al-'ilm*) and is not based on reports tenuously attributed to the Prophet.

V. The Intermediate Position (¶¶ 55–58)

Paragraph 55 begins the discussion of the doctrine of the intermediate position, on whether sinners are believers or unbelievers. Paragraph 56 raises the interesting question of why a grave sinner (fasiq) is not considered to be an unbeliever (kafir). The answer is that Islamic law, Shari'a, does not treat grave sinners as such; for example, it does not require Muslim grave sinners to pay the poll tax (*jizya*) required of unbelievers and People of the Book. Nor is the sinner a *munafiq*, a hypocrite (¶ 57), as al-Hasan al-Basri had argued. The distinction the Mu'tazilites wished to make was that hypocrites disguise their unbelief, whereas grave sinners do not.

Continuing this theme, ¶ 58 refers to Islamic lore regarding the punishment in the grave, the interrogation by the two angels, Munkar and Nakir, the Final Judgment, and walking the final path or bridge to eternal Paradise or Hellfire.[44] Manekdim adds considerable amplification to these beliefs by answering doubters' questions. For example, if there was punishment in the grave, wouldn't grave robbers and others who saw bodies after the punishment see evidence of it? Manekdim denies this, suggesting that God punishes under circumstances and in ways to which grave robbers and other human witnesses could never be party (*Ta'liq*, p. 733).

VI. Commanding the Good and Prohibiting Evil (¶¶ 59–67)

'Abd al-Jabbar's explicit discussion of the fifth Mu'tazili principle of commanding the good and prohibiting evil (*al-amr bi l-ma'ruf wa l-nahy 'an al-munkar*) occurs only in the first paragraph of this section (59). The commanding/prohibiting principle can be regarded in comparative theological terms as "Mission to the World." 'Abd al-Jabbar stresses that a proactive mission to the world is incumbent upon Muslims; not to "command the good and prohibit evil" would amount to disobeying God.

In his supercommentary, Manekdim adduces *ayat* (verses) from the Qur'an to prove that a proactive mission to the world is incumbent upon believers. He then expands on the theme somewhat, pointing out that the Muslim umma is almost unanimous on the necessity of commanding the good and prohibiting evil. An exception he mentions is a small group of the Imami Shi'a. He goes on to say that the Two Mu'tazili Masters, Abu 'Ali al-Jubba'i and his son Abu Hashim, agree on the necessity of the principle, but that Abu 'Ali had argued its necessity was known rationally (*'aqlan*) and Abu Hashim had argued that it is known by revelation (*shar'an*). Manekdim, following 'Abd al-Jabbar and the Bahshamiya generally, defends Abu Hashim's position on the matter (*Ta'liq*, p.741–742).

A.   Political Theology: The Imamate (¶ 60)

In ¶ 60 the Qadi takes up the matter of political theology, the question of the imamate. The main dispute on this issue is between the *ahl al-sunna wa l-jama'a* or Sunni Muslims and the various branches of the Shi'a. 'Abd al-Jabbar states the Sunni position, that the rightful imams or religious leaders of the umma after the Prophet were Abu Bakr, 'Umar, 'Uthman, and 'Ali. He denies that any one of them (e.g., 'Ali) was superior to the others, specifically mentioning the Imami (Twelver) Shi'a as opponents on this issue.

As we might expect, Manekdim, as a Zaydi Shi'i mutakallim, differs with the Qadi on this matter. He presents several issues on which the Zaydi Shi'a qualify the imamate. First, the reality of the imamate (*haqiqat al-imam*) is that the Imam has authority over those who hold the office of qadi (judge) and *mutawalli* (chargé d'affaires) of the community. As Manekdim puts it, his hand is above theirs (*Ta'liq*, 750: 8–16). Second, the Imam is needed to carry out and enforce divine legislation. On this the Shi'a generally (referred to in the text as *ahl al-bayt*) agree. The Imami Shi'a, Manekdim tells us, hold that the Imam is needed only to teach divine legislation. However, divine legislation is already known from the Qur'an, Sunna, etc. What the community needs is an Imam to implement the Shari'a (750: 16–751: 17). Third, the Imam functions specifically in the office of *mujtahid*, one who is entrusted with *ijtihad*, authority to decide in legal and theological matters, contrary to the Khariji position that such authority belongs to the community at large (751: 18–753:16). Fourth is the method of designation (*al-nass*) by which the Imam is chosen, contrary to the Mu'tazila and Ash'ariya (753: 17–757: 15). Fifth, Manekdim presents the Zaydi Shi'i view that the Prophet appointed 'Ali ibn Abi Talib as Imam. His sons Hasan, then Husayn, were appointed, down to the fifth Imam, Zayd ibn 'Ali, and thereafter those (and there could be more than one at a time) who followed in their path. This he contrasts with the Mu'tazili (Sunni) and Imami (Twelver) Shi'i positions (757: 16–758: 6).

B.   The Validity of Tradition (¶ 61)

Returning to our text, ¶ 61 takes up a problem that also divided the Mu'tazila from the Ahl al-Hadith and other traditionalist-minded Muslims: on what basis should reports (*al-akhbar*) be accepted as authoritative sources (along with the Qur'an)? 'Abd al-Jabbar mentions the main Sunni criterion of multiple chains of transmitters. The Mu'tazila take a more liberal position than the traditionalists on the question of whether a report by only one or two transmitters is acceptable. Against the traditionalists, he says that in the application of the Shari'a such reports can be cited if they are from a reliable source. The distinctive Mu'tazili position comes in the last sentence of this paragraph: "And that which is transmitted in conflict with scripture and rational proof we will interpret in a sound manner, just as we interpret scripture in accord with rational proof, not with that which conflicts with it." Here again we see the Mu'tazili emphasis on reason as the primary arbiter of understanding and interpreting sacred texts, the Qur'an and Hadith.

Manekdim's supercommentary expounds briefly the more philosophical discourse on reports and Hadith as propositions that must be determined as true or false. Necessarily true (*idtiraran*) are those multiple-source reports from reliable transmitters about things one hasn't seen, such as foreign countries and monarchs who rule the land. So, too, multiple-source reports on what the Prophet established by his own practice, such as the Five Pillars of Islam. True by inferential reasoning (*istidlalan*) are the report of God's unity, of the prophethood of Muhammad, and the like. These cannot be observed in the phenomenal world in the way a foreign country or monarch theoretically could be, but must be established rationally in the mind on the basis of acceptable premises.

C. *God's Decree* (¶ 62)

God's decree (*qadar*) receives brief mention in ¶ 62. Does God decree, and hence predetermine, the disposition of everything, good and evil, sweet and bitter? The Qadi replies that God determines everything as well as the prosperity or misfortune that may occur in it. In keeping with Mu'tazili theodicy, however, he goes on to say that God does not decree disobedience or unbelief. This is a refinement of the position taken by the group of mutakallimun in early Islam known as the Qadariya. Already, by the time of al-Hasan al-Basri's kalam discussions at Basra at the beginning of the eighth century, several theologians had been (or subsequently were to be) labeled "Qadarites." The issue was for them, as for the Mu'tazila later, whether God determined (*qadara*) events in the world. They held that humans are free to act out their own wills and thus to determine their own salvific destinies. The context of this debate, as Harun Nasution makes clear, in the introduction to his defense of the Mu'tazila, was early Muslim politics.

Among the Arabs and converts to Islam living during the stormy days of civil uprising (*fitna*) during 'Uthman's reign (644–656), and later during the reign of the Umayyads in Damascus (661–750), were those who were critical of the heavy-handed rule of the Umayyad regime. For some, the criticism was leveled at those Umayyads who arrogated to themselves and their deeds the quality of divine decree and guidance. Not all Muslim intellectuals opposed the Umayyads on these grounds. The poet known as Jarir said of the Umayyad rulers:

> God has garlanded you with the *khalifa* and guidance,
>
> For what God decrees (*qada*) there is no change.

His contemporary al-Farazdaq said of the Umayyads:

> We have found the sons of Marwan[45] pillars of our religion,
>
> As the earth has mountains for its pillars.[46]

Not every Muslim poet or intellectual felt as charitable toward Umayyad rule, however. The so-called founder of the Qadariya, Ma'bad al-Juhani, had joined an uprising against the Umayyads during 'Abd al-Malik's reign, for which he was executed in 704. Ma'bad held that humans, including the Umayyads, determine their own deeds and misdeeds. We have already seen that al-Hasan al-Basri had replied to a letter from Caliph 'Abd al-Malik, expressing the same view of human responsibility for one's own acts. A few years later during the reign of Umar II (*reg.* 717–720), Ghaylan al-Dimashqi urged that caliph in a letter to make certain reforms and not to claim divine guidance and decree in matters of political rule.

   Later on the Mu'tazili mutakallimun were to refine Qadari doctrine into a more systematic theodicy and theological ethic, as we have already seen. Nonetheless, they did not like being labeled "Qadari," which seems to have become a term of opprobrium, much as the term "Mujbira" (Compulsionists) was not an epithet much liked by the Ash'ariya and traditionists. Manekdim includes a whole section in his commentary on this passage in 'Abd al-Jabbar's *Kitab al-usul al-khamsa* in which he offloads the label (*laqab*) "Qadariya" back onto the Mujbira and a group known as the Mushabbiha. The former were, of course, the Ash'ariya primarily. The latter we have also encountered above as the purveyors of the doctrine of tashbih or anthropomorphism. They were primarily traditionalists like Ahmad ibn Hanbal and his followers. Manekdim says:

> Know that in our view the [true] Qadariya are the Compulsionists and Anthropomorphists, and in their view [the Qadariya] are the Mu'tazila. We hurl this label at them and they hurl it back at us. One of them is reported to have said: "The Mu'tazila have labeled us the Qadariya, so we will turn the table on them".[47]

He goes on to say that the Qadi, once at one of the sessions of disputes among intellectuals, argued that "Qadariya" was a term of blame, which applied only to the Ash'ariya (*Ta'liq*, 773: 1–3). Even more interesting is Manekdim's quoting of a Hadith in which the Prophet Muhammad is reported to have said: "The Qadariya are the Magians (*majus*, Zoroastrians) of this umma."[48] In evidence of this, Manekdim brings several arguments. Linguistically, it is the Mujbira who assert that qadar, the sole power to determine events, belongs to God, whereas the Mu'tazila absolve God of that attribute, which would compromise His being just (*Ta'liq*, 775: 19–776: 2). The most pertinent theological argument is that the predetermination of human salvation among the traditionalists and Ash'ariya is like the dualistic determinism of the Zoroastrians (*Ta'liq*, 773: 11–14; 774: 3–6).

D. *Repentance and Faith* (¶¶ 63–67)

In ¶¶ 63–67, the Qadi presents the Mu'tazili doctrine of repentance (*tawba*), which is drawn by implication from the earlier discussions of theodicy and the ethical consequences of the threat and the promise. Grave sinners, if they repent of their sins, will not be punished eternally. Conversely, if someone is a grave sinner, an act of obedience without repentance does not obviate eternal punishment, but it may lessen it (¶ 66). Manekdim identifies this as the last division of the Qadi's book (by which he meant 'Abd al-Jabbar's sharh [commentary] on the work). The reason 'Abd al-Jabbar placed this discussion last, he tells us, is because he wanted to leave the reader with the desire to repent and turn to God, which of course is a human and not a divinely determined act, according to the Bahshamiya. Manekdim identifies the Baghdadi branch of the Mu'tazila as the chief disputants over the doctrine of repentance. The Baghdadiyun had argued that the human act of repentance as such could not effect the rescinding of punishment at the Eschaton; only God by His grace may set aside the punishment when one repents (*Ta'liq*, 790: 2–3). This was a compromise position between the liberal, humanistic position of the Mu'tazila on the one side, and the harder line divine-determinist position of the Ash'ariya and traditionalists on the other. Qadi 'Abd al-Jabbar closes this last section of his compendium of Mu'tazili doctrine with a corollary of the doctrine of tawba, that faith may increase and diminish with the performance of good works or their contrary (¶ 67).

We come to the end of our discussion of Qadi 'Abd al-Jabbar's remarkable summary of Mu'tazili doctrine, the *Kitab al-usul al-khamsa*. Our intent has been to situate the text in the history of kalam and of theological discourse more generally as well as to identify some of the more pertinent work of modern scholarship, especially that which is accessible to Western readers, on particular issues. The next chapter presents a rendering of the text itself in an English style that we hope is both accurate and readable.

Notes

1. We borrow the term used by Clifford Geertz and Gilbert Ryle to refer to the uncovering of layers of meaning of a social or written text.
2. BMO 8613 39a (top). The text is a supercommentary (unidentified as to author) on Abu Rashid al-Nisaburi's additions to another of 'Abd al-Jabbar's usul works (the original text is missing), *Kitab al-usul*.
3. *Al-Mughni*, 13, 335: 8–10.
4. *Sharh*, 39: 11.
5. Throughout this chapter we frequently cite Manekdim's supercommentary (ta'liq) which, it should be recalled, was a commentary on 'Abd al-Jabbar's own commentary (*sharh*) on the work (*kitab*) translated in the next chapter.
6. This is probably 'Abd al-Jabbar, *al-Mukhtasar fi usul al-din*. On pp. 197–198 the Qadi mentions the four usul al-din as unity, justice, prophethood, and divine legislation.
7. 'Abd al-Jabbar, *Sharh al-usul al-khamsa*, 122: 14–123: 5. This work in fact is a supercommentary on (*ta'liq 'ala*) 'Abd al Jabbar's *Sharh al-usul al-khamsa* by Manekdim.
8. Reprinted in *SEI*, art. "al-Mu'tazila."
9. Helmut Ritter published the letter in German in *Der Islam* 21 (1933): 67–83. It was subsequently discussed by Julian Oberman, "Political Theology in Early Islam," and Michael Schwarz, "The Letter of al-Hasan al-Basri." Portions of the first half of the letter appear also in Rippen and Knappert, *Textual Sources for the Study of Islam*, pp. 114–121.
10. Cf. Madelung, *Der Imam al-Qasim, ibn Ibrahim*, pp. 8–9.
11. Ibid., pp. 18–20.
12. For example, a Muslim woman is not allowed to be married to a non-Muslim man. A famous case in the Egyptian courts in 1996 concerned the forcing of the wife of an Egyptian professor at Cairo University, Dr. Nasr Abu Zayd, to be divorced from her husband because he was declared to be a kafir on the grounds that his writings were critical of Islam. Interestingly, Nasr Abu Zayd is, like Harun Nasution, an exponent of Mu'tazili teaching. We will discuss his views of Mu'tazilism briefly in chapter 10.
13. 'Abd al-Jabbar, *al-Mughni*, vol. 5.
14. "Unity" is not, strictly speaking, an accurate rendering of tawhid, which carries the causative sense of "making one." The more rarely used term "unicity," which means "oneness – the state of being unique of its kind" is a better English translation.
15. We have followed W. M. Watt's translation (*Formative Period*, pp. 246–247) of al-Ash'ari, *Maqalat*, pp. 155–156.
16. *Maqalat*, 195: 10–15.

17. Al-Shahrastani, *al-Milal wa l-nihal*, 1, 46: 12–13.

18. *Maqalat*, 169: 9–14. For a discussion of Ibn Kullab's proto-Ash'ari teaching on divine attributes, see *Formative Period*, pp. 286–287.

19. *Maqalat*, 165: 5–7. For a discussion of Abu l-Hudhayl's position on divine attributes, see Frank, "The Divine Attributes."

20. *Formative Period*, p. 299. See also Allard, *Le problème des attributs divins*; and Frank, *Beings and Their Attributes*.

21. *Formative Period*, p. 300.

22. Madelung, *Der Imam al-Qasim ibn Ibrahim*, p. 8.

23. *Formative Period*, p. 234.

24. *Maqalat*, 281: 2–5.

25. *Formative Period*, p. 193.

26. Frank, *Beings and Their Attributes*, p. 195.

27. *Ta'liq*, 477: 9–11.

28. Ibid., 513: 14–19.

29. George F. Hourani, *Islamic Rationalism*, p. 3.

30. S.v. "Ibn al-Rawandi, " *EI²*, and *Theologie*, 4" (¶ 8.22, forthcoming). The identification of Ibn al-Rawandi as the originator of the fictional Brahmin critics of the Qur'an and Muhammad's prophethood was made by Kraus, "Beiträge zur islamischen Ketzergeschichte." For a different view – that Indian Brahmins may actually have been meant, see Stroumsa, "The *Barahima* in Early Kalam."

31. Madelung, "Origins of the Controversy," pp. 504–525.

32. Ibid., pp. 512–515; last quotation from p. 515.

33. See Martin, "The Role of the Basrah Mu'tazilah," pp. 179–181.

34. *I'jaz al-qur'an fi nazmihi wa* ta'lifihi (The inimitability of the Qur'an with respect to its order and composition). See Audebert, *al-Hattabi et l'inimitabilitié du Coran*, pp. 58–71.

35. *Ta'liq*, pp. 585–596. Qadi 'Abd al-Jabbar devoted an entire volume (16) of his *Kitab al-mughni* to the apologetic miracle.

36. BMO 8613, fol. 17b (bottom)–18a (top). This acephalic MS, also without colophon, appears to be the *Ziyadat al-sharh* (Additions to the commentary) by 'Abd al-Jabbar's foremost pupil, Abu Rashid al-Nisaburi, or a later commentary on it. The "sharh" in the title was the Qadi's commentary on another basic handbook of kalam by an earlier mutakallim, Abu 'Ali ibn Khallad, who had been a pupil of Abu Hashim. A translation and introduction to this text is under preparation by Richard C. Martin and Adel S. Gamal.

37. See al-Khayyat, *Kitab al-intisar*, p. 28 (Arabic text), p. 25 (French trans.).

38. See Martin, "The Role of the Basrah Mu'tazilah," pp. 187–189.

39. BMO 8613, fols. 17b–28a.

40. In addition to the works cited in note 30 above, see art. "Mulhida" in *EI²*. Josef van Ess has examined the evidence on Ibn al-Rawandi extensively and argued his view of Ibn al-Rawandi as a theological critic of kalam in *Theologie*, 4 (forthcoming). For an earlier statement of his work on Ibn al-Rawandi's place in the history of kalam,

see van Ess, "Une lecture à rebours de l'histoire de Mu'tazilisme," pp. 163–198; now reprinted with the second part under the same title by Librairie Orientaliste Paul Geunther (Paris, 1984) providing the original pagination in square brackets.

41. An excellent discussion of this doctrine in Sunni Islam is Denny, "Exegesis and Recitation."

42. Cited by Watt, *Formative Period*, p. 141.

43. According to Wensinck (*Concordance* 3: 151) this widely attested Hadith is found in the collection by al-Tirmidhi at locus "Qiyama 1100," as well as in the Hadith collections by Abu Da'ud, Ibn Baja, and Ibn Hanbal.

44. A useful study of Islamic eschatological beliefs is Yvonne Yazbeck Haddad and Jane Idleman Smith, *The Islamic Understanding of Death and Resurrection*.

45. The branch of the Umayyads that came to power with Marwan I in 684, and whose greatest caliph was the famed 'Abd al-Malik (*reg.* 685–705).

46. Cited and translated by Watt, *Formative Period*, p. 83. Watt's lengthy discussion of the Qadariya, its history, and its theological significance (pp. 82–118) is the chief source of our discussion here.

47. *Ta'liq*, 772: 14–16.

48. This Hadith is not attested in the six sound (*sahih*) collections, according to Wensinck, *Concordance*. Nonetheless, the editor of Manekdim's *Ta'liq* says it is a Hadith that is traceable to the Prophet, citing al-'Ajluni, *Kashf al-khafa'*, p. 61.

five

Kitab al-Usul al-khamsa (Book of the Five Fundamentals)

A *Translation*[1]

By the Learned Jurisconsult 'Abd al–Jabbar,
may God's blessing and favour be upon him.
In the name of Allah, the most Beneficent
and the Most Merciful[2]

[I.   First Principles]

[A.   Knowledge of God]

1. If it is asked:[3] What is the first duty that God imposes upon you? ***Say to him:*** Speculative reasoning (*al-nazar*) which leads to knowledge of God, because He is not known intuitively (*daruratan*)[4] nor by the senses (*bi l-mushahada*).[5] Thus, He must be known by reflection and speculation.

2. Then if it is asked: Why do you say that is obligatory? ***Say to him:*** Because we fear that if we do not come to know Him we will disobey Him and thus we will perish. Therefore, it is obligatory for us to know Him in order to avoid disobedience and to perform obedient acts.

3. Then if it is asked: Why did speculative reasoning become the first of the duties? ***Say to him:*** Because the rest of the stipulates of revelation (*shara'i*, pl. of *shari'a*) concerning what [we should] say and do are no good until after there is knowledge of God. Do you not see that it is no good for us to pray without knowing to whom we are to pray?

4. Then if it is asked: What is the first grace bestowed upon you by God? ***Say to him:*** That is something that I cannot account for. In general, however, He created me a living [being], and provided me with power (*al-qudra*) and physical means (*al-ala*).⁶ And He perfected my nature (*khulq*) and gave me passions and enabled me to enjoy a variety of pleasurable things. Then, He issued me commands and prohibitions so that I could attain the [requisite] level of reward and enter the Heavens. Therefore, it is incumbent on me to establish His existence and to know Him so that I can worship Him, give Him thanks and do what satisfies Him and avoid disobedience toward Him.

5. Then if it is asked: If reasoning speculatively on the knowledge of God is incumbent then on what do you speculate? *Say to him:* On evidentiary proofs (*al-adilla*).⁷

6. Then if it is asked: What are the proofs? *Say to him:* There are four: rational argument (*hujjat al-'aql*), scripture (*al-kitab*), the example [of the Prophet] (Sunna), and the consensus [of the community] (*ijma'*). Knowledge of God can only be gained by speculating with rational argument, because if we do not [first] know that He is truthful we will not know the authenticity of the Book, the Sunna and the communal consensus.

7. Then if it is asked: What is the proof by which speculative reason leads to the knowledge of God? *Say to him:* My own being (or "self" *nafsi*) and what I observe about [physical] bodies.

8. Then if it is asked: How can your own being be evidence of God? *Say to him:* Because I find my own being in a state of perfection, and it is impossible for me to create something like myself or some parts of myself. Thus, *a fortiori*, as I am unable in my original state of being a drop of sperm to create myself, I know that I have a creator and designer who is good, and who is other than me, and He is God.

9. Then if it is asked: How does this give proof of God? *Say to him:* Because I know that bodies must have motion, rest, contiguity and separation, and these things are contingent (*muhdatha*).⁸ Thus, bodies (*al-jism*) must be contingent since transitory things (*al-hawadith*) are not eternal.

[B. The Fundamentals of Religion]

10. Then if it is said: Tell me all that is necessary for one to know about the fundamentals of religion (*usul al-din*). *Say to him:* There are five fundamentals of religion: unicity (*tawhid*); justice (*'adl*); the promise and the threat (*al-wa'd wa l-wa'id*); the intermediate position (*al-manzila bayn al-manzilatayn*); and commanding the good and prohibiting evil (*al-amr bi l-ma'ruf wa l-nahy 'an l-munkar*).⁹ These are the fundamentals on which religion is based. Anyone who opposes them is in great error and may commit unbelief or grave sin because of that. But if you know these fundamentals, it follows that you will have to know about jurisprudence (*fiqh*) and divine legislation (*shar'iyat*).

11. Then if it is asked: What is [God's] unicity? *Say to him:* It is the knowledge that God, being unique, has attributes that no creature shares with Him. This is explained by the fact that you know that the world has a creator (*sani'*) who created it and that: [a] He existed eternally in the past and He cannot perish (*fana'*),[10] while we exist after being non-existent, and we can perish. [b] And you know that He was and is eternally all-powerful (*qadir*) and that impotence (*al-'ajz*) is not possible for Him. [c] And you know that He is omniscient of the past and present and that ignorance (*jahl*) is not possible for Him. [d] And you know that He knows everything that was, everything that is, and how things that are not would be if they were. [e] And you know that He is eternally in the past and future living, and that calamities and pain[11] are not possible for Him.[12] [f] And you know that He sees visible things (*mar'iyat*), and perceives perceptibles, and that He does not have need of sense organs. [g] And you know that He is eternally past and in future sufficient (*ghani*) and it is not possible for Him to be in need. [h] And you know that He is not like [physical] bodies, and that it is not possible for Him to get up or down, move about, change, be composite, have a form [. . .] limbs and body members.[13] [i] And you know that He is not like the accidents of motion, rest, color, food or smells. [j] And you know that He is One throughout eternity and there is no second beside Him, and that everything other than He is contingent, made, dependent (*muhtaj*), structured (*mudabbar*), and governed [by someone/thing else]. Thus, if you know all of that you know [God's] unicity.

12. Then if it is said: Tell me about [divine] justice (al-'adl); what is it?[14] *Say to him:* It is the knowledge that God is removed from all that is morally wrong (*qabih*) and that all His acts are morally good (*hasana*). This is explained by the fact that you know that all human acts of injustice (*zulm*), transgression (*jawr*), and the like cannot be of His creation (*min khalqihi*).[15] Whoever attributes that to Him has ascribed to Him injustice and insolence (*safah*) and thus strays from the doctrine of justice. [a] And you know that God does not impose faith upon the unbeliever without giving him the power (al-qudra) for it, nor does He impose upon a human what he is unable to do,[16] but He only gives to the unbeliever to choose unbelief on his own part, not on the part of God. [b] And you know that God does not will, desire or want disobedience. Rather, He loathes and despises it and only wills obedience, which He wants and chooses and loves. [c] And you know that He does not punish the children of polytheists (*al-mushrikin*) in Hellfire because of their fathers' sin, for He has said: "Each soul earns but its own due"

(Q. 6:164); and He does not punish anyone for someone else's sin because that would be morally wrong (*qabih*), [and] God is far removed from such. [d] And you know that He does not transgress His rule (*hukm*) and [. . .][17] that He only causes sickness and illness in order to turn them to advantage. Whoever says otherwise has allowed that God is iniquitous and has imputed insolence to Him.[18] [e] And you know that, for their sakes, He does the best for all of His creatures, upon whom He imposes [moral and religious] obligations (*yukallifuhum*), and that He has indicated to them what He has imposed upon them and clarified the path of truth so that we could pursue it, and He has clarified the path of falsehood (*tariq l-batil*) so that we could avoid it. So, whoever perishes does so only after [all this has been made] clear. [f] And you know that every benefit we have is from God; as He has said: "And you have no good thing that is not from Allah" (Q. 16:53); it either comes to us from Him or from elsewhere. [g] Thus, when you know [all of] this you become knowledgeable about [God's] justice.

13. **Then if it is said:** Tell me about the promise and the threat;[19] what are they? *Say to him:* They are the knowledge that God promises recompense (*al-thawab*) to those who obey Him and He threatens punishment to those who disobey Him.[20] He will not go back on His word, nor can He act contrary to His promise and threat nor lie in what He reports, in contrast to what the Postponers (al-Murji'a) hold.[21]

14. **Then if it is said:** Tell me about the intermediate position (al-manzila bayn l-manzilatayn); what is it? *Say to him:* It is the knowledge that whoever murders, or fornicates (*zana*), or commits serious sins is a grave sinner (*fasiq*) and not a believer, nor is his case the same that of believers with respect to praise and attributing greatness, since he is [to be] cursed and disregarded. Nonetheless, he is not an unbeliever who can't be buried in our [Muslim] cemetery, or be prayed for, or marry [a Muslim]. Rather, he has an intermediate position, in contrast to the Seceders (Khawarij)[22] who say that he is an unbeliever, or the Murji'a who say that he is a believer.

15. **Then if it is said:** Tell me about commanding the good and prohibiting evil (*al-amr bi l-ma'ruf wa l-nahy 'an l-munkar*); what are they? *Say to him:* Commanding the good is of two types. One of them is obligatory, which is commanding religious duties (*al-fara'id*) when someone neglects them (*dayya'aha*),[23] and the other is supererogatory (*al-nafila*), which is commanding supererogatory [acts of devotion] when someone omits to do them (*tarakaha*). As for prohibiting evil, all of it is obligatory because all evil is ethically wrong (qabih). It is necessary, if possible, to reach a point where evil (*al-munkar*) does not occur in the easiest of circumstances or lead to something worse, for the goal is for evil simply not to happen.

And, if it is possible to reach the point where good (*al-ma'ruf*) occurs in the easiest of circumstances, then preferring the difficult [circumstances] would be impermissible. Similarly, God has said: "If two parties among the believers fall into a quarrel, make peace between them; but if one of them transgresses beyond bounds against the other, then fight against the one who transgresses until he complies with the command of Allah; [then, if he complies, make peace between them with justice, and be fair: for Allah loves those who act fairly]" (Q. 49:9).[24] Thus, prohibiting evil is obligatory only if the view does not prevail that [prohibiting a particular evil] would lead to an increase in disobedience, and [if] a preference for what was harmful were [not] predominant. If such a view does prevail, [prohibiting evil] would not be obligatory,[25] and avoiding it would be more appropriate.

[II. Divine Unicity]

[A. Inferring God's Existence from Physical Bodies]

16. Then if it is asked: What is the proof that you yourself and all bodies are contingent (*muhdath*)? **Say to him:** Because they always have motion, rest, separateness, and contiguity [relative to one another], and all of these are necessarily transitory, so [bodies] must similarly be contingent.

17. Then if it is asked: What is the proof that bodies are produced (*muhdith*)?[26] **Say to him:** Because writing, constructing and craft (*sina'a*)[27] [are activities that] require a maker, from whence [it follows that] they are contingent (muhdath), so it is necessary for them to have a producer (muhdith), for every thing contingent must have a producer and maker.

[B. Inferring God's Attributes]

18. Then if it is asked: What is the proof that He has the power [to act] (*annahu qadir*)?[28] **Say to him:** Because an act in the visible world (*al-shahid*) can only be [the act of] one who has the power [to act autonomously] (*min qadir*), and acting is valid on God's part, so it must be said that He is qadir [has the power to act].

19. Then if it is asked: What is the proof that God is omniscient (*'alim*)?[29] **Say to him:** Because skillful acts (*al-af'al al-muhkama*),[30] such as writing and crafts (al- sina'a),[31] can only be done by one who knows [how].[32] And since it is true for God, in creating human beings, to exceed the wonders of crafts, therefore, He must be omniscient.

20. Then if it is asked: What is the proof that He is living (*hayy*)?

94

Say to him: Indeed, everyone who is powerful and knowing must be living.

21. **Then if it is asked:** What is the proof that He is hearing (*sami‘*), seeing (*basir*), and perceiving of perceptibles (*mudrik li l-mudrakat*)? *Say to him:* Because He is a living being with no deficiencies, and deficiencies are impossible for Him, and each one who has these attributes must be hearing, seeing, and perceiving of perceptibles, the same as we grasp things with our intellects in the visible world (*kama na‘qiluh fi l-shahid*).

22. **Then if it is asked:** What is the proof that He is existent (*annahu mawjud*)? *Say to him:* Because He is omnipotent, and it would not be possible for a nonexistent being (*ma‘dum*) to act, because His being nonexistent could not be related to a possible nonexistent [entity] (*bi l-maqdur*).[33] Therefore He must be existent. If not, it would open the way to much ignorance.

23. **Then if it is asked:** What is proof that He is eternal (*qadim*)?[34] *Say to him:* Because if He were contingent (muhdath) He would need someone to cause Him to exist, and that would lead to a *regressio ad infinitum* (*ila ma la nihaya lahu*). Therefore He must be eternal.

24. **Then if it is asked:** What is the proof that He is self-sufficient (ghani) and that it is impossible for Him to be in need? *Say to him:* Because one for whom pleasure, benefit and desire are possible must be [in] a physical body for which increase and decrease are possible.[35] God is not a body. Therefore He must be self-sufficient.[36]

25. **Then if it is asked:** What is the proof that He is not a [physical] body (jism)? *Say to him:* Because if He were a body then [a] He would have to be contingent, because bodies are existent things, and then [b] it would not be appropriate for Him to make bodies, the same as it is not possible for us to make bodies.

26. **Then if it is asked:** What is the proof that God is unseen (la yura)? *Say to him:* Because God has said: "vision (*al-absar*) does not perceive Him" (Q. 6:103), and the perception involved in vision is seeing (*al-ru'ya*), so He is necessarily unseen unless He is [present] in one mode but not in another, and Allah is [removed] from that, because that is the mark of being contingent (*huduth*). Therefore, He must be unseen by the sense of vision, but only seen by the heart, insight (*ma‘rifa*) and knowledge (*‘ilm*). There is His saying: "That day will faces be resplendent, looking towards their Lord" (Q. 75:22–23); its interpretation is that [those faces] are waiting[37] for God's recompense, or waiting for His mercy, according to what the Qur'an interpreters have related, so that it accords with the evidence of reason[38] and the Book.

27. **Then if it is asked:** What is the proof that He is One and has

no second? *Say to him:* If there were besides Him a second who was eternal then [the second] would have to be like Him in eternity, but the Eternal One is eternal in Himself (*li-nafsihi*). Thus, He must be omnipotent in and of Himself. If there were two beings who were omnipotent in themselves it would be possible for one of them to cause a body to move and the other to cause it to remain at rest. If that were the case[39] it would have to be so in one of three ways: Either [a] the two things they willed must both exist, which is impossible because they contradict each other. [b] Or neither of them exists, which is impossible because it implies the impotence of both, and it is impossible for the omnipotent divine being to be impotent. So [c] it must be that one of the two willed things exists, and that necessitates that one be powerful and the other be impotent, and the impotent one cannot be eternal or divine. And it establishes that He is One. On this He has said: "If there were in them a divinity besides Allah, there would have been confusion in both [the Heaven and the Earth]" (Q. 21:22).[40] On this basis the doctrine of the Dualists (al-Thanawiya) that The [God of] Light and The [God of] Darkness are both eternal is refuted. And that by which we have proved that bodies are contingent and have a creator also refutes their doctrine. And on this basis the doctrine of Christians that in God are three hypostases (*aqanim*): the father, the son and holy spirit, is refuted, for we have explained that He is One, and because it is absurd for that which is one in reality [also] to be three in reality.

[III. Theodicy][41]

28. Then if it is asked: What is the proof that God does not do that which is ethically wrong (*la yaf'alu al-qabih*)? *Say to him:* Because He knows the immorality of all unethical acts (pl. *qaba'ih*) and that He is self-sufficient without them, and it is impossible for Him to do them. For one of us who knows the immorality of injustice and lying, if he knows that he is self-sufficient without them and has no need of them, it would be impossible for him to choose them, in so far as he knows of their immorality and his sufficiency without them. Therefore, if God is sufficient without need of any unethical thing it necessarily follows that He would not choose [the unethical], based on His knowledge of its immorality. Thus every immoral thing that happens in the world must be a human act, for God transcends doing [immoral acts]. Indeed, God has distanced Himself from that with His saying: "But Allah wills no injustice to His servants" (Q. 40:31), and His saying: "Verily Allah will not deal unjustly with humankind in anything" (Q. 10:44). And even if we allowed that He did what was unethical, we would not believe that He punished the prophets and the righteous ones (*al-salihin*) and sent them to the Hellfire (*al-nar*), and we would not believe that His word was a lie and an order that could be nullified,[42] for that, then, would necessitate that we [could] not trust in His promise and threat.[43] And we do not believe that He sends prophets to the Hellfire and enemies and unbelievers to Paradise. Anyone who did such things would not command our obedience to Him because we could not be safe from His evil, and by obeying Him we would create the utmost havoc.[44] And it would necessitate the possibility that God could send to humankind one who called them to unbelief and deception, and manifest through him[45] miracles and proofs. For if it were possible for Him to do what is unethical, what would prohibit Him from doing all of [what we have just mentioned]? And saying this would lead us not to trust in the Book and the Sunna, and not to know the Shar'ia. And it would lead us to be unsure [whether] what we do is straying (*dalal*) [from the Right Path] and what unbelievers do is truth. Whoever reaches this point, his error (*khata'uhu*) is detestable and his infamy is great.

29. Then if it is asked: What is the proof that human acts are not created (*laysat bi-makhluqat*) by God but that they are done with His knowledge? **Say to him:** If they were done by God then what good would there be in His commanding those that are ethically good and prohibiting those that are ethically bad, and praising and rewarding obedience but blaming and punishing disobedience? In the same way, it would not be good for Him to command His acts in us,[46] such as color,[47] shape, health, and sickness, or to prohibit such, or lay blame for such. Moreover, if God were the agent of our acts then they would not have happened according to our purposes and motivations.[48] And moreover, [even] a wise man cannot create his own abuse, or condemn and vilify [himself]; for how could it be said that every abuse and vilification [addressed] to him is of his own doing?[49] And moreover, who ever commits injustice and transgression must be unjust and a transgressor. Thus, if God committed injustice He would be unjust, just as if He acted justly He would be just, and whoever says [otherwise] is an unbeliever. He has said: "You will see no disharmony in the creation of [God] the Beneficent" (Q. 67:3), and: "He who has made everything that He has created good" (Q. 32:7), and: "[Such is] the artistry of Allah, who disposes of all things in perfect order" (Q. 27:88). [These verses] indicate that these ethically bad acts are not created by God but that they are human acts, and on that basis they deserve blame and punishment. How can it be possible for God to create erroneous behavior in them and then punish them, thus saying: "Why do you disbelieve?" Isn't that the same as someone commanding his slave to do something, then punishing him for it? And that would clearly be corrupt.

30. **Then if it is asked:** What is the proof that the power [to act autonomously] (qudra)[50] precedes the act [itself]? *Say to him:* Because if it were simultaneous with the act then necessarily the unbeliever would not have had the capacity [power] (qudra) to have faith. And if he did not have the power for it, it would not be good for God to command it[51] because God does not impose on human beings what they do not have the power to do, according to His saying: "On no one does Allah place a burden greater than he can bear" (Q. 2:286); and "Allah puts no burden on anyone unless He has enabled him and given to him [what he needs in order to bear it]" (Q. 65:7). If it were possible for Him to impose on [His] servants what they were unable to do then it would be possible for Him to enjoin (*yukallif*)[52] the impotent to act, the disabled to run, and the blind to place the diacritical points correctly in the text of the Qur'an; and to enjoin us to climb to the roof without using stairs; all of that is clearly spurious. This establishes the fact [a] that He only enjoins on His servants what they have the power to do, and [b] that the unbeliever has the power [both] to believe and to disbelieve, so if it comes from him to disbelieve, it is by his choice. [This is] the same as if we gave a man a knife to use to his own advantage but he killed himself with it. The one who gave him the knife did him a good deed, but he harmed himself using the knife for what caused the danger, and not for what benefited himself. Likewise, God gives the unbeliever power (*quwa*), but [the latter] uses it to destroy himself and does not use it [to adopt] faith; thus it is he who destroys and does evil to himself. That which indicates that [God] does not impose upon humankind what they do not have the power to do is that it is impossible to command someone with no wealth to pay religious charity (*zakat*), because the zakat is invalid without property. Similarly, He does not command His servant to believe if he does not have the power for it, because faith is invalid without the power for it.[53] And that which indicates that the power precedes the act is that the instrument, such as the hand or foot, by which the act occurs must exist prior to it. So, too, the power [must exist prior to the act].

31. **Then if it is asked:** What is the proof that God does not will disobedience, and why do you deny that everything that happens in the world is by the will and wish of God? *Say to him:* Because we say that every religious duty (*'ibadat*) is an act that He wills and wants and consents to, and every form of disobedience He prohibits is an act that He loathes and censures and for which He threatens punishment. The proof of that is that it would be impossible for a wise man[54] to command something he loathed and to prohibit something he wanted. God has commanded [us to have] faith, so He must will it; and He prohibits unbelief, so He must loathe it. [God] has said: "And God wills no injustice for his servants" (Q. 40:31); and "I created the jinn and humankind only to worship [Me]" (Q. 51:56). And He said after He mentioned a number of disobedient acts: "All of that is evil, loathsome in [the sight of] your Lord" (Q. 17:38). That which indicates this is that a wise man would not will to do something ethically wrong, because willing something ethically wrong is ethically wrong, and wanting to do something insolent is insolence, just as willing wisdom is wisdom. Thus, if God is all-wise we know that He does not will insolence. How would it be possible [for Him] to will to curse and condemn Himself, and how could it be said that every corruption or injustice that occurred to humankind was willed by Him?

32. **Then if it is said:** If something that [God] did not will happened in the world, that would necessitate His impotence. *Say to him:* Are there not [cases] in the world where He does not command something but rather prohibits it? These do not indicate His impotence. And, in the world things happen that He does not will but rather loathes, and these do not necessitate His impotence. If it were possible for Him to will disbelief, it necessarily follows that the unbeliever as well as the believer will have done what God has willed. And if that is the case [His willing unbelief] would be beneficial, the same as it is beneficial when a slave does what the master wishes. And it would necessarily follow that He should not punish the unbeliever but send him to Paradise along with the believer, because [the unbeliever] had also done what God willed the same as the believer had done. Thus if He prohibits disobedience it is not possible for the Wise One to prohibit what He willed, just as He would not command what He loathed. **Moreover,** if it could be said that He willed disobedience, then one could also say that He loves it and is pleased with it. But He says: "He likes not ingratitude from His servants; if you are grateful, He is pleased with you" (Q. 39:7).

33. **Then if it is said:** People say: "Whatever Allah wants is so, and whatever He does not want isn't." So, it must be that everything that perishes or exists[55] is by virtue of what He wants. *Say to him:* What those people say is not an argument. If one could argue on the basis of that statement then one could argue on the basis of their statement: "God's command is inexorable" (*la maradda li-'amri llah*), meaning it is impossible to repulse what He commands. But it has been established that unbelievers do repulse God's command. Therefore, its interpretation should be that "there is no resistance to what He does." Similarly, the interpretation of their statement: "Whatever Allah wants is so" should be: "Whatever God wants to do must be."

34. **Then if it is asked:** What do you say about the affliction of the children of polytheists, do you allow that God would do it? *Say to him:*

May God protect [me] from permitting that of him, for it would be an injustice and an [act of] insolence, and He is far removed from such things. What God has said indicates this: "No bearer of burdens can bear the burden of another" (Q. 6:164, 17:15), and "for every soul to receive its reward by the measure of its endeavor" (Q. 20:15), and "Every soul earns only its own account" (Q. 6:164), and "nor would [We] send our wrath until we had sent a messenger [to give warning]" (Q. 17:15); and [anyway], messengers are not sent to children.[56] The Prophet said: "The pen is raised in three instances: a man sleeping until he awakens, a child until he reaches puberty; and an insane person until he recuperates."[57] One for whom the pen has been raised has no sin (*dhanb*) for which to be punished. **Moreover**, [divine] punishment is morally good only for one who has committed a sin, just as those who misbehave are disciplined in the visible world. Now, a child is without sin, so, how can it be said that God would punish him?

35. **Then if it is asked:** He punishes him for his father's sin? *Say to him:* It is impossible to punish someone for someone else's sin, just as, it would not be morally good to punish and beat one man for the misbehavior and injustice of another.

36. **Then if it is asked:** Has God not said: "And they will breed none but wicked ungrateful ones" (Q. 71:27)? *Say to him:* He intends [in this verse] that only those who become wicked and ungrateful, when they mature, should not breed; He does not mean that they have this attribute (*sifa*) when they are born.[58]

37. **Then if it is asked:** Is it not the case that in this world (*al-dunya*) children are virtually the same as their fathers in regard to disbelief? Hence, are they not under virtually the same rule as their fathers in the hereafter (*al-akhira*) regarding [divine] punishment? *Say to him:* If what you said were possible, one could also say that if [the father] committed adultery [the child] should be flogged[59] and if [the father] committed murder, [the child] should be killed, because he is under the same rule as his father. If that is not valid then what you asserted is faulted; he only has the same judgment as his father, however, in that which does not relate to divine punishment. As for divine punishments, God preserve us!

38. **Then if it is asked:** Does God recompense them for these diseases and sicknesses he causes, or not? *Say to him:* Verily, if He caused sickness,[60] He would turn it into greater advantage in the hereafter. If that were not so then it would not be ethically good for Him to cause animals and children to be sick, just as it would not be ethically good for us to hire somebody and work him to exhaustion without paying him his wage.

39. **Then if it is asked:** Thus, is there a lesson[61] and benefit from

these sicknesses for humans (*al-mukallafin*) or not? **Say to him:** Yes, because when a man is sick he is much more likely to be mindful of disobedience, fearing the Hellfire, and to act obediently desiring Paradise. God stated this warning: "See they not that they are tested every year [once or twice? Yet they turn not in repentance and they take no heed]" (Q. 9:126).[62]

40.   Then if it is asked: Are you saying that Allah has indicated the truth (*al-haqq*) to everyone He has created, and has He guided them to religion? **Say to him:** Yes, and the evidence for that is that if He is forbearing and merciful, it would not be possible for Him to impose on us [what He requires of us] unless He has indicated to us what He will impose; and it would not be possible for Him to prohibit us from disobedience unless He has warned us about it so that we could avoid doing it, because He has willed our well-being.   Therefore, He must explain and indicate to us the proper way (*tariqat l-rushd*) so that we can take it, and the improper way (*tariqat l-ghayy*) so that we can beware of taking it.   If He does that, and then He issues a command to a man, and the man disobeys it, the man harms himself and will perish despite clear evidence [warning him]; and if [the man] obeys, he will have done himself good and would be saved.   God is good to all of humankind (al-mukallifin), both to those who believe and those who disbelieve, just as someone who offers food to two starving men and [only] one eats it, he has been morally good to them both equally.

41.   Then if it is asked: Are you saying that every blessing [good] (*ni'ma*) we have is from God? **Say to him:** Yes, He gave us life, and empowered us, and gave us the instrumental means [with which to accomplish things], and made it possible for us to enjoy things, granted us health and vitality and sense perceptions, and provided us with various kinds of sustenance.   Then He imposed [duties] upon us, and prohibited us from [certain things] so that we would worship Him and enter the delights of Paradise; by these [we acquire] the perfection of grace in this world as well as in religion. As for the gifts, tributes, and legacies we receive from others than Him, all of them are [ultimately] from God.   Truly, God is [the one] who created [all of] that, and He made us to have possessions and advantages so that we would be gracious and giving.   Thus, every good thing we have is from God.[63]

42.   Then if it is asked: Are you saying that God bestowed favors upon us (*an'ama 'alayna*) by imposing obligations upon us and by issuing us commands and prohibitions, and that speech (*al-kalam*) is [one of] His [creative] acts? **Say to him:** Yes, because God created [His] servants, then He gave them commands and prohibitions and imposed duties upon them, just as He created them and He was good.   Just as doing the good is contingent (muhdath), so His speech is contingent.   He has said: "Naught comes to them of a reminder (*dhikr*) from their Lord but that it is contingent [or new]" (Q. 21:2). He describes the reminder as "contingent" (muhdath).⁶⁴ The reminder is the Qur'an, according to His saying: "And this [Qur'an] is a blessed message which we have sent down" (Q. 21:50), and His saying: "This is no less than a reminder and a Qur'an that makes clear" (Q. 36:69). And He said: "And Allah's command must be fulfilled" (Q. 33:37), and His command is the Qur'an. And He said: "He has sent down [from time to time] the most beautiful saying (*hadith*)" (Q. 39:23), and a saying must be contingent (muhdath).⁶⁵ And He said: "Alif Lam Ra, [This is] a Book whose verses are univocal [or plain] and then were detailed" (Q. 11:1), and this is the mark of the contingent. And He said: "And before this was the Book of Moses as a guide and a mercy" (Q. 46:12), and if something else existed before [the Qur'an] then [the Qur'an] is contingent. And moreover, the Qur'an has many suras, and is in Arabic, and is divided into two and many parts, and is heard. There is no disagreement within the community of the faithful (*umma*) that everything other than God is contingent, hence it follows necessarily that the Qur'an and the rest of God's speech is other than He, and that indeed, no one besides Him has the power to do the likes of [this], as He has said: "Say: If the whole of mankind and jinns were to gather together to produce the like of this Qur'an, they could not produce the like thereof, even if they backed up each other" (Q. 17:88).

43. Then if it is asked: Are you saying that Muhammad is a true prophet? *Say to him:* Yes, and the evidence for that is that he challenged the Arabs, who had the ultimate in pure speech (*al-fasaha*), to produce something similar to this Qur'an. We know that they were intent on invalidating his affair, for if they had been capable of the likes of this Qur'an, they would have been able to invalidate his affair. They avoided him despite their desire to make war upon him and fight against him. So, when we know that they turned to fighting and that they deserted their homeland and homes, that is evidence that it was not within their power to make something similar to the Qur'an. And we would know that God made it a miracle for His messenger so that we would know by this means that he is a true messenger, just as we know that raising the dead and healing the blind and lepers are the miracles of Jesus ('Isa), and just as [we know] that He made parting the sea and transmuting rods [into serpents] the miracles of Moses (Musa ibn 'Imran). And [additional] evidence that [Muhammad was a true prophet] is that he fed a crowd of people with only a modicum of food; and he beckoned to a tree and it stretched out [toward him] without his having pushed or pulled it; and he put his hand in a basin (*mida'a*)⁶⁶ with [little] water in it, and then it gushed from between his fingers until the people drank and performed ablution from it; and small stones swam in his palm.⁶⁷ Human beings (*al-bashar*) are not capable of any of this. Thus it establishes that he is a true prophet and that we have to accept what he commanded us to do and prohibited us from doing, and that the Qur'an is the word of God, requiring us to do according to what is in it.

44. Then if it is asked: The Qur'an consists of verses that disagree with each other (*ayat mukhtalifat*), so how can you implement what is in it? For example, His saying: "There is nothing whatever like unto Him" (Q. 42:11); and He says in another passage: "I have only created (*khalaqtu*) the jinn and humankind that they may serve me. No sustenance do I require of them, nor do I require that they should feed me" (Q. 51:56–57); and He says: "Many are the jinn and humans we have created for Hell" (Q. 7:179). *Say to him:* The Qur'an has [verses whose meanings are] univocal (*muhkam*) and [verses whose meanings are] equivocal (*mutashabiha*), just as He said: "He it is who has sent down to you the Book; in it are univocal verses; they are the Mother of the Book;⁶⁸ others are equivocal" (Q. 3:7). It is obligatory for you to carry out what accords with reason, [. . .]⁶⁹ upon that which is sound within it. Thus, judge that which accords with rational proof to be true, and bring that which contradicts [reason] into accord with it. Therefore, we say that His saying "There is nothing whatever like unto Him" (Q. 42:11) is univocal, and His saying: "And your Lord comes" (Q. 89:22) means "And your Lord's command has come." And we say that His saying: "I have only created the jinn and humankind that they may serve me" is univocal, and that He created all of them to worship Him. And His saying: "Many are the jinn and human beings we have created for Hell" is figurative (*majaz*), whose meaning is that the fate of their affair is the Hellfire. Then, [. . .]⁷⁰ the [meaning of] equivocal verses in the Book of God is indicated by univocal verses, but if not, then human intellect (*al-'aql*) is sufficient to indicate [the meaning]. God made some of the Qur'an[ic verses] univocal and some equivocal to bring humans closer to speculating (al-nazar) on its [meaning], and to [bring them to] rely on the proofs of the intellect and the arguments of the ulama and not on blind trust [in their pronouncements] (*taqlid*).⁷¹ It is obligatory for a rational person (*al-'aqil*) to base his convictions only on the univocal [verses] and on that which is indicated by reason, and to bring the equivocal [verses] into agreement with that.

[IV. Eschatology]

45. Then if it is asked: Are you saying that God has threatened grave sinners (*al-fusaq*) with Hellfire? *Say to him:* Yes, because⁷² God said: "Those who unjustly consume the property of orphans, shall consume a fire into their

103

own bodies: they will soon be enduring a blazing fire" (Q. 4:10). And He said: "Consume not your property among yourselves in vanities;[73] but let there be amongst you trade by mutual good will: Nor kill yourselves: for verily Allah has been to you Most Merciful! If any do that in rancor and injustice, soon shall we cast them into the Hellfire: And easy it is for God" (Q. 4:29–30). And He said: "If any does turn his back to them on such a day – unless it be in a stratagem of war, or to retreat to a troop (of his own) – draws on himself the wrath of God, and his abode is Hell – an evil refuge (indeed)"(Q. 8:16)! These passages indicate that those who commit sins of great magnitude (*al-kaba'ir*)[74] will be the People of Hell.

46. **Then if it is asked:** Are you saying that those [who commit grave sins] will be in Hellfire eternally and they will remain there forever, or will they be let out? *Say to him:* Indeed, they will be there eternally according to what Allah informs us in His Book: "But those who disobey Allah and His messenger and transgress His limits will be admitted to a fire, to abide therein eternally" (Q. 4:14)! And He said: "If a man kills a believer intentionally, his recompense is the Hellfire, to abide therein [forever]: and the wrath of Allah is upon him" (Q. 4:93).[75] And He said: "And the wicked – they will be in the Hellfire, which they will enter on the Day of Judgment, and they will not be able to keep away therefrom" (Q. 82:14–16). This clarifies the fact that they will not be absent from the Hellfire.

47. **Then if it is asked:** It is narrated from the Prophet in several reports (*akhbar*)[76] that a group of people will leave the Hellfire. *Say to him:* There cannot occur on the basis of reports attested unilaterally (*akhbar ahadiyya*) [. . .][77] reports that contradict their claim.[78] When they are contradicted we should refer to the Book of God, and we have just explained passages that indicate the eternity [of the Hellfire].

48. **Then if it is asked:** But God said: "Those who are wretched shall be in the Hellfire: There will be for them therein [nothing but] the heaving of sighs and sobs.[79] They will dwell therein for all the time that the Heavens and the Earth endure, except as your Lord wishes" (Q. 11:106–107). This indicates that they will not abide there forever. *Say to him:* If this indicated what you said, the following saying of His would so indicate: "As for those who are gladdened on the Last Day, they shall be in Paradise [eternally so long as the Heavens and the Earth endure, except as God wills, a gift that can't be cut off]" (Q. 11:108). If that is not an indication concerning the People of Paradise, similarly neither is what you said.[80] God intended only to make remote their departure from the Hellfire by correlating it with the duration of the Heavens and the Earth because that is remote, according the lexicographers. As the poet has said:

When crow's feathers turn gray,

    I shall go back to my family

And tar has turned into a pure milk.

49. Then if it is asked: What does His saying mean: "Allah forgives not that partners should be set up with Him; but He forgives anything else, to whom He pleases" (Q. 4:48)? *Say to him:* It means that God does not forgive polytheism (*shirk*), but that nonetheless He forgives what He wishes to, if it is among the lesser sins (*al-sagha'ir*). God has explained: "If you avoid the gravest sins (al-kaba'ir) which you are forbidden to do, we shall expiate your misdeeds from you" (Q. 4:31).

50. Then if it is asked: Has God not said: "Say: O my servants who in their prodigality have harmed themselves! Despair not of the mercy of God, who forgives all sins" (Q. 39:53). What does that mean? *Say to him:* Its meaning is that you should not despair of God's mercy when there is repentance. To this He said: "Turn to your Lord in repentance and submit to Him before the punishment comes on you" (Q. 39:54).

51. Then if it is asked: Are you claiming that there is intercession (*al-shafa'a*) and do you believe in it?[81] *Say to him:* Yes, but it is for the believers, not for grave sinners (*fasiqun*), because God has reported that He will cast the grave sinner into eternal Hellfire. He says: "The wrongdoers have no close friend and no intercessor who will be obeyed" (Q. 40:18),[82] and He says: "The wrongdoers have no helpers" (Q. 2:270). And He says: "And they offer no intercession except for those who are acceptable" (Q. 21:27).[83] All of that indicates that the grave sinner has no intercession, and that the Prophet intercedes on behalf of believers.

52. Then if it is asked: What is the use (*al-fa'ida*) of his intercession on behalf of the believers if they are the People of Paradise? *Say to him:* by his intercession for them, God will increase their level and stature in Paradise, and that is in honor of the Messenger of God, thus this is a great benefit.[84]

53. Then if it is said: Intercession is only for those who are being harmed or are in prison, thus one intercedes in order to end those things. Why then do you say: "There is no intercession for grave sinners"? *Say to him:* Intercession in the visible world (al-shahid) might concern the increase of stature and merit, just as one of us petitions someone else and thereby requests an increase in his rank and stature.

54. Then if it is asked: The Prophet said "My intercession is for the serious sinners (*ahl l-kaba'ir*) in my community (*umma*)." [85] Why don't you say that? *Say to him:* It is not possible to substitute for what is manifest in the Book of God a report whose validity cannot be decided. If [the report] were valid, it would mean that one who commits serious sins and then repents would be among the people [for whom there] was intercession, so that no one would presume that the intercession is only for those who always obeyed God, and from whom there was never any great or small disobedience.

[V. The Intermediate Position]

55. Then if it is asked: Why did you say that one who fornicates (zana)[86] and murders is a grave sinner, not a believer?[87] *Say to him:* Because our saying "believer" in Islamic law (Shari'a) is a noun of praise, for it is [in this sense] that God mentions [believer] in His Book and correlates it with praise saying: "Successful (*aflaha*) are the believers"[88] (Q. 23:1), and He says: "The believers are those only who, when God is mentioned [their hearts feel fear, and when His verses are recited to them it increases their faith, and who trust in their Lord, who perform the prayer and spend freely of that which We have given them]. They are the ones who in truth are the believers" (Q. 8:2–4). Therefore, if a man intends to praise someone else, he says: "He is an excellent believer (*mu'min fadil*)."[89] If that is valid, and it is established that the grave sinner deserves blame, cursing and scorn, it follows necessarily that we do not call him a believer, just like we do not call him excellent. When we mean [or know?][90] linguistically that a man is called [a believer], and [the one who calls him that] intends thereby that [the man] gives credence to God (*musaddiq li-llah*), then we stipulate therefore [the man's] speech. Hence, we say: "He believes in God, His Messenger and what His revelation stipulates."

56. Then if it is asked: Why did you say that a grave sinner is not an unbeliever (*kafir*)?[91] *Say to him:* If he were an unbeliever, [Islamic] legislation (*ahkam*) for unbelievers, such as the poll tax [for non-Muslims] (*jizya*), war [against non-Muslims], and prisoners [of war] would be applied to him,[92] and he could not be buried in the cemetery for Muslims, nor receive the [funeral] prayer. And if grave sin occurred after virtue (*salah*), he would have to be an apostate (*murtadd*) who is called to repent and thus repents, and if not, then killed just as would be done to unbelievers. And since [such things] are invalid according to the consensus (ijma') of the community, we know that [the grave sinner] is not [of the same status as] an unbeliever.

57. Then if it is asked: Do you say, then, that he is a hypocrite (*munafiq*)?[93] *Say to him:* No, because "hypocrite" is a name for one who hides unbelief within himself while manifesting submission [to God (*al-islam*)], and the grave sinner does not hide within himself the contrary of what he manifests, so how [can it][94] be said that he is a hypocrite? If all of that were not the case, we would know that he was a grave sinner. We name him a grave sinner only because of his exchange of friendship with God for enmity, and obedience toward God for disobedience. It is said of a mouse that she is "a tiny thing getting out" (*fuwaysiqa*)[95] when she goes out from her cave in order to cause harm and corruption.

58. Then if it is asked: What do you say about the punishment in the grave; do you believe in that? *Say to him:* Yes, because God has said that which so indicates, saying: "Our Lord! Twice have you made us die" (Q. 40:11),[96] and His saying: "They will be exposed to the Hellfire morning and evening, and on that Day when the Hour comes up, [it will be said]: 'Cast the People of Pharaoh into the severest torture'" (Q. 40:46). And many reports were also narrated from the Prophet; such as, what has been related concerning the story "Munkar and Nakir"[97] and that the interrogation will take place in the grave; and such as the narratives about the weighing of man's deeds at the Resurrection even though that is impossible because [the deeds] are past and no longer extant; and that God places a mark of light [indicating] good deeds on one pan of the scale, and mark of darkness on the other indicating bad deeds. And if the pan bearing light weighs in heavier we know that [that person] belongs to the inhabitants of Paradise; if the pan bearing darkness weighs in heavier, we know that he belongs to the inhabitants of the Hellfire. And they say that God will make them accountable and inquire [about them]. And we maintain that the Path (*al-sirat*) is a way [both] to Paradise and way to the Hellfire.

[VI. Commanding the Good and Prohibiting Evil]

59. Then if it is asked: Do you say that one who does not prohibit wrong-doing has disobeyed God? *Say to him:* That is possible for him when he knows about it and it is his view that in accepting it, it becomes incumbent [upon him], and that in omitting it, it becomes disobedience. Similar is commanding the good; if he were afraid for his [own safety], it would not be incumbent upon him. If, after that, he denounced wrongdoing and manifested the truth (al- haqq) he has done good. If not, it devolves upon him [to do so].

[A. Political Theology: the Imamate]

60. Then if it is asked: What do you say concerning the imamate? *Say to him:* We say that the Imams after the Messenger were Abu Bakr, then 'Umar, then 'Uthman, and then 'Ali ibn Abi Talib. [This is] on the basis of what is established by his statement that 'Ali ibn Abi Talib was the Imam, according to what is established by reports and traditions. As for talk about which one was superior, there is no evidence [that proves] any one of them was superior, even though those who [otherwise] are [blameless in this matter] have strong opinions and err in denouncing him, such as the Rafida[98] and the Khawarij.

[B. The Validity of Tradition]

61. Then if it is asked: What do you say about the reports that they narrate, do you accept all of them or not? *Say to him:* We declare [as true] all that is established by multilateral reports (*al-akhbar al-mutawatira*), [by] which we know what the Messenger of God has said. And that which was narrated by one or two [transmitters only], or by one for whom error was possible, [such reports] are unacceptable in religions (*al-diyanat*) but they are acceptable in the proceedings of positive law (or "branches," *fi furu' l-fiqh*),[99] as long as the narrator is trustworthy, competent, just, and he has not contradicted what is narrated in the Book, and is not subject to any proscription. And that which is transmitted in conflict with the Book and rational evidence we will interpret metaphorically[100] in a sound manner, just as we interpret the Book of God in accord with rational proof, not with that which is in conflict with it.

[C. God's Decree]

62. Then if it is asked: Do you say that God determines (*qada*) and decrees (*qaddara*) every good and evil, sweet and bitter[101] thing? *Say to him:* We say that God determines every prosperity (*al-rakha'*) and misfortune (*al-shidda*) and other things besides [in that which] He has created. As for disobedience and unbelief, God forbid that He would create, decree, and determine them, except in the sense that He informs us about them, as He has said: "And We decreed for the Children of Israel in the Book" (Q. 17:4), which means: We informed them. As for [their] saying "He decreed" means He created and enforced, that is absurd. How is it possible that He is pleased with (*radiya*) the unbeliever, then incites against him.[102] And how is it possible concerning God's determination that satisfaction [with it] does not occur, when it has been established by the umma that satisfaction with God's determination is obligatory?

[D. Repentance and Faith]

63. Then if it is asked: Do you say that whoever disobeys God and disbelieves and commits grave sin, then repents, his repentance will be accepted? *Say to him:* Yes, because God says: "Those who invoke no other god with Allah [nor take any life which God has forbidden except in righteousness, nor fornicate – for whoever does that shall pay the price. The punishment for him shall be doubled on the Day of Resurrection, and he will eternally abide therein in disdain. Save he who repents and believes and works] righteous deeds" (25:68).[103] Just as one who does evil to someone else, then he excuses [himself] with a real excuse, his plea will be accepted, and also if he repents, his repentance will be accepted.

64. Then if it is asked: What is the attribute of repentance (*tawba*)? *Say to him:* It is to repent of past disobedience because it was [one's own] disobedience. If one repented of another's disobedience, it would not be accepted, the same as when someone apologizes to someone else who wrongs him [. . .][104] and by virtue of this [he assists him (nasarahu?)][105] or [. . .][106] he profits from it, [the one to whom he apologized] is not obligated to accept his apology.

65. Then if it is asked: Are you saying that whoever repents, his punishment will be abolished and he becomes one of the People of Paradise? *Say to him:* If his repentance is valid he will be excluded from the Hellfire and he will be one of the People of Paradise, unless he returns to his disobedience toward God.

66. Then if it is asked: Do human beings profit from obedience (*ta'a*) [even] if they are unbelievers or grave sinners? *Say to him:* They do not deserve reward, although it would necessitate decreasing their punishment, just as God has said: "If you avoid the greatest [sins] which you are forbidden to do [We will pardon your evil deeds and make you to enter at a noble gate]" (Q. 4:31).[107]

67. Then if it is asked: Do you say that faith increases and decreases, and that it [consists in] the performance of the limbs and the conviction in the heart and the speaking of the tongue? *Say to him:* Yes, because every duty which belongs to faith is either the speaking of the tongue or the performance of limbs or conviction in the heart. Hence, God says: "For believers are those who, when Allah is mentioned, feel a tremor in their hearts. [And when they hear His signs rehearsed, find their faith strengthened; they trust in their Lord. Who establish the prayers and spend (freely) out of the gifts We have given them for sustenance.] Such in truth are the believers" (Q. 8:2–4). He made an increase in faith, but a decrease is possible.

The Prophet said: "One who is not trustworthy has no faith." [108] It has been established that all that we call faith increases and decreases, because religious duties performed by some worshippers are greater than [those performed] by others, and some do more than others.

This [entire] statement [above][109] is sufficient for those who wish to cover all of "unity and justice."

This is [now] complete. Praise God, the Mighty and Benevolent, and may prayers and peace be upon our Master, Muhammad.

Copied on Wednesday [. . .],[110] the third of the month of Shawwal in the year AH 1108 [1696 CE] with the help of my master, the Qadi al-'Arif Sharaf al-Din al-Hasan ibn Muhammad al-Makhidi al-Qadi al-'Arif, in the city of 'Imran,[111] may God protect it, [and may He] make him and us successful, for the appropriateness of [our] works by virtue of the truth (al-haqq) of the Prophet, the Chosen One, and his family, the pure ones, and praise God, Lord of the Worlds.

[Written] by the hand of a poor soul (*faqir*) for his Lord, confessing his sins, 'Ali Abdallah al-'Anari.

Notes

1. The text that immediately follows begins the translation. Square brackets surround titles and phrases that are not found in the Arabic original.
2. Hereafter, for the sake of brevity and clarity, the translation will not repeat formulaic praises and eulogies, stated almost invariably after the names of God and His messengers.
3. The interlocutory formula *in qila* literally means "if it is said." We have translated it "asked" here and in those subsequent paragraphs where context suggests that the statement can be read as a question. Following this first question, the Arabic formula reads: *fa-in qila*, "thus" or "then if it is asked (or said)."
4. This term and its cognates from the same Arabic root denote that which is known directly, not mediated by the senses. Hence they are often translated "necessary reason," and we will occasionally so translate it in these pages. Normally, however, we have preferred "intuitively" in the philosophical sense of that term.
5. On the Mu'tazilite theory of knowledge, see George F. Hourani, *Islamic Rationalism*, pp. 17–36.
6. Lit., instruments, that is, bodily limbs.
7. The meaning of *dalil* (pl. al-adilla) is "evidence that is or can be used to draw a conclusion." See Frank, *Beings and Their Attributes*, esp. references in Technical Terms Index – Arabic under the root *d-l-l*. In addition see George F. Hourani, *Islamic Rationalism*, pp. 17–36. Mu'tazilite epistemology and the importance of rational and physical evidence is discussed by Josef van Ess, "The Logical Structure of Islamic Theology."

8. That is, caused to be, created. The Quranic term *makhluq* is translated in this work as "created" and "*muhdath*" as "contingent," while *haditha/hawadith* is usually rendered temporal thing/s or entity/ies, following Frank, *Beings and Their Attributes*, Glossary, passim.

9. These are the five fundamental doctrines that characterize the Mu'tazili school. As indicated in chapters 2 and 4, 'Abd al-Jabbar reclassified the fundamentals of Mu'tazili doctrine throughout his career.

10. The mutakallimun distinguished between past eternity and future eternity (*fima lam yazal wa fima la yazalu baqi'*). In the pages that follow, we have usually stipulated both tenses of eternity if they are both stated in the original.

11. MS: *al-'alat*; editor: *al-'alam*.

12. This may be in reference to the Christian concept of crucifixion.

13. The editor notes a lapse in the text here and suggests *wa taswir l-jariha wa l-a'da'*, "and fashion limbs and body members."

14. The proper sense of "al-'adl", as explained in the preceding chapter, is theodicy, that is, vindicating the claim that God is just.

15. Or, . . . of His "nature" (*min khulqihi*), although it seems unlikely that a Muslim mutakallim would assert that God has a "nature," as the Christian mutakallimun did.

16. This principle of theodicy is based on: "Allah never places a burden on someone greater than he can bear" (Q. 2:286), and "Allah puts no burden on anyone unless He has enabled him" (Q. 65:7). For a discussion of this principle in Islamic thought, see Ormsby, *Theodicy in Islamic Thought*.

17. The editor of the Arabic text suspects a lapse occurs here in the text.

18. MS: *ila al-safah*; editor: *ilayhi al-safah*.

19. The Mu'tazila used this formulaic phrase to refer to eschatological doctrine: the promise of divine reward in Paradise for obedience to God and the threat of punishment in Hellfire for disobedience. See the discussion in chapter 4.

20. MS: *wa-tawa'ada li l-'iqab bi-man 'asahu*; editor: *wa-tawa'ada min al-'iqab man 'asahu*.

21. The sect known as the Murji'a is discussed in chapters 2 and 4.

22. The sect known as the Khawarij is discussed in chapters 2 and 4.

23. In the strong sense of neglect, that is, doing away with religious duties, in contrast to the case of simply omitting to do supererogatory acts, which is the purpose of the second type of Commanding the Good.

24. The rest of the verse, missing in the original, is given for context.

25. MS: *lam yajuz*; editor: *lam yajib*.

26. The notion of bodies brought into being or being contingent (*muhdath*, passive participle) implies that which brings them into being (*muhdith*, active participle) or a maker (*fa'il*). The Arabic says literally: bodies have a producer (or creator).

27. Editor: perhaps *siyagha*, "fashioning," "forming."

28. In the case of God, power or capacity (qudra) has the connotation of divine omnipotence, although, as the following passage indicates, establishing qudra as a divine attribute takes precedence here over the moral limits of God's power,

which is taken up in the section on theodicy (al-'adl) below.

29. God's knowing is "omniscience."

30. The passive participle of *ahkama*, which means to do something or act with precision, such as learning a language.

31. Editor: or *al-siyagha*, "fashioning"; a cognate of al- sina'a, however, occurs later in the sentence.

32. The knowledge associated with skillful pursuits (*al-af'al al-muhkama*) resembles the distinction made by the British philosopher Gilbert Ryle between "knowing how" and "knowing that." To Ryle, knowing "how" to do things – being able to perform intelligently – is logically independent of any interior theorizing. Therefore, it involves a display of intelligence that others can witness. See *Encyclopedia of Philosophy* (New York: Macmillan and The Free Press, 1972), vol. 7/8, s.v. "Ryle, Gilbert."

33. Frank, *Beings and Their Attributes*, pp. 108, 195 translates and explains *maqdur 'alayhi* as "the possible whose existence can be brought to actuality by an agent."

34. That is, eternally preexistent.

35. That is, mutability.

36. The claim in this and the next paragraph that God is not a corporeal being is made against the doctrines of corporealism (*tajsim*) and anthropomorphism (*tashbih*). In addition to our discussion in the preceding chapter, see *Formative Period*, pp. 248, 290, et passim.

37. 'Abd al-Jabbar finesses the literal implication of this passage (that humans might see God in the visible world) with an etymological interpretation, by saying that the Quranic term for "looking" (*nazira*) should be understood by the eighth-form verb (*yantaziru*) from the same root, meaning "waiting." The Mu'tazila rejected the Ash'ari and popular Sunni view that God can under certain circumstances be seen by human beings in the visible world.

38. MS: *al-'aqli*; editor: *al-'aql*.

39. MS corrupt; editor suggests: *idha kana ka-dhalika*.

40. Standard Sunni commentary, as reflected in *Tafsir al-imamayn al-Jalalayn*, identifies "both" as Heaven and Earth, whereas the sense of 'Abd al-Jabbar's use of the quotation is that the two divine beings would be in logical and practical conflict.

41. Or, justice: the doctrine of the justification of God's *operatio ad extra*. See ¶ 12.

42. MS: *'amr batilan*; editor: *'amran batilan*.

43. Discussed in the text at ¶ 13 above and ¶ 45 below.

44. The editor notes that the phrase in the MS is unclear: *wa-an yablughana fi ta'atihi kulla mablagh*.

45. MS: *'alyhim*; editor: *'alayhi*.

46. That is, to order humans to do what only God can perform.

47. MS: *al-lawn*; editor: *kal-lawn*.

48. MS: *da'wiyana*; editor: *dawa'ina*.

49. Or, "the All-Wise One cannot create His own abuse, or condemn and vilify [Himself]; for how could it be said . . ."

50. Throughout this passage and elsewhere, qudra and its cognates are translated as "power," but also as "capacity," or "ability," depending on the most felicitous English usage.
51. MS: *ajarahu* [he rewarded it]; editor: *amarahu* [he commanded it].
52. Lit., imposes, obligates.
53. According to Islamic law, children who have not reached the age of puberty, as well as the insane and slaves, are exempt from the full force of divine legislation, that is, the Shari'a. See Schacht, *An Introduction to Islamic Law*, pp. 124–133.
54. As in ¶ 29 above, this could also be translated as "the All-Wise [One]," referring to God, although the passage seems to refer to an example of an intelligent person doing something stupid.
55. MS: *halik ka'in*; editor: *halikan ka'inan*.
56. MS: *rusul* (pl.), with *rasul* (sing.) written over it, editor.
57. The reference is to the divine record of human performance of the religious duties. This Hadith is widely attested. See Bukhari, *Sahih al-Bukhari*, vol. 6 (Book 90, ch. 7), p. 2499; English translation, vol. 8 (Book 82, ch. 800) p. 527.
58. In other words, he is punished because it is he himself who chooses unbelief and error, not his parents. See the gloss on this by Manekdim, *Ta'liq*, p. 481.
59. See Qur'an 24:2, where one hundred stripes are prescribed for both the man and the woman discovered in adultery. However, to some jurists, the punishment mentioned above is for fornication, since for adultery (committed by married persons), the prescribed punishment is stoning to death.
60. MS: *maruda*; editor: *amrada*.
61. MS: *i'tibaran*; editor: *i'tibar*.
62. 'Abd al-Jabbar, following literary custom, here and elsewhere wrote "to the end of the aya" to abbreviate the rest of the verse, which his students and readers would know by heart.
63. In his defense of the Mu'tazila in chapter 9 (II, G), Harun Nasution quotes the famous phrase of D. B. MacDonald that the Mu'tazila were "daring and absolutely free-minded speculators." This statement of divine providence must qualify such a blanket characterization.
64. That is, in so far as God continually recreates the world and all that is in it, everything is continually renewed, which is to say, created (muhdath).
65. The widely consulted Sunni commentary *Tafsir Jalalayn* gives *qur'an* as a synonym for Hadith in this passage, i.e., "beautiful saying" means "beautiful Qur'an." The Qadi, however, plays on the sense of Hadith as something new, produced, thereby locating the concept of contingency in the text of the Qur'an.
66. The basin at the mosque used for ritual ablutions prior to prayer.
67. 'Abd al-Jabbar discusses Muhammad's miracles other than the inimitable Qur'an in *al-Mughni*, 16: 407–23; the miracles discussed here are discussed on pp. 413–414.
68. *Umm al-kitab*; in Quranic cosmology this is the heavenly prototype of the Book, sometimes also called the Well-Preserved Tablet, *al-lawh al-mahfuz*.

69. MS: *qadiyatahu?* (MS unclear.)
70. MS: blank space.
71. The Mu'tazila were early critics of blind acceptance of the authority of the ulama; as we shall see in more detail in subsequent chapters, this criticism was advanced by both modernists and later traditionalists alike.
72. MS: *'anna* or *'inna*; editor: *li'anna*.
73. MS: *bi-l-batil baynakum*; editor: *baynakum bi l-batil*.
74. The term is synonymous with fisq, "grave sin."
75. The legal consequence is under the rule of *qisas* (Q. 2:178). That is, a life should be taken for a life destroyed, on the scale of equality. For an accidental murder, one is enjoined to free a slave or to perform fasting in two following months (*Tafsir Jalalayn,* at Q. 2:178).
76. "Akhbar" here is a plural synonym of Hadith, the prophetic tradition. The technical point being made is that according to the Ash'ariya and Hanbaliya, for a Hadith to be well attested is a greater guarantee of its soundness than its content per se. The Mu'tazila gave a greater role to the rational meaning of the content of a Hadith.
77. MS: blank space. In *Ta'liq,* 672: 10, the Qadi (or Manekdim) impugns the validity of reports attested only unilaterally, saying the Mu'tazili method is to address a problem by way of knowledge *(tariq al-'ilm).*
78. In *Ta'liq,* p. 673, the Qadi mentions several Hadiths that counter a single report. Then, he offers the interpretation that "People who will leave the Fire" refers to those who will leave the wrongdoing of the People of the Hellfire.
79. The sobs and sighs correspond to the two-part braying of an ass, a simile that refers to the folly of the arrogant and wicked who do not realize the punishment they bring upon themselves.
80. MS: adds *da'iman,* "forever," which the editor suggests should be ommitted.
81. See the discussion of this point in chapter 4. The Mu'tazila differed pointedly with the Murji'a on this issue as well as among themselves.
82. That is, evildoers will have no one through whom to petition God's mercy.
83. In the context of the preceding verses, the reference is to the Christian belief that Allah has begotten a son, and to the pre-Islamic Arab belief that the angels were daughters of Allah. In the Islamic worldview, the prophets and angels are servants of Allah, along with human beings. They deserve respect, but not worship.
84. MS: *al-'azima*; editor: *la-'azima* (lam with fatha).
85. Al-Tirmidhi, *Sunan al-Tirmidhi* 4: 45, Hadith 2552.
86. Unlawful sexual intercourse, including adultery.
87. The Murji'a argued that punishment and condemnation of sin must be postponed until God's Judgment; therefore, the sinner is a believer. The Mu'tazila opposed this position, arguing that the grave sinner at least is not a true believer.
88. Following Pickthall's translation. On the interpretation of *falah,* see Rahman, *Major Themes of the Qur'an,* p. 63.
89. MS omits "mu'min", which is required by the preceding discourse.

90. MS: *'aradna*; editor suggests *'arafna*.
91. The argument now turns against the Khawarij, who condemned the grave sinner here and now as an unbeliever who must be forced to repent or be expelled from the community.
92. That is, if the Khawarij were correct, then grave sinners would have to be treated as prisoners of war.
93. This was the middle ground that al-Hasan al-Basri (d. 728) tried to strike between the Murji'a and the Khawarij — that the grave sinner is neither a believer (the Murji'a) nor unbeliever (the Khawarij).
94. MS: blank space; perhaps it originally read *yumkin an* "is it possible to?" or in this context, "can it?"
95. A diminutive feminine form of *fasiqa* (wanton sinner), which Lane, *Arabic–English Lexicon* identifies as an epithet for a mouse, perhaps because of the destruction she is able to accomplish when she gets out of her lair.
96. The sense of this passage is given in Qur'an 2:28: "How can you reject faith in Allah? — seeing that you were without life, and He gave you life; then He will cause you to die, and will again [at the resurrection] bring you to life; and again to Him will you return."
97. The persecuting angels of the grave. Qur'an 47:27: "Then how [will it be with them] when the angels gather them and strike their faces and backs?" Refer to *SEI*, s.v. "Munkar wa Nakir."
98. "Turncoats," the derogatory term used by Sunni Muslims for the Imami (Twelver) Shi'a. On the development of Imami Shi'a doctrine of the Imamate during 'Abd al-Jabbar's lifetime (tenth and early eleventh centuries) see Sachedina, *Islamic Messianism*.
99. Literally, the "branches" of legal reasoning, as opposed to the foundations (usul) of legal reasoning. In other words, weaker Hadiths may be used in arguing cases, but not in establishing the foundations of what is legal.
100. MS: *ta'awwalna*; editor: *ta'awwalnahu*.
101. MS: *man*; editor: *murr*.
102. The meaning of this passage is not clear.
103. The text within the square brackets is abbreviated in the text.
104. MS: blank space and whiteout of part of a word. The original meaning is difficult to reconstruct.
105. There is not enough context to understand the word used here.
106. Editor: word illegible here.
107. The crucial passage in square brackets was left out of the quotation in the text.
108. Wensinck locates the Hadith in Ibn Hanbal, *Al-Musnad*, 3: 135, 153; 21: 251.
109. That is, the sixty-seven paragraphs that comprise this compendium of Mu'tazili doctrine.
110. MS: a word here is unreadable.
111. A city in the region of Hamdan.

II

Harun Nasution *and* Modern Mu'tazilism

six

The Persistence *of* Traditionalism *and* Rationalism

The 1980s and 1990s have witnessed avid public interest around the globe in the revival of traditional religions, particularly Islam. The resurgence of religion in contemporary Islamic societies is extremely broad and varied, however. It cuts across political movements, social classes and ethnic boundaries. It finds sympathetic support among both the middle and the working classes – among university students and faculty, engineers, physicians, and other professionals as readily – indeed, often more readily – than it does among the traditional ulama. Nonetheless, because it is sometimes associated with violence, the resurgence of Islam is viewed by Western media as well as many academics as a potential threat to non-Muslim societies.[1] The code word for Islamic resurgence as "threat" to Western and Westernized societies is "fundamentalism" – a term that has come to connote "extremism" in common parlance. The concern with fundamentalism dominates contemporary discourse – public as well as academic – about modern Islam. That concern creates a distortion of contemporary Muslim theology that we turn now to correct in the remaining pages of this volume. We will continue to develop the argument that Islamic rationalism is also an aspect of Islamic resurgence, in dialectical tension with resurgent traditionalism, as it has been throughout much of Islamic history.

Our aim is to show that the rational and critical spirit of Mu'tazili theology, found in such texts as the one by 'Abd al-Jabbar translated in chapter 5, is still alive in Harun Nasution's debates about Islamic rationalism with traditionalists and modernists, and this has intellectual overtones throughout modern Islamic thought. We will also argue that the opponents of Islamic modernism, the traditionalists, are not "irrationalists," but rather they are proponents of a scripturalist rationalism, a rationalism put solely in the service of revelation.

The resurgent interest in renewing the Islamic spiritual and intellectual heritage is in fact quite diverse and complex. Moreover, it is not very new. It is true that many who urge the revival and implementation of Islamic teachings in modern society – "Islamists" (Ar. *islamiyun*) as they are often called – are inspired by the traditionalist interpretation of Islam by figures like Ahmad ibn Hanbal, whom we have already discussed, and the fourteenth-century Hanbali reformer Ibn Taymiya, whom we will discuss in more detail below. Others, however, have drawn from different or additional resources in the rich heritage of Islamic thought, including the Mu'tazili *mutakallimun*. Some modernists have found the Mu'tazili doctrines too heterodox; many of these have nonetheless opted against the social and confessional exclusivism of traditionalists by subscribing to the more orthodox rationalism held by the Maturidi *kalam madhhab*. On the whole, however, modernist interpretations of Islam have been eclectic in their appropriation of ancient and modern texts and intellectual currents. In particular, modernist Muslim theologians have applied the spirit of rationalism, formerly ascribed to Mu'tazili mutakallimun, to broader social and political issues affecting Islamic societies today. It is in this broad sense, which is not focused narrowly on specific doctrines, that the classical Mu'tazili teachers and their works have become referents in the writings of many modernist (and postmodernist) Muslim intellectuals.

One of the characteristics of both modernist and traditionalist theology is that both "madhhabs" challenge the claim of the ulama to be the sole legitimate interpreters of Islamic sacred texts. In a speech before several thousand faculty, students and ulama in 1943, the Shaykh (Rector) of al-Azhar, Mahmud Shaltut, advanced the argument that the medieval ulama had been true scholars of Islam, who did not blindly follow the opinions of their teachers; rather, they thought independently.[2] Both modernist and traditionalist (including Islamist) theologians have emphasized that each Muslim has a right and a duty to employ independent reasoning (*ijtihad*) in interpreting and deploying Islam in the world. On the other side, both trends in interpretation have condemned the antonym of ijtihad, namely, *taqlid*, blind reliance on tradition or on the interpretation of the ulama. The dialectical tension between modernists and traditionalists, then, has little to do with which texts should be read and who has the authority to interpret those texts. Qur'an and Sunna are among the essential texts of Sunni and Shi'i modernists and traditionalists alike, and both groups believe that every Muslim in principle has a right and a duty to interpret and implement these texts.

For traditionalists, however, ijtihad is based on the hermeneutical conceit that all interpreters must find a single, original meaning in the sacred texts of Qur'an and Sunna. Modernists interpret ijtihad to mean that Muslims must find the contextual meaning of Qur'an and Sunna for changing historical and political situations. The difference between the two groups is not over texts but rather interpretation. And, as in the age of Ahmad ibn Hanbal and his opponents among the Mu'tazila, a chief concern is whether revelation judges reason or reason judges revelation.

Modernist writers diverge in their approaches to these issues. In the next three chapters, we will focus on how Harun Nasution has attempted to persuade modernist Muslims of the need for Mu'tazili rationalism, indeed, Mu'tazili kalam, in contemporary Islamic societies. In the latter part of this volume, we will assess the views on rationalism held by other modernist Muslim thinkers, such as Fazlur Rahman (Pakistan/United States), Mohammed Arkoun (France), Hassan Hanafi (Egypt), and the feminist Fatima Mernissi (Morocco), none of whom would say, with Nasution, that they were Mu'tazilites, but all of whom have valued in one way or another the contribution of the Mu'tazila to Islamic intellectual history. Interestingly, few modernist Muslim theologians discuss particular Mu'tazili doctrines. The actual doctrines that Mu'tazili mutakallimun debated with their enemies, then, are not always the issues that are debated in modern Islam. Rather, it is the first principle of Mu'tazili kalam that has attracted the attention of most modernists to Mu'tazili thought. Let us recall the opening argument of *Kitab al-usul al-khamsa*, where 'Abd al-Jabbar restates the traditional first principle of theological reflection as follows:

> If it is asked: What is the first duty that God imposes upon you? Say to him: Speculative reasoning which leads to knowledge of God, because He is not known intuitively nor by the senses. Thus, He must be known by reflection and speculation.[3]

When asked how, in the absence of knowing that God exists, one comes to know that speculative reasoning is the first duty imposed by God, the Mu'tazili mutakallimun offered a circular argument (see chapter 5, ¶ 2). It is perhaps for this reason that many modernist Muslim theologians are not prepared to argue that God can be known, apart from revelation, by human reason alone. Nonetheless most would contend that the human intellect (*'aql*) must be put in the service of divine truth and the determination of human social responsibility. Traditionalists since Ibn Taymiya have also stressed the importance of reason in understanding divine revelation.

A distinguishing aspect of the difference between rationalists and traditionalists in modern Islamic thought is related to the Mu'tazili insistence on the ability of the human mind to grasp the divine moral imperatives, as well as their insistence on individual responsibility for all human acts. The role of theology in determining social and political action in the world is an issue with which contemporary Muslim theologians have grappled, as we shall see throughout the remainder of this volume. In a recent work on war and peace in Western and Islamic traditions, John Langan argues that the traditional Christian construction of theological warrants for the "just war" has evolved in modern times into the moral problem of how to eliminate war. In Langan's words, it "ceases to be a problem about God and history and becomes a problem about ourselves and our failure to do what our situation requires."[4] So, too, modernist Muslim theologians are more concerned to develop rational Muslim responses to the challenges of the modern world than to attack the theological creeds of opponents, whether Muslim or non-Muslim. In this respect also, modernist and postmodernist Muslim theologians differ from their traditionalist opponents. "Doing theology" more broadly across religious traditions rather than within a single tradition seems to be characteristic of modernist theologians in the late twentieth century. Some would argue that this is characteristic of a postmodern theological activity.

The remainder of this chapter will explore further the revival of interest in theological rationalism in modern Islamic theology. We begin with the critique of blind (irrational) adherence to tradition mounted by the fourteenth-century traditionalist Ibn Taymiya, and revived in eighteenth-century Arabia by Muhammad ibn 'Abd al-Wahhab. The severe communal and ritual boundary lines drawn between Muslims and non-Muslims (or fallen Muslims) by contemporary traditionalists often contain discourses and interpretations of Islam that bear the name of Ibn Taymiya but reflect the stringent interpretations of Ibn 'Abd al-Wahhab. We then consider the revival of rationalism and the formation of modernist Islamic theology in the person and writings of Muhammad 'Abduh (d. 1906), who sought to accommodate the reasoning of Islamic theology to modern science. This, along with the discovery of Mu'tazili manuscripts in Zaydi Shi'a archives in Yemen convinced some Europeans that the end of nonprogressive forms of Islamic traditionalism was in sight – a conclusion and an understanding of Hanbali traditionalism that this book seeks to correct. Our purpose at this stage of the argument is not to provide a comprehensive history of modern Islamic thought, but rather to identify a trend that is often overlooked.

The Revival of Traditionalism: Ibn Taymiya (d. 1328)

Abu l-'Abbas Ahmad ibn 'Abd al-Halim ibn Taymiya, known honorifically as Taqi al-Din, "devout in religion," was born in the Mesopotamian city of Harran in 1263, just five years after the Mongol warlord Hugalu had destroyed the Abbasid capital, Baghdad – not that far away, even in the thirteenth century. Ibn Taymiya's family soon moved to Damascus, and there he studied Islam with his father and other teachers, eventually becoming a recognized Hanbali jurist and teacher of religious sciences. Later he traveled to Egypt and other urban centers of Islamic learning. He gained public attention as a vigorous Hanbali polemicist and soon made enemies among scholars of the other madhhabs, especially the Shafi'i scholars. His scholarly career was frequently punctuated by political intrigues and reprisals arising from his own abrasive style as well as the instability of the Islamic world in the post-Abbasid Age.[5]

The disarray of the Islamic world in Ibn Taymiya's time is summarized under three major headings by Victor E. Makari: (1) the internal fragmentation of the Islamic world, especially evident in the collapse of the *Pax Islamica* of the Abbasid caliphs after 945; (2) the invasion of the central Muslim lands from the east by the Mongols in the thirteenth century, destroying the last vestiges of rule by the Abbasid caliphs; and (3) the invasion of Palestine and Syria from the west by the Christian Crusaders, bringing considerable violence to Muslim lives and property in that region.[6] As an activist politically and theologically, Ibn Taymiya was directly involved in rousing public opinion to raise a jihad in Egypt against Mongol troops in Syria. On more than one occasion he was publicly censured, and even jailed, for his outspoken views, which he urged the public to adopt and to act upon. For example, shortly before his death, he was imprisoned in Damascus by order of the sultan for having earlier issued a fatwa (nonbinding legal opinion) which held that the Shari'a forbids the visiting of the tombs of saints and prophets – a popular practice in Muslim, Christian, and other Middle Eastern religious communities. In 1293, he urged Damascene Muslim society to execute a Christian who had been accused of insulting the Prophet Muhammad.[7] He devoted numerous fatwas and polemical treatises to trenchant criticism of the Ash'aris, Shi'a, and popular Sufis, as well as non-Muslim confessional communities. When it was found that he continued to advance his views in writing while in prison, his books and writing materials were confiscated. He soon fell ill and died in 1328, reportedly a broken man.

To regard Ibn Taymiya as a Hanbali reformer is not to categorize him as a champion of irrationalism. Despite his sharp criticism of the Mu'tazili rationalists (usually referred to as the Qadariya in his writings), Ibn Taymiya urged Muslims to utilize the faculty of rational knowledge in order to achieve intellectual certainty about the meaning of revelation. Recall that 'Abd al-Jabbar stressed that the role of reason was to bring rational human beings to faith in God, to wit, Islam. For 'Abd al-Jabbar, reason precedes faith.

Rationalism in the service of faith, on the other side, is evident in Ibn Taymiya's characteristic stress on ijtihad, independent reasoning, and his criticism of blind reliance or devotion (taqlid) to the traditional teachings and interpretations of the ulama. Starting with revelation (the Qur'an) and the Sunna of the Prophet as an epistemological condition *sine qua non*, Ibn Taymiya urged individual reasoning over against blind acceptance of the authority of the ulama to interpret the Qur'an and the Sunna. In this respect he was even critical of Hanbali traditionalism, for if any scholar's teaching was accepted without question it placed unwarranted power in the hands of that person or madhhab. Ibn Taymiya sought to destroy the divisive results of factionalism that arose out of sectarianism.

Equally important to Ibn Taymiya, tradition had become encrusted with popular innovations in practice, such as visits to saints' tombs – even Christian and other non-Muslim shrines.[8] Hanbali reformers like Ibn Taymiya declared such practices to be innovations (sing. *bid'a*) that were condemned by the Sunna of the Prophet Muhammad and absent in the practice of the Salaf, the pious first three generations of Muslims who had transmitted the genuine Islamic tradition. Like Protestant Christian reformers two centuries later in Europe, Ibn Taymiya placed the rational responsibility for reforming and purifying religion on the individual believer, for he lost faith in the ability of the established religious authorities to reform themselves. In this respect, Ibn Taymiya's concerns about the dead weight of tradition on reform and renewal is echoed in the writings of modernist and postmodernist theologians, as we shall see.

Rationalism bound by servitude to the claims of revelation, however, is not the rationalism of the early Mu'tazila, nor is it comparable to the theological and political criticism by Muslim modernists and postmodernists. Ibn Taymiya's project, which reflected the Hanbali élan more generally, was to revivify the Muslim umma and strengthen its position over against its cultural enemies, by establishing its identity separate from non-Muslim communities and practices. The traditionalist instinct for communal survival through social and cultural separation can be seen in Islamist theological discourse today.

For Ibn Taymiya, as for many jurists and theologians, the political history of Islamic rule presented a problem. The caliphate had fallen to the Mongols in 1258, just before his birth. Effective control over Abbasid lands beyond the capital city of Baghdad had been seized by Buyid (945) and Seljuq (1055) warlords, among others. In what sense could Muslims of either traditionalist or rationalist outlook any longer speak about the centrality of the Qur'an and the teachings of the Prophet Muhammad in societies ruled by nominal Muslims and even non-Muslims? This was the problematic that Ibn Taymiya labored to resolve in a book titled *al-Siyasa al-shar'iya* (loosely, "Revelational politics" or "Politics according to revelation").[9]

In *al-Siyasa al-shar'iya*, Ibn Taymiya argued that all human society must be governed by a ruler who must extract obedience from his subjects, by force if necessary, to avoid social anarchy; in Sunni Islam, in order to have a more or less stable social order in which the requirements of the Shari'a can be carried out, it is worth putting up with nominal Muslim rulers, such as the Mamluks who ruled Egypt in Ibn Taymiya's time. The best Muslim polity in the Islamic mythos was the one instituted by the Prophet and made mighty by the rightly guided caliphs of the first generation. The breakup of the caliphate into numerous Islamic dynasties and kingdoms did not change the basic human social need for government. Specifically, Ibn Taymiya sought to accommodate the *Realpolitik* of the slave-soldier Mamluk government of Egypt to the central role he believed Islam should play in the growing cultural and religious pluralism of Egypt in the fourteenth century. Politically, the Mamluk state was governed by Turks and Caucasians, while guidance in religious and other local matters came from Arabic-speaking Egyptian ulama. The classical tension between the ulama and the ruling power in the Abbasid Age evolved into a conflict between the ulama and multiple, changing, and often non-Muslim governments with the rise of nationalism in the twentieth century.

The political state that Ibn Taymiya envisioned was to be governed in all aspects by the Shari'a. In exchange for just rule according to the Shari'a, Muslims would have to submit themselves to the ruler – even one who fell below or possessed virtually none of the ideal qualities of the Prophet Muhammad and his successors, the rightly guided caliphs of the next generation. Central to this argument was the role of *maslaha*, "public welfare," which is a key ingredient of Islamic jurisprudence and legal theory. Ibn Taymiya accommodated the Shari'a-minded conservatism of Hanbali traditionalism to the political vicissitudes of his time by arguing that the real intention of the Shari'a was the public good, maslaha. In all matters where the commands and prohibitions of the Qur'an and Sunna of the Prophet were silent or unspecific, the principle of maslaha could be considered identical to the intent of Shari'a.[10]

In effect, Ibn Taymiya was arguing for a polity, even if that should be a quasi- or non-Muslim state, that would transcend competing sectarian and confessional political interests. This is the troublesome issue of *wilaya*, the power and authority of the state to uphold the word of God. This issue lies at the heart of the traditional contest between the caliphate and the ulama, and the struggle between modern government(s) (*hukuma*) and the Islamiyun over legitimacy.

Ibn Taymiya's legacy today can be measured in part by the popular revival of interest in his works since the 1960s.[11] This was the same period in which Mu'tazili works were edited and published in Arabic in great number. In the case of Ibn Taymiya, new editions and new printings keep appearing. Was Ibn Taymiya, then, the spiritual ancestor of contemporary Islamic fundamentalism, as so many analysts have argued? The answer to that question is a complicated *sic et non*.

Our conclusion is that Ibn Taymiya was a more rational and independent-minded thinker than many of his later interpreters seem to have appreciated. The harder line of separation between a strict Hanbali interpretation of Islam on the one side and Sufism, Shi'i Islam, popular cult practices, and non-Muslims on the other was the work of Ibn 'Abd al-Wahhab, the eighteenth-century reformer who turned Ibn Taymiya's theology into political action far more successfully than Ibn Taymiya had been able to do.

The Political Enforcement of Traditionalism: Muhammad ibn 'Abd al-Wahhab (1703–1787)

Muhammad ibn 'Abd al-Wahhab was born in 1703 in the Najd, the eastern region of Arabia which is nowadays associated with petroleum. This was a century before Napoleon landed with a platoon of French Orientalists in Egypt. Ottoman political order (wilaya) in the Gulf region was nonetheless in decline. Ibn 'Abd al-Wahhab's early education was under Hanbali teachers, whose madhhab predominated in the Najd. Later, he studied Islamic science in Mecca, Medina, Damascus and Basra. Like so many Muslims in the late Middle Ages and early modern times, he had gained some of his early religious education from teaching Sufis, whose spiritual qualities seem to have impressed him, but whose popularized cultic practices he soon came to see as an abomination of the true Islam. The latter he defined as the Mu'tazila and the Sufis had done, each in their own distinct way, according to the doctrine of divine unity (*tawhid*). Hence, his followers referred to themselves as the Muwahhidun, the purveyors of divine unity. (It will be recalled that the Mu'tazila, by the time of 'Abd al-Jabbar in the tenth century, referred to themselves as the *ahl al-tawhid wa l-'adl*, "the People of [divine] Unity and [divine] Justice.") 'Abd al-Wahhab and his followers are known outside his movement as the Wahhabiyun, in English: "the Wahhabis."

Ibn 'Abd al-Wahhab's theological and political project was to rid the Muslims of the Najd of local popular cultic practices that had crept into the Islamic religious ethos and that were tolerated by the absent political land-lords, the Ottoman sultans, and even the local Hanbali ulama. In this, he was carrying out the theological agenda of Ibn Taymiya and the Hanbaliya more generally. The term "puritanism" is often applied to the Wahhabi movement, but one must do so with a caveat. The desire for purity and simplicity of religious practice was a desideratum of seventeenth-century Puritan refugees in North America, as it was of the eighteenth-century Wahhabis in Arabia. The political circumstances were different, however. British Puritans were not driven by a reformist political agenda.

Like Ibn Taymiya, Ibn 'Abd al-Wahhab soon ran afoul of financial beneficiaries of local shrine establishments, as well as the ulama and others committed to maintaining the religious status quo. He was forced to flee his home town of al-Uyayna and make a *hijra*, as it were, to al-Dar'iyya. There he converted the local prince, Muhammad ibn Sa'ud, to the Hanbali doctrine of Ibn Taymiya that Islamic revival is a necessary ingredient of successful political rule. It was in this political and intellectual marriage of reformer and ruler that the modern state of Saudi Arabia had its gestation. Modern scholarship has also attributed the rise of Islamic fundamentalism to Wahabbi/Saudi origins in the eighteenth century.[12] The problem with this view, however, is that for some scholars it is formed by looking backwards, from a contemporary concept of "fundamentalism" as religious reactions to modernity, to an Islamic movement that was largely unaffected by the European Enlightenment, secularization, and other cultural trappings of modernity. If Ibn Taymiya and Ibn 'Abd al-Wahhab are the spiritual mentors of contemporary Islamiyun, it has to do more with their ability to wage culture wars with traditional opponents within Islamicate societies; the discourse against more modern enemies – the West, secularism, communism, etc. – is largely an extrapolation from disputes with the Shi'a, Mu'tazila, local popular religions, and Christians, among others.

A more accurate view is that the Hanbali élan, from Ibn Hanbal himself, Ibn 'Aqil in tenth-century Baghdad, Ibn Taymiya in fourteenth-century Egypt, and Ibn 'Abd al-Wahhab in eighteenth-century Arabia, was their ability to lead periodic critiques of vested political and religious interests and to unify popular sentiment against what they vividly identified as non-Islamic accretions in Muslim religious practice. It was a form of theological rationalism that began with revelation as the indisputable source of religious and political identity, and cultivated legal and scriptural reasoning in defense of that identity and as a tool for bringing fallen Muslims back to a narrowly defined fold. Hanbali traditionalism, like the modernism we are about to discuss, can be seen as another form of rationalism: reasoning from texts and received truths that society generally accepts, but that require periodic reauthentication.

The Revival of Mu'tazili Rationalism in Modern Islam

In his 1957 article on the revival of Mu'tazilism in Islam, Rudi Caspar noted the ironic reversal of fortunes of the school. The Mu'tazila had begun in the eighth and ninth centuries as champions of Islam against non-Muslim enemies, as we have already seen. Mu'tazilism was defeated by a rising tide of traditionalism, which accused the Mu'tazila of doctrinal innovation (bid'a) and even unbelief (*kufr*).[13] For two more centuries the Mu'tazila contended with traditionalists as well as the newer Ash'ari and Maturidi madhhabs. From the late eleventh to the early twentieth century, however, the Mu'tazili madhhab was declared to be anathema in most Islamic locales, and only the Ash'ari and Maturidi madhhabs of kalam were regarded acceptable in Sunni Islam.[14] Within Sunni Islam, Hanbali traditionalism and Ash'ari kalam continued to be contentious. A rising tide of modernist criticism of traditionalism emerged in the late nineteenth century, in movements led by such figures as Muhammad 'Abduh in Egypt and Sayyid Ahmad Khan (1817–1898). Modernist interest in the Mu'tazila developed even further at mid-century, as we saw in earlier chapters, when an Egyptian team of scholars microfilmed a cache of Mu'tazili manuscripts in Yemen. This soon led to the discovery and publication of several important Mu'tazili works. Caspar (and others) viewed the renewed interest in Mu'tazilism among Muslim intellectuals as a trend that would turn the tide against Islamic traditionalism (and its postmodern offspring, fundamentalism).

Caspar linked the earlier twentieth-century revival of Mu'tazilism with the liberal intellectual and literary (Arabic) renaissance (*nahda*) of the late nineteenth century. The Nahda came in response, as Caspar thought, to the challenges of "the progressive but irresistible invasion of modern civilization imported from the Occident," which had the effect of attacking traditional Islamic thought, frozen in conservatism.[15] Mu'tazilism appeared to some modern intellectuals as an indigenous but long-neglected Islamic response to historical change and external challenges. To others, the ancient Mu'tazili mutakallimun were nothing short of people with vain passions (*ahl al-hawa*), who could be accused of the concept of grave sin (*fisq*) which ironically the early Mu'tazila had introduced into Islamic theological discourse (see chapter 5, ¶¶ 45–46). The Muslim theologian who perhaps contributed most to the renewed interest in the Mu'tazili madhhab was the Egyptian theologian, educator and jurist Muhammad 'Abduh (d. 1906). Like Ibn Taymiya and Ibn 'Abd al-Wahhab, Muhammad 'Abduh responded to perceived threats to Islam from social and political change. The difference lay in Shaykh 'Abduh's attempt, reminiscent of the Mu'tazila, to articulate a view of Islam at home in a world of change and non-Muslim intellectual challenges. 'Abduh faced challenges that differed from those that 'Abd al-Jabbar and his predecessors had encountered in so far as the late nineteenth century brought to Islam the challenges of modernity and the politically and economically powerful "West."

Theological Modernism: Shaykh Muhammad 'Abduh (d. 1906)

Caspar's belief that Islam was, like the West, progressing toward a more rational form of religion may have been based in part on Muhammad 'Abduh's rationalist predecessors in Egypt, such as Shaykh Rifa'a al-Tahtawi. Al-Tahtawi (1801–1873) had been influenced by his teacher, Hasan al-'Attar, one of the first Egyptian intellectuals to visit France and to appreciate the positive impact that knowledge of science might have on Egyptians. Al-Tahtawi came, as his name indicates, from a family of ulama in the Upper Egypt city of Tahta. He was among the scholars sent by Muhammad 'Ali, the Turkish ruler of Egypt, to study in Paris. He was actually sent as an imam for the other Egyptian students, but after five years, from 1826 to 1831, he returned to Egypt a scholar of European philosophical and scientific thought. After his return to Egypt, he dedicated himself to translating French historical, philosophical and scientific works into Arabic. He had a politically troubled, but nonetheless influential, life as an educator and translator.[16] Al-Tahtawi was followed by other nineteenth-century Muslim intellectuals, most of whom came from ulama families and received a traditional religious education but who were drawn to the new European thought becoming available in Arabic. Although the number of Muslim scholars so influenced was not large, it was clearly a trend. The most important figure in this trend by the end of the century was Shaykh Muhammad 'Abduh.

Muhammad 'Abduh was born in a village in Lower Egypt in 1849. His education was in the traditional Islamic mode, beginning in the Nile Delta city of Tanta and ending formally at al-Azhar University. He left al-Azhar in 1870 after four years of study, however, because of its archaic curriculum and pedagogy, which lacked the study of philosophy and theology. In the next year he met the religious reformer and controversialist Jamal al-Din al-Afghani (d. 1897), with whom he studied and with whom he later collaborated in bringing about reform in Egypt. The concept that many reformers such as al-Afghani and 'Abduh followed was that Islam could not meet the challenges of modernity (and the West) unless Muslims received a modern education that included science and other "rational" sciences. In his second book, published in 1879, while he was still strongly under the influence of al-Afghani, 'Abduh showed his Mu'tazili intellectual leanings in a commentary on the theological creed of a famous Ash'ari mutakallim, 'Adud al-Din al-Iji (d. 1355).[17]

'Abduh was later to face down considerable opposition in seeking the reform of the curriculum at al-Azhar University. He believed, as one Western biographer has pointed out, "that, if the Azhar were reformed, Islam would be reformed."[18] 'Abduh received from al-Afghani instruction in the rationalism of early Islamic thought, which al-Azhar and other institutions would not teach. Even as a younger man, however, ideas of reforming Islam forced 'Abduh into exile.

'Abduh's exile from teaching at al-Azhar came not from conflict with students – many of whom were attracted by his probing intellectual style and methods driven by rational inquiry into the meaning of texts – but rather from the tradition-bound ulama who were then teaching on the faculty. One such was over a text that the young 'Abduh introduced to his class on kalam at al-Azhar. 'Abduh chose to use "The Creed of al-Nasafi" (*al-'Aqa'id al-nasafiya*) by al-Taftazani (a Maturidi mutakallim who had died in 1389), which was strongly Mu'tazili and critical of Ash'ari doctrine in its orientation. One elderly and reactionary Azhar professor, Shaykh 'Ulaysh, publicly challenged 'Abduh, asking "if he had given up Ash'arite teaching to follow the Mu'tazilite." 'Abduh replied: "If I give up blind acceptance (taqlid) of Ash'arite doctrine, why should I take up blind acceptance of the Mu'tazilite?"[19] The tenacious emphasis on intellectual independence to read and think about Mu'tazili ideas, yet the insistence that Muslims should avoid doctrinaire acceptance of any, including the Mu'tazili, creed (*'aqida*, pl. *'aqa'id*) is characteristic of most modernist Muslim theologians, as we shall see in this and the following two chapters.

Muhammad 'Abduh spent 1885 in exile in Beirut. Reminiscent of Mu'tazili intellectualism and free thought in the early centuries, it is said of 'Abduh in Beirut that

> [h]e took advantage of the throngs of the common people of all sects and nationalities, Sunnis, Shi'ites, Druses, Christians, Jews, who came to his house, to give expression to his views on religious matters. He treated all

with impartial courtesy, but never said anything except what he believed, whether in regard to religion or learning, customs or social affairs. He won the regard of all by his learning, his conduct, and his eloquence.[20]

The lectures on Islamic theology (kalam) he delivered in Beirut were subsequently published under the title *Risalat l-tawhid* (Treatise on [divine] unity).[21] In this work we see how profoundly Shaykh 'Abduh felt the need to restore rationalism, earlier championed by Mu'tazili mutakallimun, to the intellectual ethos of Islamic societies. In the first edition, he apparently defended the Mu'tazili doctrine of *khalq al-qur'an*, "the creation of the Qur'an." A few years earlier, in the commentary (*Hashiya*) on al-Iji's Ash'ari creed, mentioned above, he again indicated his support for the traditional Mu'tazili position. Interestingly, 'Abduh removed mention of it in subsequent editions of the *Risala* when it proved to be too controversial. It remained for later figures like Mohammed Arkoun, whose style has been less irenic toward Islamic traditionalism, to challenge the Sunni dogma of the eternity of the Qur'an directly, as we shall see in chapter 10.[22] Nonetheless, virtually every modernist Muslim has had to confront the problematic of the nature of the Qur'an, in one way or another.

Of particular importance to 'Abduh's appreciation of the Mu'tazila was the conflict between religion and reason that had raged in Europe since the publication of Charles Darwin's *The Origin of Species* in 1859. Writing less than three decades later, 'Abduh held, as he said, that "we Muslims are fortunately under no necessity of disputing with science or the findings of medicine regarding the corrections of a few traditional interpretations [of the Qur'an]. The Kur'an itself is too elevated in character to be in opposition to science."[23] In this respect, Abduh's modernist rationalism departed from the Mu'tazili physics and metaphysics; most of the Mu'tazila up to beginning of the eleventh century, when 'Abd al-Jabbar flourished, had showed little direct influence from or curiosity about the Greek scientific treatises that were increasingly available in Arabic translation.[24] Along with certain trends in Christian theology (as well as the theory of Quranic interpretation later adopted by Fazlur Rahman, which we shall discuss in more detail below), 'Abduh also applied reason to textual interpretation and to the larger task of seeing the whole message of a text and not just the meaning of an isolated verse used as a narrow proof text.

In an important passage in the *Risala*, 'Abduh argued that reason (al-'aql) could not be disparaged in comparison to religion (*al-din*), because reason guides humans in following and submitting to that which religion reveals.

If that be so,

> [h]ow then can reason be denied its right, being, as it is, the scrutineer of evidences (*adilla*) so as to reach the truth within them and know that it is Divinely given? Having, however, once recognized the mission of a prophet, reason is obliged to acknowledge all that he brings, even though unable to attain the essential meaning within it or penetrate its full truth. Yet this obligation does not involve reason in accepting rational impossibilities such as two incompatibles or opposites together at the same time and point. For prophecies are immune from bringing such follies. But if there appears something which appears contradictory reason must believe that the apparent is not the intended sense. It is then free to seek the true sense by reference to the rest of the prophet's message in whom the ambiguity occurred, or to fall back on God and His omniscience. There have been those who have chosen to do either one or the other.[25]

'Abd al-Jabbar and the Mu'tazila, of course, did not "fall back on God and His omniscience" as the traditionalists did; nor did Muhammad 'Abduh and the modernists. By opening the door to accepting traditionalist theological interpretations as legitimate alternatives within *dar al-islam*, Muhammad 'Abduh attempted to set a modernist course of open dialogue with theological opponents.

As the debate between postmodernists and Islamists has sharpened in more recent times, the quality of open dialogue has been harder to effect. The intrusion of outside voices in this debate (Orientalism), which has often been seen as excavating and reconstructing the very Islamic past to which Muslim reformists appeal, has destabilized the intra-Islamic character of the conflict. Theological discourse has become global in the postmodern world. This "new" situation recalls for some modernists the Mu'tazili disputes in the Abbasid court with Christians, Jews, philosophers, atheists and others. The task of neo-Mu'tazilism is to challenge modern opponents of Islam on their own intellectual grounds.

Many of the same arguments adduced by Muhammad 'Abduh, as we have seen, were advanced and debated by Mu'tazili mutakallimun, like 'Abd al-Jabbar, writing some 850 years earlier. This had led Harun Nasution to conclude that Shaykh 'Abduh was a Mu'tazilite, not an Ash'arite. For example, the importance of reasoning from evidences (*al-adilla*), which include scripture, is argued in ¶¶ 1–9 (chapter 5 above). Muhammad 'Abduh's *Risalat al-tawhid* was an exercise in kalam that in many passages reflected the rationalism of the earlier Mu'tazila. Yet in other passages of his work, 'Abduh reflects the Islamic puritanism of Ibn Taymiya and Ibn 'Abd al-Wahhab, a reading of 'Abduh that Nasution did not appreciate, as we shall see in the following chapters. Like these fourteenth- and eighteenth-century tradition-alist reformers, 'Abduh sought to rid Islam of popular superstitions and undue outside influences. However, he did so, as we have shown, with less iconoclasm and more openness to dialogue with non-Islamic thought. In this respect, his approach was more in keeping with the spirit of Mu'tazilisim.

Was Muhammad 'Abduh a modern-day Mu'tazilite, a champion of rationalism and liberalism in Islamic thought, or a traditionalist in the mode of Ahmad ibn Hanbal and Ibn Taymiya? The answer has to be an ambiva-lent yes: he was both. The question itself is based on a dichotomy in the study of Western historical theology between liberalism and fundamentalism in the early twentieth century. Western historians of Islamic thought, such as Caspar and Adams cited above, viewed the "'Abduh movement,"[26] we sug-gest, in light of the struggle against Protestant liberalism by Christian groups in Britain and America calling themselves "Fundamentalists." Such spectac-ular American religious controversies as the Scopes trial in Tennessee in 1925, over the teaching of the scientific theory of evolution in a high school science class, served to dramatize this conflict, which has dominated the tax-onomies of religious groups by Western historians and social scientists ever since. It is still the claim of some educated Americans that scriptural cos-mogonies should be taught in science classes as alternative scientific theories.

Caspar in particular saw in Shaykh 'Abduh's rationalism a trend toward accommodation to the religious liberalism and social progressivism that characterized European thought from the late nineteenth century through the first half of the twentieth. There was not yet in 1957, when Caspar wrote, just five years after the Free Officers' revolution in Egypt led by Gamal Abdel Nasser, much reason to believe that Egyptians, at least, were not following a course laid out by 'Abduh toward greater modernism and lib-eralism in Islamic theology.

The studies by Charles C. Adams and Albert Hourani, on the other side, emphasize different aspects of Shaykh 'Abduh's thought. With many Europeans, 'Abduh came to believe in a social philosophy of progress. He traveled to England especially to meet the philosopher Herbert Spencer, whose writings he admired and one of which, on education, he translated into Arabic. He also held in esteem the great Russian literary figure and crit-ic of the Russian Orthodox Church hierarchy Leo Tolstoy, to whom 'Abduh wrote on the occasion of the latter's excommunication from the Church.[27] 'Abduh's rationalism and philosophy of progress was not put forth as an attempt to model Islam on liberal Christianity, however; it was rather an attempt to demonstrate to Muslims, as well as to Europeans, that Islam was the most advanced religion of humankind.[28]

'Abduh argued for the inherent rationalism of Islam and its compatibility with, and even anticipation of, modern science. Like the early Mu'tazili mutakallimun, but also like the Islamist groups of today, Shaykh 'Abduh worked to arm Muslims with arguments that would be effective in the modern world in defense of Islam from external (European, Christian) attacks. And like the Islamiyun of today, he argued that the true Islam knew no national or political boundaries. A rationally based Islam was, for Shaykh Muhammad 'Abduh, as for his publicist and dedicated follower, Rashid Rida, an Islam that educated its ignorant masses, brought them up from the poverty to which they were currently subjected, and thus restored the world greatness that once was Islam.

Shaykh Muhammad 'Abduh had many followers in the next two generations of Egyptian (and other Muslim) intellectuals who sought to reincorporate aspects of Mu'tazili rationalism into modern Islamic theology. The particular history of neo-Mu'tazilism in Egypt is a fascinating topic that will require further research.[29] In our survey of the influence of Mu'tazilism on the modern Muslim world we simply note, as we turn to later Muslim figures, that like Shaykh 'Abduh himself, several rationalist modernists were shaykhs of al-Azhar. Like 'Abduh, Shaykh Muhammad Mustafa al-Maraghi sought to modernize Islam through administrative and curricular reform of al-Azhar University. 'Abduh's most studied successor in this regard was Shaykh al-Azhar Mahmud Shaltut.[30] In 1943, Shaykh Shaltut delivered a lecture that was popularly received before a large audience of several thousand students, faculty and ulama at al-Azhar's College of Usul al-Din. Zebiri summarizes his remarks as follows:

> Like al-Maraghi . . . Shaltut began by praising the Azhar's work in the Middle Ages in preserving the Islamic religion and the Arabic language. He particularly commended the fact that at that time the law was taught according to the various *madhahib* rather than just one, and the curriculum included several mathematical and rational sciences. He went on to explain that the situation deteriorated with the spread of the practice of *taqlid* . . . The spirit of sectarianism grew and people were obliged to confine themselves to a single *madhhab*. All this obstructed real intellectual progress, and the Azhar became increasingly isolated from the Muslim community.[31]

We can only speculate on what might have happened if Muhammad 'Abduh and his followers in authority at al-Azhar University had been successful in persuading more conservative Azhari ulama to accept their reforms. As matters turned out, the theological debate about these reforms, and thus about modernism and rationalism, was superseded by President Gamal Abdel Nasser's decision to impose a drastic Reform Law on al-Azhar in 1961. Zebiri points out that the earlier theologically based visions of modern Islam were replaced by secular, governmental policy. Perhaps there is a pattern to be seen here that is reminiscent of Caliph al-Ma'mun's attempt in the ninth century (discussed in chapter 2 above) to impose doctrine that suits the purposes of the ruler?

Islamic Traditionalism and Rationalism in South Asia

If Egypt was the primary Middle Eastern country in which Islamic modernism and traditionalism would contend with each other in the late nineteenth and early twentieth centuries, India was the region of Asia that spawned similar trends. Both regions – the Middle East and South Asia – were subjected to European colonialism, from which they emerged in the twentieth century as "Third World" nations. There were important differences between these two centers of Islamic learning and revival, however. Egypt, like many Middle Eastern countries, has always been predominantly Muslim. India has always been predominantly non-Muslim (primarily Hindu, but also Sikh, *inter alia*), but nonetheless ruled by Muslims during the Mogul dynasty, which lasted from 1526 to 1858. Islam in India has always been a minority religion, yet South Asia has the largest number of Muslims of any geographical region. Some rulers in India, notably Akbar (*reg.* 1542 1605), were innovative in removing boundaries between Muslim and non-Muslim religious practices and communities.

The tendency toward religious pluralism in South Asian societies also produced opposite tendencies toward Islamic reform and the purification of Islam from non-Muslim, especially Hindu, accretions. Indeed, Wahhabism and non-Hanbali forms of traditionalism had parallel expressions in the South Asian environment, as did modernist expressions of Islamic thought. The traditionalist temperament to return to the Islam of the Salafiya and to remove all non-Islamic accretions from Hinduism and local popular religion was spearheaded by Shah Wali Allah al-Dihlawi (1702–1762), a contemporary and remarkably parallel figure to Muhammad ibn 'Abd al-Wahhab. He lamented the decline of Islamic political power and religious unity in India, and he attacked the religious syncretism that in some ways could be seen as the heritage of Akbar's broad, almost boundaryless vision of religion. South Asian Islamic traditionalism intensified under the leadership of Ahmad Brelwi (1786 1831). Brelwi's theologically driven refusal to share religious and cultural space with Hinduism and Indian popular religion got him killed in 1831 while he was attempting to form a separate Islamic state and lead a jihad against the rest of India.

Islamic modernism in India was led by Sayyid Ahmad Khan (1817–1898), an older contemporary of Muhammad 'Abduh. Ahmad Khan had worked for the British East India Company as a young man and had come to believe that Muslims in India would have to come to grips with modern science and the more productive aspects of Western thought. In this regard he said: "If people do not shun blind adherence, if they do not seek that light which can be found in the Qur'an and the indisputable Hadith, and do not adjust religion and the sciences of today, Islam will become extinct in India."[32] He therefore set about to have Western works translated into Indian languages. He founded the Muhammadan Anglo-Oriental College in Aligarh which, until this day, has been the center of Islamic modernism in India.[33] That Ahmad Khan justified modernism and rationalism in the Islamic tradition of kalam can be seen in the following passage, quoted by Fazlur Rahman: "Today we are, as before, in need of a modern theology (*'ilm al-kalam*), whereby we should either refute the doctrines of modern sciences, or undermine their foundations, or show that they are in conformity with Islam."[34] Like 'Abduh, Khan believed that Islamic teaching was compatible with modern science and thus he favored the latter alternative. Indeed, he seems to have come much closer than 'Abduh to the epistemological position of the Mu'tazila and of European rationalism, that reason precedes faith. His metaphysical framework, however, was inspired more by the emanationist doctrines of medieval Islamic philosophers, who spoke of God as First Cause. As the twentieth-century Pakistani modernist Fazlur Rahman (to whom we turn in chapter 10) notes:

> Yet, such individual interpretations are not to be decried. They are not only statements of personal faith and expressions of the principles of liberalism but provided a leaven and fertilization of ideas for an eventual formulation of the Faith, and in this process they are necessary moments.[35]

The modernist viewpoints of Muhammad 'Abduh and Sayyid Ahmad Khan were articulated in Islamic environments that had been created, in part, by British colonialism. During the next century, the twentieth C.E., the British and other European empires were to fall. This, we have argued, allowed the older debates between traditionalism and rationalism to reemerge. In the following chapters, the story of Islamic modernism and neo-Mu'tazilism continues, this time in Indonesia.

Notes

1. This Western view of Islam as a threat is analyzed and confuted by John L. Esposito, *The Islamic Threat.*

2. On Shaltut's reformist modernism, see Zebiri, *Mahmud Shaltut and Islamic Modernism,* p. 23 et passim.

3. See ¶ 1 of the text in chapter 5 below.

4. Langan, "The Western Moral Tradition on War," p. 87.

5. The most important work on Ibn Taymiya has been done by Henri Laoust; see especially his *Essai sur les doctrines sociales et politiques de Taqi-al-Din Ahmad b. Taimiya.* In English, see idem, "Ibn Taimiyya," *EI².*

6. Makari, *Ibn Taymiyyah's Ethics,* p. 7.

7. Mentioned in Lapidus, *Islamic Societies,* p. 184.

8. His famous treatise on the Islamic critique of popular religion, *Kitab iqtida' al-sirat al-mustaqim mukhalafat ashab al-jahim,* has been loosely translated by Muhammad Umar Memon in his *Ibn Taimiya's Struggle Against Popular Religion.* Memon's Introduction is a useful source of information about Ibn Taymiya.

9. Translated by 'Umar Farrukh, *Ibn Taymiyyah on Public and Private Law.*

10. Albert Hourani discusses Ibn Taymiya's political theology in his *Arabic Thought in the Liberal Age,* pp. 18–22.

11. See the list of Ibn Taymiya's works in Arabic (and a few titles of works in English translation) in Makari, *Ibn Taymiyyah's Ethics,* pp. 227–231.

12. See, for example, Voll, *Islam,* pp. 59–60.

13. Caspar, "Un aspect de la pensée musulmane moderne."

14. We showed earlier that isolated pockets of Mu'tazilism survived the so-called "Triumph of Ash'arism" in the late eleventh century, mainly among the Ithna 'Ashari (Twelver) Shi'a in Iran and the Zaydi (Fiver) Shi'a strongholds in the Caspian region and in Yemen.

15. Caspar, "Un aspect de la pensée musulmane moderne," p. 142. Hassan Hanafi, discussed below in chapter 10, has analyzed a concept of "Occidentalism" as an Islamic counterpoise to "Orientalism."

16. See Hourani, *Arabic Thought in the Liberal Age,* esp. pp. 68–85 on al-Tahtawi; and Livingston, "Western Science and Educational Reform."

17. 'Abduh, *Hashiya 'ala sharh al-Diwani.*

18. Adams, *Islam and Modernism in Egypt,* pp. 70–71.

19. From *al-Manar,* 8: 391; cited by Adams, *Islam and Modernism in Egypt,* pp. 42–43. *Al-Manar* was the Egyptian journal published by 'Abduh's disciple Rashid Rida. On Shaykh 'Ulaysh, see Adams, p. 30.

20. Adams, *Islam and Modernism in Egypt,* p. 64. Adams cites *al-Manar* 8: 463–464.

21. Muhammad 'Abduh, *Risalat al-tawhid* (Beirut: Dar Ihya' al-'Ulum, 1986). The *Risala* was first published by 'Abduh in Cairo in 1897. Muhammad Rashid Rida published a revised second edition in 1908. The fifth Cairo edition in 1926 was further revised, chiefly with added notes. The English translation is *The Theology of Unity,* trans. Ishaq Musa'ad and Kenneth Cragg (London: George Allen & Unwin, 1966).

22. Hourani, *Arabic Thought in the Liberal Age*, pp. 142–143 interprets this as an example of 'Abduh's eclecticism and his tendency to "evade difficult questions." We think such a judgment is too facile and fails to comprehend the deep theological conflict surrounding any attempt to question the doctrine of the eternity of the Qur'an.

23. 'Abduh, *al-Manar* 9: 334–335, quoted and translated by Adams in *Islam and Modernism in Egypt*, p. 138.

24. The influence of Greek philosophy on the development of Islamic thought is a historiographical problem still under dispute among historians. See the works by Fakhry, Watt (*Formative Period*) and Wolfson in the bibliography.

25. 'Abduh, *Theology of Unity*, pp. 107–108 'Abduh, *Risala*, pp. 115–116.

26. Or "Manar Party." These terms are used by Charles C. Adams to designate the many Egyptians and other Muslims who, as he put it, "have been influenced by the teachings of Muhammad 'Abduh and have identified themselves more or less openly with the movement which he inaugurated" (idem, *Islam and Modernism in Egypt*, pp. 180, 205–268).

27. Ibid, p. 95.

28. The claim that modernity is in fact a product of Islam and that Islam is better suited than Christianity and other religions – or is in a position now to stand alongside or even to replace Christianity as the predominant world religion of modernity – has resonated among twentieth-century Muslim modernist and postmodernist thinkers, especially Hassan Hanafi, whose work we shall consider in chapter 10.

29. Neo-Mu'tazilism in Egypt from Muhammad 'Abduh to the present is the subject of a study by Ahmad 'Arafat al-Qadi, "Falsafat al-tarbiya 'ind al-mu'tazila wa l-ash'ariya" (The philosophy of education of the Mu'tazila and Ash'arites).

30. On Shaltut and Islamic modernism in Egypt more generally, see Zebiri, *Mahmud Shaltut and Islamic Modernism*, esp. chapters 2 and 3.

31. Ibid., pp. 22–23; summarized by Zebiri from Muhammad 'Abd al-Mun'im al-Khafaji, *al-Azhar fi alf 'am*, 2nd ed., 3 vols. (Beirut and Cairo, 1988), 3: 14–16.

32. Quoted by Rahman, *Islam*, pp. 216–217, from Sayyid Ahmad Khan, *Khutabat-i Sir Sayid* (Badalun, 1931), p. 55.

33. Voll, *Islam*, pp. 112–113.

34. Quoted by Rahman, *Islam*, p. 217, from *Letters ka Majmu'a* (n.p., 1890), p. 2101.

35. Rahman, *Islam*, p. 218.

seven

The Significance *of* Mu'tazilism *in* Indonesia

Mu'tazili *kalam* has been known in Indonesia since at least the sixteenth century. *The Admonitions of Seh Bari*, the manuscript of a Javanese mystical text brought to Holland in the late sixteenth century, includes an extensive discussion of God's creative acts, and raises the question of whether or not there was a time when He did not create. Much of the text takes the form of a series of conversations, invented in the text, between Imam Ghazali (d. 1111) and a series of heretics. When questioned concerning his teachings about creation, one Sufi shaykh replies: "Imam Ghazali! It is not my opinion that my words: the Lord did not create, should be taken at their face value. They should be interpreted as the utterance of the mystic whose being, sight and speech are submerged by the being of God, and therefore I say: God the most high did not create." [1] To this Imam Ghazali replies: "You are an infidel according to the four schools, because your doctrine detracts from the attributes of the Lord. Because you attribute non-existence to or minimize the attributes of the Lord your words have been branded as heretical . . . [Y]ou are tainted by the heresy of the Mu'tazila." [2]

Islam came to Indonesia at a time when Sufism, not kalam, dominated intellectual discourse in the Muslim world. The theological debates that influenced the development of Islam in Indonesia and the other Muslim societies of Southeast Asia concerned the nature of mystical experience and the relationship between the essence of God and the soul of the mystic and the related issue of the role of the Shari'a in the practice of Sufism. From the beginning, Indonesian Muslims appear to have accepted Ash'ari kalam, almost without question. To the extent that Mu'tazili thought was known at all, it was simply one of a series of "heresies" known only from polemics borrowed from South Asian and Middle Eastern sources. There is no evidence that Mu'tazili thought was ever taken seriously prior to Harun Nasution's return from McGill University in the mid-twentieth century. Prior to that time "rationalism" was associated primarily with Western learning and with modernist Islamic organizations, among which the Muhammadiyah is the largest and most influential.

In this chapter we shall examine the place of rationalism as a category in Indonesian Islamic thought. We shall focus on the Muhammadiyah, the organization through which Harun Nasution first experienced Islamic modernism, and on the thought of contemporary neo-modernists like Nurcholish Madjid, who have been influenced by Nasution's rationalism.

Serious discussion of rationalism and some of the issues related to Mu'tazili thought emerged as important themes in Indonesian Muslim discourse in the early years of the twentieth century. This discourse was initially motivated not so much by theological concerns as by the intellectual, political and economic dominance of the Dutch colonial state and the perceived need for economic and intellectual development in the Muslim community. At that time, an important debate within the Muslim community centered on the role of "Western education" and Western rationalism in a Muslim society. The question of the legality (in Islamic terms) of Western education was motivated not so much by the content of Western secular knowledge per se as by the colonial context in which it was conveyed. Prior to the establishment of the so called "Ethical Policy" in 1900, Western education was available only to Europeans, Eurasians and a very small number of native Indonesians from aristocratic and/or wealthy families. Until the very end of the colonial period, the Dutch educational system was overtly anti-Islamic. Students in Dutch-language schools were discouraged, if not actually prohibited, from acquiring more than a minimal understanding of Islam. They were taught that the "authentic" Indonesian culture was that of the pre-Islamic past, and that traditional Islamic learning was, as the great Dutch Orientalist Snouck Hurgronje so bluntly put it, "medieval rubbish which Islam has been dragging along in its wake for too long."[3] The Dutch educational system presented students and their families with clear alternatives. They could choose to pursue "modern" studies at the cost of secularization or choose the path of Islamic learning at the cost of social and economic marginalization.[4] The Muhammadiyah and other modernist organizations argued for the development of an Islamic educational system in which the study and practice of Islam was combined with that of "general", i.e. secular, subjects. Their purpose was to create an educational system which combined the scientific and technical aspects of modern Western knowledge with Islamic values and piety. More conservative Muslims held that anything Western, including education, was *haram* (forbidden). This debate was not resolved until the establishment of the Indonesian Republic, when an agreement between the Ministry of Education and the Ministry of Religion allowed for religious instruction in government schools and the incorporation of elements of the modern secular curriculum into Islamic educational institutions.

Clifford Geertz and most subsequent students of Indonesian Islam have used the dichotomy between modernity and tradition to characterize religious variation in the Indonesian Muslim community.[5] Organizations like the Muhammadiyah and Persatuan Islam are generally classified as modernist while the more conservative Nahdlatul Ulama is described as traditionalist. The category "modern" is associated with what Geertz calls a "scripturalist" religious orientation and with a concern with rationality, economic development and Western education. Traditional Islam has been described as mystical, syncretic, rural and otherworldly. The modernity/tradition dichotomy is based on ethnographic research conducted in the 1950s and reflects the social and political orientations of theologically defined Muslim communities of that period. In this chapter we shall pursue more generally the argument of this book that, as important as it was in the late colonial period and the formative years of the Indonesian Republic, the modernity/tradition dichotomy is increasingly difficult to maintain. Contemporary Indonesian Muslim intellectual debates focus on how modernity and development can be achieved – themes that we encountered among the early modernist Muslim intellectuals discussed in the last chapter. Debates concerning the nature of modernity and Islamic rationality make the study of Mu'tazili kalam increasingly significant for Indonesian Muslim intellectuals.

The Intellectual Background of Indonesian Modernism

Indonesian modernists place themselves in the lineage of *tajdid* (renewal) movements we discussed in the last chapter, beginning with the fourteenth-century reformer Ibn Taymiya and twentieth-century Middle Eastern modernists including Jamal al-Din al-Afghani, Muhammad 'Abduh and Rashid Rida. In this respect they share a common intellectual genealogy with Islamic modernists writing in the Middle East and the West. These four thinkers in particular contributed to the rise of Indonesian modernism in the early decades of the twentieth century.[6] Indonesian modernist movements concentrated their efforts on purifying Islamic thought from what were considered to be historical and cultural influences, which were described as unlawful innovation (*bid'a*) and superstition (Ind. *khurafat*).[7] They also advocated the elimination of the Sunni legal schools (Ind. *mazhab*, Ar. *madhhab*) and the exclusive use of the Qur'an and Sunna of the Prophet Muhammad as sources of Islamic law.

The Muhammadiyah developed a rationalist Islam, if by rationalism we mean only an understanding of the natural world based on empirical observation. The organization does not in any sense endorse a rationalist understanding of God or Islam. Indeed, a theological conservatism bordering on fundamentalism lies at the heart of the Muhammadiyah's understanding of the faith. One of the central principles of the Muhammadiyah's theology is that God and Islam can be known only from the Qur'an and Hadith. Human reasoning can be used to understand the natural world, but not God or the nature of Islam. The Muhammadiyah retains a traditional Ash'ari understanding of God's attributes, the Qur'an and predetermination. This theological perspective is clearly stated in official Muhammadiyah texts.

Muhammadiyah Sebagai Gerakan Islam (The Muhammadiyah as an Islamic movement) by Kamal, Yusuf and Sholeh includes an explicit denunciation of Mu'tazili thought.[8] The authors describe this as being derived from the question of whether someone who professes to be a Muslim, but who committed a grave sin, is properly understood as a believer (Ind. *mukmin*) or a *kafir*.[9] Their summary of the Mu'tazili position on this and other theological questions, including the use of reason in making moral judgments and the ability of humans to act independently in the world with powers given them by God, accurately reflect basic Mu'tazili positions.

The opposing Ash'ari positions on these and other issues are described as those of the People of the Tradition (of the Prophet Muhammad) and the Community (*ahl al-sunna wa l-jama'a*). The authors cite the conversation between al-Ash'ari and al-Jubba'i concerning the positions of the believer, the kafir and the young child in the afterlife as a refutation of the Mu'tazili position.[10] They state explicitly that the Ash'ari position is that of the People of the Tradition and the Community, which is one of the Muhammadiyah's most common self-designations. The text also takes a strong Ash'ari line on the uncreated nature of the Qur'an, the attributes of God, and predetermination. The authors explain that the Qur'an is the speech of God, that it is: "eternal with the characteristic of eternalness." The Qur'an in its eternal sense is distinguished from the letters and sound of the text which are described as "new things."

The Ash'ari nature of Muhammadiyah theology is more fully developed in texts on theology and law. In *Kitab Tauhid* (The book of the unity of

God) the Muhammadiyah scholar Hadikusuma describes the books of God, including the Torah, the Psalms and the Gospels, as well as the Qur'an, as being among the attributes (*sifat*) of God. He describes both speech (kalam) and the speaker (*mutakallim*) as being attributes which are united with the essence (Ind. *dzat*) of God. He describes all of the attributes of God as being eternal. He also distinguishes between the speech of God (kalam Allah), which is eternal, and the sounds and letters of the text, which are not. The books of God are those portions of His speech which He has chosen to reveal to His prophets.[11] Another Muhammadiyah text, *Himpunan Putusan Tarjih* (Collected decisions), prepared by the central leadership of the organization, explains that because relationships between the attributes and essence of God cannot be understood by human reason, it is not allowable to speculate about them. Both texts maintain that Quranic statements concerning the seemingly anthropomorphic attributes of God must be taken literally. As a whole, these texts are expressive of the view that the Qur'an is uncreated, that in its heavenly form it constitutes one of the attributes of God, and that knowledge of God can be obtained only through revelation.

Kitab Tauhid also includes a lengthy discussion of divine determinism which, while maintaining an Ashʿari position, allows for the efficacy of human action within a range determined by God.[12] This enables Hadikusuma to conclude that God rewards human efforts. A similar understanding of divine determinism is often expressed in sermons at Muhammadiyah mosques in which the expression "God helps those who help themselves" is often quoted in Indonesian, Dutch or English. Hadikusuma's text reads as follows:

Qadar is derived from the [Arabic] term qadara which means "to determine" in the sense of to establish within fixed limits. For example, God determines that a particular person will be wealthy and fixes the limits of his wealth. This determination is the result of a clear plan.

Qadla [Ar. qada] means to "cause" or to "carry out." The meaning is to carry out that which had already been determined within the limits of qadar.

Faith in qadar and qadla requires the conviction that at the begining of time, prior to the creation of [human and other] beings, God had already determined the nature, characteristics and time of the beings to be created. This is called qadar or takdir [Ar. taqdir]. God created each being in accordance with its individual destiny.

Every faithful Muslim, in accord with the type of faith explained above, believes that all of the events and movements of the world, including the destiny of humanity as a whole, as well as that of the individual, were determined by God at the beginning of time. The course of human life is the unfolding or *qadla* of his destiny which, however, *can not be known* before it is manifest as *qadla*.

If a person has an incorrect understanding of *qadla* and *qadar*, it is easy for him to slip into the incorrect view that it is not necessary for him to make serious efforts, because what use could it be if everything has been determined in advance by God? Poverty is determined by God, as is wealth. One becomes lowly or exalted because of *takdir*. God determines that some people will be unbelievers (*kafir*) and others pious Muslims [*mukmim*, Ar. *mu'min*]. Why is it that people who are unbelievers (*kafir*) or polytheists [*musyrik*, Ar. *mushrik*] or evil because of God's *qadar*, should be sent to Hell? If this is true is God really good and just? A person who holds such views has slipped to the point of denying the justice of God and destroying his faith.

What follows is an explanation of how we are to understand *qadla* and *qadar* correctly so that we do not slip, but rather receive a great lesson and blessing.

Takdir is the secret work of God. We have no way of knowing about it before it unfolds. Certainly, knowledge that it is our destiny to be poor would give rise to the feeling that it is not necessary to make efforts to prosper because they are bound to fail. But how are we to know that it has been determined that we are to be poor? If we choose not to exert ourselves because of presumed knowledge of *takdir*, which limits us, it would be to presume that human thought has the same capacity as that of God. In such a case it would be as if thinking as humans, we understand that we must exert ourselves, but if we presume to think as God, we understand our actions as determined because of our knowledge of *takdir*. This is not natural and cannot be allowed.

Exertion, such as that to maintain oneself and to meet one's needs, is a basic characteristic of created beings from the moment of birth. A mouse that has been caught in a trap makes an effort to escape. A cat that sees a mouse will try to catch it. People who notice something dangerous will attempt to avoid it. Even a person who thinks that it is pointless to exert himself because of *takdir* will attempt to escape from danger and meet his basic needs. He can not act upon the conclusions of his thought because exertion is a basic characteristic of created beings.

God's *takdir* is variable and reversible. It may be determined that today someone will be rich, and that he will become poor tomorrow, and that he will find great fortune again next year. One can be sick today, take medicine and be healthy again next week. Things like this happen every day and show that there certainly is hope and that every effort is worthwhile. A *kafir* can become a *mukmin* as the result of hearing the call of religion. A Muslim may lose his way because of passion and desire.

Knowledge of *qadla* and *qadar* is reserved for God alone. It is not our affair. We can not know *takdir* before it unfolds. Our lack of knowledge gives us the freedom and courage to exert ourselves. What is our affair is to work and to exert ourselves and to choose the road of the good life and to reject the path of evil.[13]

Hadikusuma concludes his exposition of qadla and qadar with a discussion of the social and psychological benefits of faith in divine determinism. He repeats his previous statement that it is not necessary to become disheartened with failure because of the potentially changing nature of takdir. He asserts that one need not be afraid of the danger of acting on the basis of truth because the consequences of such actions have already been determined; that these teachings instill a sense of humility in the powerful, provide solace for those who suffer in the path of truth, and encourage people to treat the poor with compassion and justice. There are two reasons for this. The first is that poverty is the result of takdir. The other is that by providing assistance to them the poor will be able to "escape their destiny and move forward to a better one." He concludes that "*Takdir* is changeable and established only by God, but that no human can understand it. This establishes a wide space for human efforts. God establishes and regulates *takdir*."[14]

Geertz suggests that Muslim modernists are inclined towards a neo-Mu'tazili view of the doctrine of takdir (predetermination). He draws a contrast between traditional Muslims who, he claims, attribute everything to the will of God and modernists who attribute success or failure in the material aspects of life to human action.[15] The Muhammadiyah's theology cannot, however, be associated with Mu'tazilism in a doctrinal sense. Members of the Muhammadiyah and other Indonesian modernists propose a combination of Ash'ari theology, fundamentalist approaches to legal and ritual questions, and an understanding of the natural world rooted in Western scientific rationalism.

Traditionalist Indonesian Muslims hold similar theological views, but have rejected the modernist denunciation of mysticism and simplified forms of ritual practice. They argue that Muslims are obligated to follow the teachings of one of the four recognized Sunni legal schools (Hanafi, Shafi'i, Maliki or Hanbali) and one of the two Sunni theological traditions (Ash'ari or Maturidi) and to practice the mysticism of al-Junayd of Baghdad (d. 911).[16] While modernists claim that only those ritual practices that can be clearly linked to the Prophet Muhammad are allowable, traditionalists maintain a broader understanding of Sunna, according to which ritual practices associated with the first generation of the Prophet's Companions, including the four rightly guided caliphs, are incumbent upon subsequent generations of Muslims. As far as kalam is concerned, the Muhammadiyah and Nahdlatul Ulama have almost identical views. Texts written by Nahdlatul Ulama scholars describe the Mu'tazila as one of a number of heretical sects that deviate from the teachings of the Qur'an and the practice of the Prophet Muhammad and his Companions. Thoyfoer, for example, is particularly critical of Mu'tazili teachings of the created Qur'an and freedom of human action. He states: "They state that the Qur'an is not the speech of God but rather the creation of God" and "they do not believe in divine determination, but rather that humans determine their own destinies." Thoyfoer concludes that while Mu'tazili rationalism has sometimes been popular among government officials, it is properly understood as being among the major causes of discord and conflict in the Muslim community.[17]

Both modernists and traditionalists considered themselves to be the community of the Sunna of the Prophet Muhammad (Ahl al-Sunna wa l-Jama'a). During the early decades of the twentieth century, disputes between the two communities were exceedingly bitter. Each considered the other to have departed from the straight path of Islam and to have fallen into unbelief.[18] While, particularly with regard to ritual practice, the distinction between modernists and traditionalists can still be drawn, it has in recent years become increasingly less useful for characterizing Indonesian Islamic thought. There are several reasons for this. The first is that, in reality, the two groups differ on what contemporary Muslim intellectuals consider to be minor or derivative points (*al-masa'il al-furu'iya*) such as the verbal articulation of the statements of intent (*niya*) required in ritual performance and soulful Quranic prayer (*qunut*) recitation, the visitation of graves (Ind. *ziarah*) and the precise direction of prayer (*qibla*).

These and other questions concerning ritual performance continue to be debated and to play a significant role in defining local Muslim communities.[19] They are not, however, the primary concerns of contemporary Indonesian Muslim intellectuals. Since Indonesian independence, the focus of Islamic theological discourse has shifted from ritual performance to a search for Islamic solutions for social, economic and political problems. As this new set of questions has come to occupy the attention of Muslim intellectuals the intensity of the modernist/traditionalist debate about ritual performance has diminished. There is at present a sometimes grudging and uneasy truce between the two communities. Many traditionalist scholars, including those affiliated with Nahdlatul Ulama (or N.U. as it is commonly known), acknowledge the Muhammadiyah as a pseudo-mazhab, while N.U.

is often described by the Muhammadiyah as an organization for those members of the Muslim community who are "not yet ready for Muhammadiyah." Some have gone so far as to propose joint membership in the two organizations which as little as thirty years ago dencounced each other as "nonbelievers."[20] Again, we find strong parallels with the Islamic modernism of Muhammad 'Abduh at the beginning of the twentieth century.

From the 1950s until the establishment of the New Order in Indonesia following the abortive communist coup of 1965, the question of the role of Islam in the Indonesian political system dominated Islamic discourse.[21] This was the era of ideology. The dominant question was: should Indonesia be a secular nationalist, communist, or Islamic state or, as envisioned by Indonesia's first president, Sukarno, a state based on a combination of principles drawn from each of these philosophical systems? Within the Islamic community, there was considerable debate about what exactly was meant by an Islamic state and how best to achieve it. In the late 1960s many Muslim leaders expected that the collapse of the Communist Party would lead to the establishment of a more explicitly Islamic Indonesia. This was not to be.

Since 1965, the Indonesian government has had a consistent policy of limiting the role of organized Islam in the political process. It was apparent to many Indonesian Muslims that the government was intent on distancing itself from the self-consciously Islamic component of Indonesian society.[22] These developments led many to conclude that despite the fact that Indonesia has the world's largest Muslim population, Islam had been ignored in the process of national development and that pious Muslims were increasingly unable to compete with Chinese, Christians and other minorities in the economic sphere. The view that pious Muslims were somehow "suspect" because of the association of Islamic piety with political Islam was also common. In short, the end of the era of ideology required Muslim intellectuals to come to new understandings of the role of Islam in Indonesian society.[23]

Some modernists, among whom Amin Rais, chairman of the Muhammadiyah during the 1990s, has been perhaps the most vocal, continue to call for a more explicitly Islamic Indonesia, if not for an officially Islamic state. Nonetheless, most Muslim intellectuals have become disillusioned with political Islam.[24] There are several reasons for this development. One is that the failure of Islamic political parties to establish an Islamic state in the 1950s and 1960s has led many to the conclusion that the dream of an Islamic Indonesia is unrealizable. Others argue that the very notion of an Islamic state is a romantic, utopian ideal that has yet to be realized, even in nations like Pakistan and Iran that describe themselves as Islamic republics. Still others have pointed to the "Islamophobia" of the nationalist elite and the need to work within the existing system to accomplish the Islamicization of Indonesian life.[25]

Contemporary Islam in Indonesia

Indonesian Muslim intellectuals are increasingly concerned with the questions of the proper role of Islam in national development and how Islamic values can be reconciled with Western rationalism, rather than with the nature of an Islamic state. Routine religious questions in theology (kalam) and Islamic law (*fiqh*) are still debated but are not among the central concerns of contemporary intellectuals.

More significant for them is what they refer to as "Theology of Development" and what the controversial scholar Nurcholish Madjid terms the "Renewal of Religious Thought Movement."[26] Madjid's use of the term "renewal" (Ind. *pembaharuan*) and his frequent references to Ibn Taymiya establish symbolic links between what has come to be known as neo-modernism and the concept of tajdid.

What distinguishes thinkers associated with this movement from earlier modernists is the combination of empirical and historical approaches they employ in formulating a vision of an Islamic society. It contrasts sharply with the approaches of earlier modernists, and many contemporary Indonesian Muslims associated with the Muhammadiyah and other modernist organizations, which are essentially apologetic. Early modernists emphasized rationality in their denunciations of traditional religious practice and argued that Islam not only allows for but requires modernity. This much Shaykh Muhammad 'Abduh had also contended, as we saw in the last chapter. In this discourse in Indonesia, modernity is tacitly defined in technological and scientific terms. Because early modernism combined scientific and technological rationalism with Islamic scripturalism, religious questions were excluded from the domain in which rationality could operate. This meant that the modernist conception of an Islamic society was limited to the literal understanding of the social teachings of the Qur'an and Hadith.

Nurcholish Madjid's most important contribution to the development of Indonesian Islamic discourse has been his attempt to decouple modernism from scripturalism. Fachri Ali and Bahtiar Effendy point out that in contrast to earlier modernists, Madjid provides a more realistic appraisal of how Muslims should approach modernity.[27] In a controversial speech delivered on 2 January 1970, Madjid stated that: "Indonesian Muslims are again experiencing inertia in thought and the development of Islamic teachings." He explained that the need for the renewal of thought was more pressing than the need for maintaining the intellectual consensus of the community. He described modernist organizations such as the Muhammadiyah as having "become rigid, probably as a result of not being able to capture the spirit of dynamism and progressiveness of the idea of renovation itself." [28] Madjid called for an end to sectarian debate and championed the cause of reason, even in the analysis of religious phenomena.

It is at this juncture that Mu'tazili kalam becomes significant in contemporary Indonesian discourse. Harun Nasution turned to Mu'tazili kalam because it allowed for the use of reason in religious as well as worldly matters. With the exception of Nasution and his closest followers, most contemporary Indonesian Islamic thinkers are careful to place themselves within the Sunni tradition. Proponents of the Renewal of Religious Thought Movement founded by Nurcholish Madjid and the neo-fundamentalists of the Muhammadiyah and Persatuan Islam link their understandings of Islam with classical Sunni thinkers such as Ibn Taymiya. The term neo-Mu'tazili is used by neo-fundamentalists to denounce Madjid and his followers. In this sense it remains in Indonesia a term of opprobrium, much as it was in the tenth and eleventh centuries among Ash'ari and other centrist Sunni madhhabs. Among modern Indonesian Islamic theologians, only Harun Nasution has declared himself to be a "neo-Mu'tazila." Even Madjid has taken pains to distance himself from Nasution's position.[29]

While contemporary Indonesian Islamic thinkers emphasize rationality, they use the concept primarily in the analysis of social and economic phenomena and, unlike the classical Mu'tazili thinkers, retain the traditional Sunni view that scripture is the primary means through which knowledge of God can be obtained. The first principle of Mu'tazili thought, which differentiates it from other Islamic schools, is the primacy of speculative reasoning (*nazar*). For the Mu'tazila, speculative reasoning is essential in order to know God, to understand His justice, and, thus, to obey Him. Apart from the way Mu'tazili theologians perceived the results of their reflection and speculative reasoning, which stands prior to scripture as an evidentiary proof (*dalil*, see chapter 5, ¶ 6), the approach itself can be figured as follows:

1. Speculative reasoning is an effort that Mu'tazili theologians perform in order to understand religious matters. It, in other words, is the antithesis of scripture's dogmatic role, which is the Sunni standpoint.

2. However, since humans are not absolute beings, all that is produced by them is conditional.

3. Therefore, human truth is relative (Ind. *zanny*) and temporal. This uncertainty is an essential quality of all human intellectual activities, including "speculative reasoning."

Nurcholish Madjid in the preface of *Islam, Kemodernan dan Keindonesiaan* (Islam in the context of modernity and Indonesia), confirms that, in his life, he is trying to fulfill the principle of what he calls "an endless effort of finding the Truth." He believes that God is the Absolute Truth. Thus, all human effort has to be directed toward Him.[30] But, because of His being absolute, no human being will ever reach Him, including the Messenger of God who, during his miraculous Night Ascent from Jerusalem into the Seven Heavens, was only able to get to *sidrat al-muntaha*, interpreted as "the Final Tree of Truth," not God Himself.[31] This idea of a human duty to find truth, by means of reason, is constrained by the assumption that any conclusion is relative (zanny) and historically and socially located. Madjid underlines this by stating that: "None is justified to absolutize himself in discovering a 'truth,' just as if it would be forevery [sic] true, because that would be ended with an act challenging God." This is characteristic of contemporary Indonesian Islamic thought which attempts to distinguish between the eternal religious truths of Islam and the historically conditioned Muslim social and ritual systems. In this regard, the position taken by Nurcholish Madjid is similar to that of Hassan Hanafi, the Egyptian philosopher whose views we shall discuss in chapter 10 below.[32]

Madjid and other Indonesian Islamic thinkers argue that social and ritual systems are the products of human cultures. Madjid states that:

Except for the fundamental value of *taqwa* [fear of God] which grows out of faith in God and worship of Him, there are no fixed values. [Most] values are cultural values which have, of necessity, to develop continuously in accordance with the laws of change and development. Therefore the values of Islam are those which conform to humanity's true nature or to universal truth and are supported by *taqwa* towards God. Those values are Islamic if they do not contradict *iman* or *taqwa*, and are good according to humanity and its development.[33]

Madjid's rationalism, and that of other Indonesian neo-modernists, is historical and sociological. Their purpose is not to come to an understanding of God through speculative reasoning, but rather to use reason to arrive at Islamic answers to questions concerning the contemporary human problems of national development, a theological approach which is also called "Theology of Development."[34] Tolerance and the acceptance of religious pluralism (internal and external) are among the central themes of contemporary Indonesian Islamic discourse. Tolerance of diversity is a logical consequence of the view that Muslim social systems are socially and historically constructed interpretations of eternal Islamic truths. It is also considered to be an essential condition for establishing social and political stability, which is, in turn, thought to be necessary for national development.

Thus, as in the case of the early modernists we reviewed in the last chapter, the use of reason as a means of coming to a knowledge of God does not figure significantly in Indonesian Islamic theology as an explicit aim. Instead, Indonesian Islamic thinkers concentrate on phenomenal (*al-dunya*) goals, in particular the question of how to make religious ethics contribute to worldly development. Speculative reason is restricted to the analysis of the affairs of this world and is not used in the discussion of otherworldly (*al-akhi-ra*) matters.[35] God's absolute justice is not discussed in relation to punishment and reward in the hereafter.

Contemporary Indonesians discuss God's absolute justice in sociological terms; human freedom to determine courses of action and the responsibility to act in accordance with principles of social-economic justice and egalitarianism.[36] The fundamental Islamic (and central Mu'tazili) social doctrine of Commanding Good and Prohibiting Evil has taken the form of responsibility (*taklif*) to eliminate poverty and oppression and the requirement that Muslim organizations compete in goodness, in order to better the world, al-dunya. In this regard, Nurcholish Madjid and other modernists like him are reinterpreting an important principle of classical Mu'tazili kalam. The Mu'tazila had argued that the ritual and ethical obligations (taklif) that God (*al-mukallif*) enjoins upon humans (*al-mukallafun* – those under divine obligation) are inherently good, because they provide the grounds for humans to be obedient to God and thus to earn reward in the hereafter.[37] The Ash'ariya, in contrast, denied the benefit of divinely imposed taklif. Al-Ghazali (d. 1111 – almost a century after 'Abd al-Jabbar) asked:

> How can any intelligent man say that there is benefit in a creation where *taklif* exists? Benefit has meaning only if *taklif* is absent. For *taklif* is in its essence the imposition of constraint (*ilzam kulfah*), and that is pain.[38]

Modernists accept the Mu'tazili concept of taklif, but they do so in a broad and general ethical sense of the need to do social good, not in the narrow sense of obligation to perform specific liturgical and ethical acts prescribed in by ritual (*'ibadat*).

In chapter 2 above, we saw that the anti-predestination party in Islam, the Qadariya, was one of the formative movements that preceded the Mu'tazila in espousing human responsibility and freedom to act in the world. In this regard, it is interesting to find that Fachri Ali and Bahtiar Effendy note that a Mu'tazili element exists in the thought of Abdurrahman Wahid, one of Indonesia's most prominent Muslim spiritual leaders and intellectuals. They call attention to his remark about predestination (Ar. taqdir): "God's predestination established that humans must be able to survive with the available natural resources and their capacity to act."[39] Wahid's statement is an example of the influence of Mu'tazili thought on Indonesian Islamic social thought and of the ways in which it has been transformed. Worldly injustice, which Hanbali traditionalists and the Ash'ariya perceived as one's predestiny, has been replaced by human duty to shape individual and social destiny, by use of the capacity (*qudra*) to act in the world.[40] This formulation of the problem is more clearly a Mu'tazili conception. On the other side, Wahid and others have shifted Mu'tazili emphasis on God's otherworldly justice or theodicy (*al-'adl*) to the task of formulating concepts of social and economic justice.

Reflecting on Islamic Rationalism, Past and Present

Contemporary Indonesian Islamic thinkers resemble the classical Mu'tazili theologians in their emphasis on speculative reason as a means of resolving religious problems. They differ in respect of the questions to which speculative reason is applied. Classical Mu'tazili theologians like 'Abd al-Jabbar used reason to bring humans to the first principle of faith, that God exists. Like the Indonesian thinkers discussed in this chapter, the branch of the Mu'tazila to which 'Abd al-Jabbar belonged, the Bahshamiya, believed that revealed knowledge (*'ilm shar'i*), and therefore scriptures and prophets, are nonetheless necessary.

In the Bahshamiya/Mu'tazili construction, revealed knowledge is necessary in order to teach those humans who submit to God (*al-muslimun*), and who therefore are responsible (al-mukallafun) to Him, about the benefits of the religious duties (the Five Pillars of Islamic practice), and other aspects of knowing God's self-revelation in the texts and interpretive processes of the Shari'a.[41] This information cannot be known by human reason. Nonetheless, along with the classical Mu'tazili tradition, Harun Nasution argues in *Kaum Mu'tazilah* that God in His goodness makes such knowledge available through religion (*din*). Such revealed knowledge is in addition to what humans can know through intelligence (*'aql*) of God's existence and of their moral responsibilities to one another in society. The chief difference between the Bahshamiya/Mu'tazili and the Sunni/Ash'ari and Maturidi theologies, therefore, is the much larger role of reason in theological reflection and in determining ethical and political action in the world – a role that some traditionalist Sunni Muslims have sought virtually to eliminate. In this regard, the modernist thinkers of Indonesia appear to be closer to historical Mu'tazili than to historical traditionalist positions.

The contemporary Indonesian thinkers discussed above, by contrast with the Mu'tazila, are content to rely solely on scripture as the basis for knowing God. Nonetheless, they insist on the primacy of reason as a means of arriving at Islamic solutions to social problems in the world, al-dunya, as we have seen. It is this primary concern to develop a practical theology, which can provide Islamic interpretations of social and political realities, that distinguishes the classical rationalists, the Mu'tazila, from modernist theologians in Indonesia. Seen in this way, the difference between the Mu'tazili and modernist theologians may be more a matter of emphasis than heretofore noticed.

In addition to the more practical social and political implications of theology among Indonesian modernists, they also differ from the Mu'tazila in their emphasis on the interior, experiential aspects of din. Neither the *Kitab al-usul al-khamsa* nor its later commentaries demonstrated any concern to explore the spiritual side of religion. That is not the task of kalam. Moreover, the Indonesian modernists, in keeping with traditional Sunni thought, emphasize that scripture still holds the key to knowledge of God and the hereafter (al-akhira). Nurcholish Madjid put it this way:

> There is still something, however, which cannot be tackled solely by intelligence, that is, the comprehension of matters related to the spirit or life after death, in other words religious questions, including knowledge of God. Revelation, the instruction which comes direct from God to man through the instrumentality of His Messengers, is therefore man's final equipment for life. Such is the teaching of religion, particularly Islam. As to the existence of revelation and its content, man's acceptance of that is not the result of the exercise of his intellect; it belongs properly to the question of God's guidance.[42]

At the last sentence only of Professor Madjid's statement does it seem to us that 'Abd al-Jabbar would have demurred. With the rest he could easily have agreed.

With this general background of Islamic modernism in Indonesia, our next task is to assess the life and work of Harun Nasution, a contemporary self-proclaimed Mu'tazilite in Indonesia.

Notes

1. Drewes, *The Admonitions of Seh Bari*, p. 77.
2. Ibid.
3. Hurgronje, *Mekka in the Latter Part of the Nineteenth Century*, p. 79.
4. Indonesian ulama feared that Western education would lead to division within the Muslim community and even conversion to Christianity. Their fears proved to be correct, especially among the Javanese elite. In the eighteenth and most of the nineteenth centuries, the sons of the Javanese elite were educated in traditional

Islamic schools (*pesantren*) where they studied such basic elements of Islam as Qur'an recitation, ritual and family law. They were also exposed to ritual and social dimensions of pesantren culture, and came to know the children of the ulama, many of whom would ultimately continue their studies of the Islamic textual tradition in Mecca and Medina. In the first decades of the twentieth century, the children of the elite were sent to live with Dutch colonial officials at an early age. Many recall being forbidden to perform Islamic ritual and hearing that Islam was a backward, perverse and barbarous religion. While most remained Muslims, significant numbers converted to Christianity and became affiliated with mystical cults inspired by the Theosophical Society, which were popular in Dutch colonial society at the time. It was in this way that Dutch educational policy contributed to the development of what Geertz, mistakenly, described as a primordial distinction between *priyayi* (elite) and *santri* (Islamic) religious orientations.

5. Geertz, *The Religion of Java*, esp. pp. 56–89.

6. Yusuf Abdullah Puar provides a clear account of the relationships between Indonesian, South Asian and Middle Eastern modernist movements, particularly the ways in which Middle Eastern and South Asian modernism contributed to the development of the Muhammadiyah. He shows that the journal *al-Manar* published by Muhammad 'Abduh and Rashid Rida inspired the Singapore journal *al-Iman*, which in turn inspired the Padang (Sumatra) journal *al-Munir*, which was widely read throughout Indonesia. The modernist theology of *al-Manar* contributed significantly to the development of Indonesian tajdid movements. The revivalistic and sometimes intolerant character of Indonesian modernism can be attributed largely to the influence of Rashid Rida, who seems to have had a greater and more direct influence on the founders of Indonesian modernism than his teacher Muhammad 'Abduh. See Puar, *Perjuangan dan Pengabdian Muhammadiyah* (The Struggle and Dedication of Muhammadiyah), p. 41.

7. Modernists mention two reasons for the prevalence of innovation and superstition in Indonesian Islam. The first is that Indonesian cultures are accommodative and have a tendency to incorporate received traditions into preexisting cultural systems. The result of the accommodative process was a syncretism of animism, Hinduism and Islam. The second is the dominant role of Sufi mysticism in Islamic thought at the time of its introduction to Indonesia. Modernists consider any form of Sufism to be innovation. See Abdullah, *Pemikiran Umat Islam di Nusantara: Sejarah dan Perkembangannya Hingga Abad ke-19* (Islamic thought in Southeast Asia: History and development through the nineteenth century), pp. 94–117. See also Ali and Effendy, *Merambah Jalan Baru Islam: Rekonstruksi Pemikiran Islam Masa Orde Baru* (Understanding the new path of Islam: the reconstruction of Indonesian Islamic thought in the New Order), p. 41.

8. Kamal, Yusuf and Sholeh, *Muhammadiyah Sebagai Gerakan Islam*.

9. Muhmmadiyah texts generally use the term *mukmin* (Ar. mu'min), to refer to those Muslims who hold theological positions similar to those of the Muhammadiyah.

10. The dialogue between al-Ash'ari and al-Jubba'i is narrated by al-Subki, *Tabaqat al-*

shafi'iya al-kubra, 6 vols. (Cairo, 1903), 2: 250f. and discussed in Watt, *Formative Period,* p. 305. The dilemma posed by al-Ash'ari to his former Mu'tazili teacher is as follows: there are three brothers, one a believer, one an unbeliever, and one who dies before having had a chance to believe or not. Between the first two, the Mu'tazila held, as we have seen, that Paradise is for those earn it through their belief. Only the first, the one who believes, can be admitted; the unbeliever cannot escape the punishment of the Fire. An implication of the Mu'tazili view is that the third brother, the infant, must necessarily be excluded from Paradise, which seems patently unfair. Later, al-Ghazali also used the story to criticize Mu'tazili eschatology and theodicy.

11. Hadikusuma, *Kitab Tauhid,* pp. 47–49.

12. This relates to the Ash'ari doctrine of *kasb,* the human "acquisition" from God of the power to perform each act. See the discussion of *qudra,* "power" in chapter 4 above.

13. Hadikusuma, *Kitab Tauhid,* pp. 62–64.

14. Ibid., p. 66.

15. Geertz, *The Religion of Java,* pp. 150–152.

16. This position is articulated in Kyai Haji Bisyri Musthafa's *Risalah Ahlussunnah wal Jairi'ah* (History of the People of the Sunna and Community), cited in Dhofier, *Tradisi Pesantren* (The pesantren tradition), p. 149.

17. Zamakhsyari Thoyfoer, *Mutiara Khittah Nahdatul Ulama 1926* (The pearl of the 1926 Charter of Nahdat al-Ulama) (Surabaya: Persatuan, 1987) pp. 69–70.

18. See Geertz, *The Religion of Java,* pp. 148–161.

19. Questions concerning the details of ritual performance remain the subject of a significant body of popular religious literature. See K. H. Siradjuddin 'Abbas, *40 Masalah Agama* (Forty religious questions), 4 vols., Jakarta: n. p., 1985, for an example of a popular "traditionalist" ritual manual. A "modernist" approach to similar questions can be found in a collection of homilies by the later Muhammadiyah leader A. R. Fachrudin entitled *Pak A.R. Menjawab dan 274 Permasalahan dalam Islam* (Pak A .R. answers 274 questions about Islam).

20. These observations are based on interviews with leaders and other members of the Muhammadiyah and N.U. conducted in 1995 and 1996.

21. For a detailed account of the politics of Islam in Indonesia see Boland, *The Struggle of Islam in Modern Indonesia.*

22. See Bresnan, *Managing Indonesia* for on overview of the political system of New Order Indonesia.

23. For overviews of recent developments in Indonesian Islamic thought, see Taufik Abdullah, "The Formation of a New Paradigm? A Sketch on Contemporary Islamic Discourse," in Woodward, *Toward a New Paradigm,* pp. 47–88; and Federspiel, *Muslim Intellectuals and National Development.*

24. Amin Rais is the first of the new generation of Muslim intellectuals to lead Muhammadiyah. Like others of this group he is not an *'alim* in the usual sense of the term. He is a longtime Muhammadiyah activist and professor of Political

Science at Gadjah Mada University in Yogyakarta. His understanding of the social and political roles of Islam is articulated in "The Muslim Brotherhood in Egypt" and in numerous Indonesian publications, including *Cakrawala Islam: Antara Cita dan Fakta* (Islamic horizons: between ideals and reality) (Bandung: Mizan, 1987).

25. For a discussion of recent attempts to understand Islam as a system of piety and social ethics see Woodward, "Textual Exegesis as Social Commentary." For an exposition of the view that Islam does not mandate a particular political structure and that the currently fashionable concept of the "Islamic State" is socially constructed and historically conditioned, see Munawir Sjadzali, *Islam dan Tata Negara: Ajaran, Sejarah dan Pemikiran* (Islam and the political system: doctrine, history and philosophy) (Jakarta: University of Indonesia Press, 1990). Sjadzali is a pious traditionalist Muslim who served for many years in the Indonesian diplomatic service. He was Minister of Religion from 1983 until 1993. *Islam dan Tata Negara* is based in part on his M.A. thesis from Georgetown University in Washington, D.C.: "Indonesia's Muslim Parties and Their Political Concepts" (1959). The Indonesian text includes laudatory introductions by Nurcholish Madjid and Harun Nasution, both of whom have expressed similar views. Given Sjadzali's position as Minister of Religion, the work can be understood as a semi-official political theology.

26. See Madjid, *Islam: Doctrin dan Peradaban* (Islam: doctrine and civilization), a collection of Madjid's major works. For an English-language discussion of his early works, see idem., "The Issue of Modernization Among Muslims in Indonesia." The clearest English statement of Madjid's theology can be found in his article "In Search of Islamic Roots for Modern Pluralism: The Indonesian Experiences" in Woodward, *Toward a New Paradigm*, pp. 89–116.

27. Ali and Effendy, *Merembah Jalan Baru Islam*, pp. 175–177.

28. Madjid's speech was translated by Hasan, *Muslim Intellectual Responses to "New Order" Modernization*, p. 197.

29. On Nasution's theology and Madjid's reservations concerning it, see Nurcholish Madjid's contribution to the commemorative volume for Nasution titled *Refleksi Pembaharuan Pemikiran Islam 70 Tahun Harun Nasution* (Reflections on the renewal of Islamic thought: the seventy years of Harun Nasution), ed. Panitia Penerbitan Buku dan Seminar 70 Tahun Harun Nasution Berkerisama dengan Lembaga Studi Agama dan Filsifat (Publication committee for the book and seminar commemorating the 70th Birthday of Harun Nasution) (Jakarta: Lembaga Studi Agama dan Filsafat, 1989).

30. Compare to the first paragraph of the text translated in chapter 5: "If it is asked: What is the first duty that God imposes upon you? Say to him: Speculative reasoning which leads to knowledge of God."

31. Madjid, *Islam, Kemodernan, dan Keindonesiaan*, p. 8.

32. Hassan Hanafi has lectured in Indonesia, and some of his work has been translated into Bahasa Indonesian, for example, *Agama Ideologi dan Pemdangunan*, trans. Shonhaji Sholeh (Jakarta: P3M, 1991). The translation of some of Hanafi's works, most of which are published in Arabic, would not be necessary for scholars like

Madjid, but is nonetheless useful for wider dissemination among younger Indonesians and the many others who are not fluent in Arabic.

33. Translation by Muhammad Kamal Hasan in *Muslim Intellectual Responses to "New Order Modernization"*, p. 197.

34. Abdurrahman Wahid, the General Chairman of N.U., interprets the "theology of development" as a profound understanding of the complexity that humans face in developing worldly life. This implies a possible conflict between established religious norms and human needs, for which either judgment or justification can take place, and postponement is a necessity. In this case Wahid seems to locate himself between Murji'i and Mu'tazili concepts of the intermediate position (see ¶¶ 55–58, chapter 5 above). See Abdurrahman Wahid, *Teologi Pembangunan, Meinbangun Teologi* (Theology of development and developing a theology: in the lighted intuition/heart) (compiled from Pelita's religious column), p. 182.

35. Madjid, "Sekularisme Bertentangan dengan Islam" (Secularism is against [the fundamentals of] Islam). In this article, Madjid explains that his main purpose in raising the issue of secularization was to motivate Muslims to pay greater attention to issues concerning life in this world (dunya) rather than focusing primarily on preparation for the hereafter (akhirat).

36. M. Dawam Rahardjo, Adi Sasono and A. M. Saefuddin, whose educational backgrounds are in economics, frequently raise this issue, even with quite distinct approaches. See Fachri Ali, *Merambah Jalan Baru Islam* (Clearing away the new path of Islam) (Bandung: Mizan, 1986).

37. The Mu'tazili position is discussed by 'Abd al-Jabbar in *al-Mughni* 14: 137ff. It is referred to but not discussed above in chapter 5, ¶¶ 12, 39–40.

38. Al-Ghazali, *al-Iqtisad fi l-i'tiqad* (Ankara, 1962), p. 176, as cited and translated by Ormsby, *Theodicy in Islamic Thought*, p. 55. For an incisive discussion of taklif, see George F. Hourani, *Islamic Rationalism* pp. 28–29, 56–57, 119–121.

39. Ali and Effendy, *Merambah Jalan Baru Islam*, p. 189.

40. On qudra, see chapter 5, ¶¶ 4, 12, and 30.

41. This concept of benefit through divine revelation is discussed in the text below in chapter 5, ¶ 12, especially subsections (e) to (g).

42. Emphasis in the original Indonesian text, translation in Hasan, *Muslim Intellectual Responses to "New Order Modernization"*, pp. 205–206.

eight

Harun Nasution's Defense
of Mu'tazilism

The text translated in chapter 9 is a modern Muslim overview of Mu'tazili thought by the Indonesian scholar Harun Nasution. Nasution is among a relatively small number of contemporary Muslim intellectuals to espouse Mu'tazili *kalam* openly. He is, in a very real sense, a modern Mu'tazili *mutakallim*. Nasution was first attracted to Mu'tazili thought during his student days in Cairo in the late 1930s. For more than half a century he has advocated Mu'tazili teachings of human freedom and responsibility and the concept of natural law. In Nasution's view, the revival of the Mu'tazili theology is an essential component of a larger program of political, social and cultural rationalization.

Harun Nasution and Fazlur Rahman:
Convergences and Divergences

In this respect, Nasution's thinking resembles that of the Pakistani scholar Fazlur Rahman, especially as expressed in the latter's book, *Islam and Modernity*.[1] Despite the facts that Rahman's works have been translated into Indonesian and are well known among Indonesian intellectuals, and that one of Nasution's close friends and associates, Nurcholish Madjid, studied with Professor Rahman at the University of Chicago, there is no evidence that Rahman directly influenced the development of Nasution's theology. Nasution's books and articles contain no references to English or Indonesian editions of Rahman's works. In part because his ideas proved to be unacceptable in his native Pakistan, Rahman is far better known in the West than

Nasution, almost all of whose writings are in Indonesian. However, because of the more tolerant political and religious climate in Indonesia, and because he has not emphasized controversial doctrines such as that of the created Qur'an, Nasution's impact on Islamic education has been far greater than that of his more famous contemporary. Curiously, Rahman mentions the development of Islamic higher education in Indonesia as an example of promising developments in the Muslim world, but fails to note the pivotal role that Nasution has played in this process.[2]

The reasons for this mutual intellectual avoidance are not entirely clear, particularly given the fact that the two scholars share a common educational and political agenda: both encouraged modern Islamic education while rejecting political radicalism and the call for explicitly Islamic states in their respective countries. The reasons are perhaps theological. Nasution holds that the revival of Mu'tazili thought is essential for the modernization of Islam. Rahman, as we shall demonstrate in chapter 10, was strongly, and at times harshly, critical of Mu'tazili thinkers, arguing that the Mu'tazili doctrine of human responsibility "denied God's role totally" and that their understanding of the "weighing" of human actions on the Day of Judgment "did grave violence to religion."[3] Nasution is clearly Rahman's equal as a scholar in both the Islamic and the Western sense. The facts that he has published almost exclusively in Indonesian and the failure of Rahman and others to mention or cite Nasution's English-language M.A. thesis at McGill University have meant that an important development in modern Islamic thought has passed almost unnoticed by Western Islamicists and Muslims outside the Malay/Indonesian-speaking world. One of our purposes in presenting an English translation of his summary of Mu'tazili thought is to begin to fill this lacuna in Islamic studies.

Nasution and Rahman share the opinion that the rationalization of Islamic theology is an essential component of a larger program of modernization in Muslim societies. Both scholars have emphasized the development of educational institutions and pedagogies which are simultaneously Islamic and modern, though Nasution, unlike Rahman, had the opportunity to put his theories into practice. Nasution's goal is the development of an Islamic modernity capable of competing with Western modernities on an equal footing, but retaining the deeply pious attitudes characteristic of traditional Islam. His strategy for realizing this goal has included the reformulation and rationalization of Islamic thought, the development of Islamic higher education and the diminution of agitation for an explicitly Islamic state.

To understand Nasution's fascination with Mu'tazili rationalism, and the nature of his own contributions to the tradition of Mu'tazili kalam, it is necessary to consider the intellectual and political contexts of which his life and works have been a significant part.[4]

Harun Nasution: An Intellectual Biography

Nasution was born in South Sumatra in 1919. His father was a traditionally minded ulama (Ar. *'alim*). Both his parents had spent time in Mecca, spoke and read Arabic. Nasution's father was appointed *penghulu* or chief Islamic religious official in the district of Simalungun by the Dutch colonial government. Like many of the ulama of his day, he was also engaged in commerce, which in Sumatra meant importing or, in Dutch parlance "smuggling," goods from Singapore. The position of Nasution's father as a government official gave him the opportunity to send his children to Dutch-language schools, which provided a vastly superior modern education to that of the native Malay-language schools. Dutch schools, however, actively discouraged the study of Arabic and Islam. This was a cause of considerable controversy and concern in Nasution's family. Despite the fact that his grandmother strongly opposed it, Nasution spent seven years in a Dutch school, which he describes as having very strict discipline and high academic standards. The conflict with his grandmother on the language and form of education is indicative of the point we wish to emphasize about the contexts of tradition and change in Nasution's background.

Nasution states that his grandmother once said: "Do not study the Dutch language. It is the language of unbelief. In Heaven they speak Arabic. If you speak Dutch in the afterlife you will go to Hell." This view was typical among conservative Muslims of her generation. Nasution mentions inspections of his hands and nails as examples of this discipline. Indonesians of his generation have a grudging respect for Dutch educators, most of them stressing the combination of mental and physical discipline they imposed. One of the primary purposes, from the Dutch perspective, of modern education for "natives" was to build a social and political elite with strong ties to Dutch language and culture. This policy, known as "associationism," was formulated by the great Dutch Islamicist Snouck Hurgronje as an antidote to Indonesian nationalism and Islamic radicalism. It succeeded in creating a remarkable generation of Western-educated Indonesians capable of confronting the Dutch on their own terms. Thus, following van der Veer's analysis of Orientalism in India, which we discussed in chapter 1, Dutch Orientalism promoted, rather than retarded, both secular and Islamic nationalisms. Through Dutch training, educated Indonesians became increasingly aware of the inequalities and injustices of the colonial system as the result of contact with democratic European intellectual traditions. Almost all the leaders of the pre-Second World War nationalist movement and of the early decades of the Indonesian republic were products of this system.

Nasution was initially attracted to a combination of the natural sciences. From an early age he hoped to become a teacher. In addition to his formal schooling, Nasution received home-based instruction in Arabic and Malay, and in Qur'an recitation from his father. Nasution describes his mother as a strict disciplinarian who required him to do numerous household chores in addition to his secular and religious studies. In general, he describes a very highly disciplined upbringing which emphasized a balance between work and the study of secular and religious subjects. The remainder of his autobiography builds on these themes of discipline and study, and the implied contrast between the traditional world of Islamic piety and the modern world of rational, empirical knowledge. Nasution describes both his academic career and his life as an attempt to reconcile these opposing currents.

When he graduated from primary school, Nasution planned to continue his studies at the Dutch-language high school, which would have led to a career in law, medicine or the colonial administration. His parents had other ideas. They insisted that he had acquired enough general knowledge and that he should continue his education in an Islamic school. As a compromise, the young Nasution was allowed to attend an Islamic high school which taught secular as well as religious subjects. Nasution was not content with his first choice of schools, however; in part because of poor material conditions and in part because of the very traditional nature of the religious curriculum. He mentions as particularly frustrating the debates about whether or not one who has not performed the *wudhu* (Ar. *wudu'*), "ritual cleansing," can touch the Qur'an.[5] He came to differ with his father on several similar issues. He subsequently planned to attend a Muhammadiyah school in Surakarta in Java, but again his parents had other plans. This was a period in which relationships between the Muhammadiyah and other modernist Islamic movements and Islamic traditionalists were exceptionally bad. Each side routinely denounced the other as unbelievers. Many communities, including Nasution's, were sharply divided between the two groups. Nasution's father was among the leaders of the traditionally minded ulama and did not wish his son to be influenced by what he saw as the corrupting influences of the Muhammadiyah.

So it was that the young Nasution was sent off to study in Mecca, which was still, at that time, the chief center of traditional Islamic learning. Nasution was not at all happy with the experience. He describes Mecca in the 1930s as being "the middle ages in the modern world." He complains

161

about the lack of chairs and desks, the dirtiness of the city, and its general backwardness.

The issue of the appurtenances of study is worth elaborating. Chairs and tables were important symbols of modernity in colonial Indonesia. They were first introduced at the insistence of Dutch officials as a way of asserting their status and avoiding the patterns of deferential behavior required in Javanese and other Indonesian royal courts, but were quickly adopted by the courts themselves as a means of asserting their own status in the colonial political order. The use of modern, Western furniture soon spread from the courts to the larger society. Even today, many Indonesians prefer to sit on mats or carpets, but invariably use chairs and tables on formal occasions, with the notable exception of Islamic ritual. While "official" business is always conducted sitting in chairs, sermons, religious lectures and other Islamic events are still conducted in the traditional manner. One can distinguish between a seminar on Islamic studies and an Islamic sermon or lecture by the seating arrangements. If participants sit in chairs the event is an academic seminar. If they sit on the floor it is a prayer service, no matter what the content of the address. The use of chairs and desks also serves as marker of the tradition/modernity dichotomy in Islamic education. Modernist schools have western-style classrooms. In traditional Javanese *pesantren* (religious schools), instruction is conducted in the mosques where students sit on the floor at the feet of a teacher. In pesantren where "general" as well as religious subjects are taught, however, religious instruction requires sitting on the floor, while students engaged in general subjects sit on chairs.

Nasution also complains that, despite the fact that Arabic was the sole language of instruction, it was impossible in Saudi Arabia to find a good Arabic language teacher. Here Nasution was suffering the consequences of his early secular education. Had he studied in a traditional Islamic school he would have acquired a very high level of proficiency in classical Arabic by this point in his student career. At the same time, Nasution felt that his knowledge of Islam was insufficient to study classical texts in the Great Mosque of Mecca. He longed to go to Cairo to pursue more modern studies, but was unable to do so without his parents' permission and financial support. Nasution describes this period as a year during which he frequented coffee shops and studied informally with other Indonesians. In exchange for lessons on "general subjects," Nasution received instruction in Arabic and the Islamic religious sciences.[6] While this type of informal education was quite common among Indonesian students of his generation, Nasution found it both frustrating and boring. Finally, he sent his parents an ultimatum. He would either go to study in Egypt or refuse to return to Indonesia at all, spending the rest of his days as a driver in Mecca. His parents eventually consented.

When he first arrived in Cairo in 1938, Nasution still had difficulties understanding lectures at al-Azhar. He arranged for private instruction in classical Arabic and Islamic law, but he spent much of his time enjoying the student life of the time. This included going to the cinema and hanging out in coffee houses with Indonesian and Malaysian students. Eventually he was admitted to the Faculty of Usul al-Din, "Foundations of Religion," at al-Azhar (not the more traditional curriculum of *fiqh*, Islamic law). This pleased Nasution immensely because some of the courses, particularly those on philosophy, ethics and psychology, were taught in English or French, both of which Nasution had mastered. Nasution did very well in his classes at al-Azhar, but complains that he did little more than memorize facts and felt that he actually understood very little.

Nasution's formal studies were interrupted by the Second World War, the Indonesian revolution, and a seemingly promising career in the Indonesian diplomatic service. However, his anti-communist views crystallized just at the time the power of the Indonesian Communist Party was waxing in the late 1950s. Thus, his position in the diplomatic service became increasingly problematical. In 1960 he was dismissed from his position as First Secretary of the Indonesian embassy in Brussels and was officially blacklisted. A diplomatic note from the foreign ministry in Jakarta advised other embassies in Brussels not to grant him a visa.

Personal connections with the Egyptian embassy enabled him nonetheless to obtain an entry visa. He spent much of the next two years studying in Cairo. It would seem that at this point many of what were to become Nasution's basic philosophical principles began to emerge. He had spent considerable time reading books on Islam in European languages during his years in Belgium. It was during this period that he acquired an interest in, and the beginnings of an understanding of, the history and variety of Islamic ideas and civilizations. During his second residence in Cairo, he studied at the private Islamic Studies Institute al-Dirasat al-Islamiya, which he describes as being similar to a Western Islamic Studies institute. He attended seminars on Islamic history, philosophy and economic development. While he studied traditional subjects like *tasawwuf* and fiqh, he approached them from a rationalist historical perspective.

In 1962 Nasution began his studies at the Institute of Islamic Studies at McGill University. This was possible largely because of the efforts of a fellow Indonesian, H. M. Rashidi, who was a faculty member at the Institute at the time. He reports being thrilled with the rational approach to the study of Islam on which the Institute's curriculum is based, contrasting it to what he saw as the irrationality of Islam in Indonesia, Mecca and al-Azhar. Nasution was most strongly attracted to history and to the works of Western Orientalists, initially finding little of value in works by Muslim authors. However, Nasution strongly denies that he was in any way subverted by Orientalism. He reports coming to the conclusion that there was a fundamental difference between studies of Islam conducted from within the Islamic tradition and those rooted in the assumptions of rationalist historiography. He also found the history of Islam to be quite different from, and more interesting than, classical legal and theological texts. He saw a dynamism in Islamic history which he found lacking in the classical texts. This is one of the basic assumptions of contemporary Indonesian neo-modernism. Nasution developed the idea in his M.A. thesis, which argues that the concept of an "Islamic state" is a strictly contemporary one which, in Indonesia at least, was the product of constitutitional debates between Islamic, nationalist and communist groups. This theme is also developed in the works of Nurcholish Madjid, Abdurahman Wahid, and other neo-modernist thinkers.

Nasution describes his doctoral work, which concerned the theology of Muhammad 'Abduh, as the result of an inspiration to seek for a rational theory of knowledge within the Islamic tradition. He was particularly concerned with the influence of the Egyptian reformer Muhammad 'Abduh on the development of Islamic modernism in South Asia, the Arab world, Turkey and Indonesia. Nasution reports the problem posed to him by his advisors regarding his proposed dissertation research: "All of this time you have been concerned with modernism and renewal in Islam, but now you are going to study kalam?" To which he replied: "I am moving [the study of] kalam because of its modernity." He goes on to explain that:

> My purpose was to understand Muhammad 'Abduh as a modern thinker. I became a modernist because of 'Abduh. Not from the Ash'arite position. I have not abandoned the position I have held all of this time: modernism. I most certainly want to study modernism, but in the context of a modern kalam.

Nasution understood his project as a combination of classical and modern Islamic thought, the purpose of which was to explore the extent to which 'Abduh had been influenced by Mu'tazili teachings. He states that if 'Abduh was, as he suspected, actually a Mu'tazili mutakallim, then he could continue to influence the development of Islamic thought, but that if, as the Muhammadiyah and other modernist movements claimed, his views were basically Ash'ari, then they would ultimately come to naught. It is clear from this statement that Nasution hoped to use 'Abduh and Mu'tazili kalam as the basis for establishing a modern, rationalist Islamic philosophy and theology.

Nasution describes his project as the culmination of a lifelong quest for a way to unite the rationalist and Islamic halves of a divided self. He describes himself as having been since his youth both a rationalist and a pious Muslim. His life and intellectual development is portrayed as a journey to join the two halves of himself. This project was mapped out in his doctoral dissertation at McGill, in which he argued that the Egyptian reformer Muhammad 'Abduh was actually a proponent of Mu'tazili kalam. From this, Nasution concluded that if Islamic societies are to come to terms with modernity it is essential that Ash'ari kalam be replaced with Mu'tazili. Nasution also argued that rationalism is among the central themes of the Qur'an and that the Islam of the Prophet Muhammad and his early Companions was rationalist in nature. Nasution's hermeneutic resembles that of his teacher Toshihiko Izutsu, as well as that of the late Fazlur Rahman. Unlike most classical and contemporary interpreters, he does not conduct his exegesis by seeking to discern the meaning of individual verses, but rather by discerning common themes in a large number of verses. In Nasution's case, the most striking theme was rationality. His exposure to both Islam and Western rationalism seems to have sparked a quest to find both a rational Islam and an Islamic modernity.

Because of his deeply felt Muslim piety, Nasution found it essential to root an Islamic rationalism directly in the Quranic text. While he often cites Islamic theological and philosophical texts from the classical period, Nasution turns primarily to the Qur'an to support his contention that rational thought is among the prime sources of religious and secular knowledge. In his *Akal dan Wahyu dalam Islam* (Reason and revelation in Islam), he cites no less than thirty passages from the Qur'an in which, in his view, humans are commanded to employ rational thought in the quest for knowledge of God and the world. He argues that the Qur'an teaches the basic Mu'tazili doctrines of free will, free act and human responsibility. His basic teaching is that humanity is God's rational creation. This view is explained in a paper first published in 1975:

> According to the truth of Islam, humanity is God's creation. The capacity for reason God gave to humanity establishes it as the greatest of his creations. Reason enables humanity to establish great civilizations and cultures. It leads to developments in science and technology. Science and technology enable humans to control the environment and establish health and prosperity now and in the future. It is reason which makes humans different from animals.[7]

Nasution is strongly critical of the doctrine of divine compulsion (*jabr*), associated with the Ash'ariya in particular. In his view, this doctrine denies human rationality and choice, and also leads to a fatalist mode of thought which renders political, economic and social development impossible. His strong position on this issue may be, at least in part, a reaction to traditional Javanese concepts of social order which are commonly described as feudalistic. Traditional Javanese social and political thought relied heavily on the doctrine of divine determinism (Javanese *titah*) to justify a rigid, hierarchical social system. The Javanese concept of *nrima*, which means passively to accept one's fate in hope of heavenly reward, is closely associated with the teaching of determinism. Most modern Indonesian intellectuals and political thinkers strongly oppose these elements of traditional thought, believing that they make the intellectual and political dynamism necessary for national and economic development impossible to attain. Nasution's advocacy of Mu'tazili kalam can be understood at least in part as an attempt to find a countertext to these teachings inside the Islamic tradition.

Nasution's reliance on the text of the Qur'an links his understanding of Islam and his mode of argumentation with other Muslim modernists who seek to use what anthropologist Clifford Geertz calls "scripturalism" as the basis for modernity.[8] Unlike most other Muslim modernists, Nasution explicitly rejects the modernist position that the Qur'an is a "complete and perfect text" including all that is required for the development of modern society, scientific thought and technology.[9] His view is that the Qur'an establishes basic moral themes but does not mandate a particular social or legal system. Nasution is also of the opinion that Allah has not only given humans the capacity for rational thought, but that He has commanded them to use it in the formulation of moral and legal choices. In other words, the text of scripture is a necessary tool for thinking about what it means to be Muslim in a changing society, but it is not a complete guide to an Islamic way of life for all times and places.

Nasution recalls that his research program encountered considerable resistance at McGill and later in Indonesia. He recounts a conversation with Charles Adams and Toshihiko Izutsu in which he claims that Adams stated that his research agenda was "dangerous" because it might lead to rumors that McGill had become an active proponent of Mu'tazili thought. He credits Izutsu with convincing Adams that the project was worthwhile. Adams recalls this conversation somewhat differently. He describes Nasution as having been a mature scholar, with firmly established and strongly held opinions at the time he entered the graduate program at McGill. He explained that his questions about Nasution's project did not concern the thesis that 'Abduh held essentially Mu'tazili views. Rather, Adams was concerned with the historical claim of Nasution's more fundamental thesis that something like Mu'tazili rationalism was among the fundamental doctrines of the Qur'an and that the Prophet Muhammad and his Companions could be understood as rationalist thinkers in the modern sense of the term.[10]

Nasution's advocacy of Mu'tazili kalam, and particularly his insistence that the rationalist perspective is central to the message of the Qur'an, have always been controversial. He reports that Mohammad Hatta, Indonesia's first vice-president; Mohammad Natsir, who was leader of the Islamic political party Masyumi and a prominent modernist thinker; and other Muslim leaders were shocked to learn of his conclusion that their beloved model, Shaykh 'Abduh (who is revered, as we have seen, in Indonesia and elsewhere, as the founder of Islamic modernism) was actually a Mu'tazili theologian. This reaction led Nasution to delay the publication of an Indonesian translation of his thesis, which was completed in 1968, until 1986. In the Introduction to the Indonesian edition, Nasution explains that he found it necessary to delay publication until such time as Indonesian Muslim intellectuals had come to understand the diversity of Islamic theology and philosophy.

Nasution's prudence probably contributed to the advancement of both his own career and his educational agenda. Had he published his thesis immediately upon its completion it is likely that he would have met with a fate similar to that of Fazlur Rahman, described below in chapter 10. Until very recently, the adjective "Mu'tazili" has been used only in the most derogatory manner. It is often used by conservative traditional Muslims to denounce the supposed secularism of modernists who, not surprisingly, utterly reject the designation. Had Nasution proclaimed his own Mu'tazilism and claimed Muhammad 'Abduh as his inspiration it is likely that he would have been denounced by the entire Muslim leadership. This would almost certainly have prevented him from playing an active role in the politics of Islamic education. This is particularly likely in light of the fact that, since the foundation of the "New Order" following the abortive coup of 1965, the diminution of religious conflict and controversy has been among the cornerstones of the religious policy of the Indonesian government. Nasution published a number of other books in the period between 1968 and 1986 which, ironically, may have helped pave the way for public reception of his study of Muhammad 'Abduh.

In essence, what Nasution wants to do is find a basis for modernity, pluralism and democracy within the Islamic tradition. He does not see "modernism" in the conventional senses we have described heretofore as being of much help to his cause. He has influenced a large number of people by making the diversity of Islam and the Islamic kalam tradition public knowledge and by making the "rational" study of history almost a "source of Islamic law."

The Literary Context of Nasution's Writing

The text translated in the next chapter is included in a collection of Nasution's Indonesian-language works prepared by Mizan Press in 1995, titled *Islam Rasional: Gagasan dan Pemikiran* (Rational Islam: ideas and thoughts). The collection includes fifty-eight articles, many of which were originally published in Indonesian daily newspapers or as journal articles.[11] Others are the written texts of speeches and seminar presentations. The collection and the articles it includes are typical of the public nature of Indonesian scholarship. Almost all Indonesia's prominent Muslim thinkers publish regularly in the popular press as well as in mass-circulation Islamic journals, which include news articles as well as theological essays. Muslim intellectuals are also frequently invited to address general audiences, give sermons or speeches in mosques, and to participate in seminars, the proceedings of which are often published in popular print media. Prominent and prolific individuals regularly publish collections of their works as books.

Edited collections that feature the writings of groups of scholars with similar interests and theological orientations are also popular. Examples of what might be called the "public theology" genre are *Islam Doktrin dan Peradaban: Sebuah Telaah Kritis tentang Masalah Keimanan, Kemanusiaan, dan Kemoderenan* (Islam, doctrine, and culture: a critical study of the problems of faith, humanity, and modernity) (Jakarta: Yayasan Wakaf Paramadina, 1992), a collection of the works of Nurcolish Madjid; and Ramlan Mardjuned, *K. H. Hasan Basri 70 Tahun, Fungsi Ulama dan Peranan Masjid* (The 70 years of K. H. Hasan Basri: the function of the Ulama and the role of the mosque) (Jakarta: Media Da'wah, 1990). Madjid is a younger associate of Nasution and one of Indonesia's most creative and controversial Muslim theologians. Basri was general chairman of the Majelis Ulama Indonesia (The Indonesian Council of Ulama) between 1985 and 1990.

The first generation of scholars of independent Indonesia, known as the "Generation of 1945," has been particularly honored with felicitation volumes offering tribute to and commentary on their works. The term refers to those Indonesians who participated in the struggle for independence from the Dutch following the Second World War. They are regarded, in an almost mystical sense, as the founders of the nation and the embodiment of the spirit of the revolutionary struggle. They were, in fact, a remarkable generation, among whom was a large number of highly productive and creative intellectuals, as well as social, political and religious visionaries. The accomplishments of this generation can be attributed in part to the fact that many, including Harun Nasution, were very deeply committed to the pursuit of modern education as well as the preservation and transformation of traditional culture and religion. Among the accomplishments of this generation are the development of a national identity, the establishment of Indonesian as a national language, more than thirty years of sustained economic growth, significant strides in reducing population growth, and increases in agricultural productivity. Extremely influential among these accomplishments has been the development of an Islamic theological discourse which emphasizes rationality, modernization, and tolerance at a time when religious xenophobia and radicalism have exerted powerful influences elsewhere in the world. Against this background, the collection titled *Islam Rasional* can be understood as a companion volume to the previously published Festschrift for Nasution, *Refleksi Pembaharuan Pemikran Islam*.[12]

The public nature of Muslim intellectual discourse reflects popular interest in and concern with theology. This interest serves to shape public opinion through regional and national media. Writing for the popular press is also among the means by which Muslim intellectuals are able to enhance their meager university or government salaries.[13] The style and content of this public theology differ significantly from more technical works written for theological students and the ulama. Indonesian public theology employs the conventions of Western journalistic and academic writing rather than those of traditional Islamic scholarship. In public theology, Arabic terms are used sparingly and almost always followed by Indonesian glosses. Even the text of the Qur'an is quoted in Indonesian translation, often without the Arabic original. Generally speaking, this genre focuses on particular social, political and ethical themes rather than on the exegesis of classical works. While the Qur'an, Hadith and classical theological works are cited, they are used as proof texts for the position the author assumes rather than as the subject of traditional commentary. All of Harun Nasution's writings are of this type. He is among the earliest of the new-style Indonesian Muslim intellectuals who are neither ulama, in the traditional sense of the term, nor secular scholars. He is rather an example of the modern Muslim intellectual who employs the methods of historical and critical scholarship to accomplish the traditional Muslim goal of constructing a religious worldview that is rooted in an understanding of God's creative power and His love for His human subjects. In this sense, he exemplifies the notion we introduced in chapter 1 and remarked upon earlier in this chapter, that the modern Muslim intelligentsia in

Indonesia and elsewhere are in many ways a byproduct, and extension, of Orientalism. Critics like Egypt's Hassan Hanafi call for the deconstruction of Western Orientalism, which has seeped into the Islamic world, through the development of an "Occidentalism" (*'ilm al-istighrab*).

Nasution's public style differs greatly from that employed in technical works and translations of Arabic classics as well as from the exegetical strategies used in the pesantren and those established by modernist organizations such as the Muhammadiya; in other words, what we have termed "traditional" Islam. In these works, the original Arabic text is reproduced, often in Arabic script, followed by a romanized transliteration and a translation into Indonesian. Commentaries include copious direct references to classical sources, as well as the author's exegesis. These texts presume a knowledge of classical Arabic. They make extensive use of technical terminology, which is often not translated, and of Indonesianized Arabic vocabulary, and even of Arabic syntax.

These works are difficult even for educated Indonesians to read, unless they have been trained in theological schools. They often include Arabic words that are not in common use in spoken or written Indonesian, and which are not found in any of the standard dictionaries. In many respects, they resemble Javanese- and Malay-language texts commonly known as *kitab kuning* (yellow books) from the premodern period, and Persian commentaries on Arabic classics written and read in Iran and (premodern) South Asia. They present enormous difficulties for Western scholars because the tasks of translation and commentary require a combination of expertise in Islamic theology, classical Arabic, Indonesian, and the complex and variable orthographic conventions (or lack thereof) for the transliteration of the Arabic employed by the ulama.[14] It should be noted, however, that many of the authors and translators are more comfortable writing in Arabic than in modern Indonesian. Although such works carry on a long-established tradition of exegetical scholarship and continue to play an important role in theological education, they have less influence among the broader Muslim literate population because of the high demands they place on readers. Increasingly, it is the broader group of Muslim intellectuals, among whom Nasution was one of the first and most influential, rather than the traditionalist and modernist ulama, who are the shapers of Muslim popular opinion.

The Text of *Kaum Mu'tazilah dan Pandangan Rasionalanya*

Of the fifty-eight works included in the collection titled *Islam Rasional*, only thirty-two are dated. Of these, the earliest was written in 1972 and the latest in 1993. Although the *Kaum Mu'tazilah* is dated, a printing error makes it impossible to determine exactly when it was written. The citation at the end of the text reads: "I.A.I.N. Jakarta, Ciputat, 31-5-7." The I.A.I.N. Jakarta designation suggests that the text dates from the period when Nasution was rector: 1974–1982. This would mean that the text would have been composed some time in the mid- to late 1970s, a period during which Nasution was extremely active as a scholar and public lecturer.

Evidence internal to the text indicates that it was originally delivered as a lecture, probably to an audience consisting of I.A.I.N. students and elements of the Muslim public. The style is colloquial in a manner common among the older generation of Indonesians. There are numerous incomplete sentences. Most of these are predicates, the subject of which is stated in a previous clause or sentence. The text does not employ the elaborate, somewhat artificial structure of contemporary formal Indonesian. This latter style is more common among younger speakers and writers for whom Indonesian is more nearly a native language than it is for Nasution's generation. In translating the text, we have endeavored (and at times struggled) to put it into grammatically correct English. A more literal translation, preserving the grammatical style of the original, including the extensive use of the passive voice, would be difficult to follow for a reader unfamiliar with the grammatical and stylistic conventions of Indonesian. It would also detract from the power and importance of Nasution's ideas.

The text employs many of the conventions of Western scholarship on Islam. It is based on a historical overview of Mu'tazili kalam. It includes numerous footnotes that reference classical Islamic texts as well as studies by contemporary Arab and Western scholars. These have been included in the translation although the form of references has been made consistent with that used throughout this book. We have edited many of Harun Nasution's notations and added several of our own in order to provide the reader with complete bibliographic reference information wherever possible. It should be kept in mind that at the time he wrote this paper, Nasution did not have access to a library collection comparable to those found in Western universities. He probably relied extensively on notes taken during his days in Egypt and Canada and on his extensive, but necessarily limited, personal library.

Western scholars may take exception to some of Nasution's historical arguments and his use of classical Arabic sources. His claim that Mu'tazili teachings preserve the original message of the Qur'an, from which other Islamic theologies have deviated, is particularly controversial among Muslim as well as Western historians. It is at this point that the reader must keep in mind the public and political context, described briefly above, in which

Nasution prepared this text. Nasution writes and speaks as a modern Muslim intellectual. He is a constructive public theologian who uses Western historiography and textual analysis to make *theological* arguments. Chief among these is the teaching that God created humans as rational beings. As such they have both the right and the duty to use their rational capacities in the pursuit of well-being and happiness in this world and in the next. In this sense, Nasution is a modern Mu'tazili mutakallim. Both the complexity of his thought and his tireless efforts to bring it to the attention of a mass audience establish Harun Nasution as among the stellar figures of this ancient and venerable (and controversial) tradition of theological scholarship.

Outline of Text

The text of Nasution's treatise in defense of Mu'tazilism follows in the next chapter. The outline below represents headings and subheadings we have added in order to grasp the organization of the treatise. The headings are otherwise somewhat arbitrary, serving mainly the purpose of being able to refer the reader to particular sections and paragraphs in the text.

   I. *The Problem of Major Sin*
       A. The First *Fitna*
       B. The Question of Faith (*iman*)
       C. The Khawarij (Seceders)
       D. The Murji'a (Postponers)
       E. The Compromise Position in the Circle of Hasan al-Basri

  II. *The Rise of the Mu'tazila*
       F. The Name "Mu'tazila"
       G. The Mu'tazila Are Misunderstood in Indonesia

 III. *Mu'tazili Teachings*
       H. Sin and Free Will
       I. Divine Attributes
       J. Abu l-Hudhayl and Greek Influence
       K. The Question of the Good (Theodicy)
       L. The Role of Reason
       M. The Role of Revelation
       N. The Apparent Conflict of Reason and Revelation
       O. Mu'ammar and the Doctrine of Creation
       P. The *usul al-khamsa* (Five Basic Teachings)
           1. *al-tawhid*
           2. *al-'adl*

3. *al-waʿd wa l-waʿid*
4. *al-manzila bayn al-manzilatayn*
5. *al-amr bi l-maʿruf wa l-nahy ʿan al-munkar*

IV. *Conclusion: A Case for Modern Muʿtazilism*

Textual Notes and Comparisons

For easier comparison we repeat here the outline of ʿAbd al-Jabbar's *Kitab al-usul al-khamsa* (chapter 5), which we first presented in chapter 4:

I. *First Principles*
    A. Knowledge of God (¶¶ 1–9)
    B. Fundamentals of Religion (¶¶ 10–15)

II. *Divine Unicity*
    A. Inferring God's Existence from Physical Bodies(¶¶ 16–17)
    B. Inferring God's Attributes (¶¶ 18–27)

III. *Theodicy* (¶¶ 28–44)
IV. *Eschatology* (¶¶ 45–54)
V. *The Intermediate Position* (¶¶ 55–58)

VI. *Commanding the Good and Prohibiting Evil* (¶¶ 59–67)
    A. Political Theology: the Imamate (¶ 60)
    B. The Validity of Tradition (¶ 61)
    C. God's Decree (¶ 62)
    D. Repentance and Faith (¶¶ 63–67)

Readers of Nasution's text will readily note the great difference in style in comparison to ʿAbd al-Jabbar's text, even though the theological positions of these two Muʿtazili intellectuals are remarkably congruent. We need to recall that, because he was writing in the highly charged theological atmosphere of Buyid Iran under Shiʿi rulers, ʿAbd al-Jabbar did not hesitate to cite Qurʾan verses, sometimes several, for many of his responses to the rhetorical interlocutor. Hadith reports attributed to the Prophet are also given. The discourse of argument for kalam, like fiqh and the rendering of nonbinding legal opinions or "fatwas," rested heavily on *loci probates* from sacred texts (and often from events in early Islamic history as well). Nasution's text, as we noted above, has a much freer, less structured style. The tight formalism of dialectical exchange with an interlocutor is absent. Qurʾan citations are less frequent than in the Qadi's text. Hadith references are even more rare, reflecting perhaps the textual privileging of divine word over prophetic practice among many modernists and reformers. ʿAbd al-Jabbar wrote (or dictated) his text in the highly formalized literary form of a disputation. It was meant to be memorized by students – mutakallimun preparing to dispute doctrine with theological opponents. Nasution most likely delivered his text originally as a general lecture. Finally, many mutakallimun argued strongly against doing theology in public, in front of the common folk (the *'awamm*); disputing theological differences carried danger of social disruption. For Nasution and for modern Muslim intellectuals in many parts of the world, theological discourse is public and popular. These differences are well reflected in the two texts.

In chapter 1 we cited Alister McGrath's argument that the construction of theological doctrine articulates a commitment to community and the need to establish religious identity. Those needs were quite different for 'Abd al-Jabbar in late tenth-century Iran and for Harun Nasution in twentieth-century Indonesia. We have tried to situate both texts and their authors in the two different historical and political contexts in which they wrote. Before we present the second Mu'tazili text, Nasution's *Kaum Mu'tazilah*, it will be useful to note some commonalities and differences.

'Abd al-Jabbar framed his outline of Mu'tazili teachings, as did most Mu'tazili mutakallimun in the Middle Ages, in the "five principles" structure (*al-usl al-khamsa*). As we saw in chapter 4, by the time of 'Abd al-Jabbar, systematically discussing Islamic doctrine within the framework of al-usul al-khamsa was like pouring new wine into old wineskins: the five principles no longer worked as inclusive categories for all the problems at issue between the Mu'tazila and their opponents. Of the sixty-seven paragraphs of the *Kitab al-usul al-khamsa*, the first fifteen and the last seven seem to fall outside the scheme. Of those that fall outside it, the most interesting in comparison to Nasution's *Kaum Mu'tazilah* are the opening paragraphs. 'Abd al-Jabbar began (¶¶ 1–9) with the duty of reason: it is incumbent on all human beings to know through the exercise of their intellects that God exists. Harun Nasution also discusses the primary role of reason, but only midway through the text, in section II, G. Nasution chooses to begin his lecture on the Mu'tazila with a discussion of the theological fallout from the first fitna, the civil strife that erupted over the murder of the third caliph, 'Uthman ibn 'Affan (d. 656). Why does Nasution choose a different doctrinal entry into essentially the same theological system?

Two reasons emerge as likely explanations. First, Nasution, as we have just shown, rediscovered the Mu'tazila in part through personal and literary contact with Western scholars and the Orientalist tradition of scholarship, which in some ways he has admired and has sought to emulate. Whereas 'Abd al-Jabbar and other mutakallimun had constructed and followed a logical framework, Western scholars like D. B. MacDonald and A. J. Wensinck (whose names appear in Nasution's annotations) explained the Mu'tazila in terms of political history.[15] The traditional religious history of origins within the teaching circle of al-Hasan al-Basri, to which Nasution turns in section I, E, is regarded, as it is in most modern histories of kalam, as a consequence of a lengthy political dispute that was at once theological as well. Did Caliph 'Uthman deserve to be murdered by other Muslims? On what grounds? Could there be a rational way out of the impasse between the two sides that emerged (Sunni and Shi'a) as well as the more extreme positions of the Khawarij and Murji'a? Nasution constructs as his introduction to Mu'tazili thought a well-known conflict in the nascent Islamic community and then fastens on the fact that the Mu'tazila provided (then, as now) a compromise response to Khariji and Murji'i extremism (sections I, E and II, F). He asserts, by structurally rearranging the kalam system, that Mu'tazilism is the solution to contemporary theological conflict in Indonesia and modern Islam more generally.

A second point of comparison reveals a profound difference between the Mu'tazilism of Qadi 'Abd al-Jabbar and that of Harun Nasution. The Qadi's project was to systematize and defend against numerous enemies a body of well-established theological doctrine. This was no mere intellectual game of arguing how many angels could dance on the head of a pin. "Doctrine," as the quotation from Alister E. McGrath in chapter 1 above asserted,

> entails a sense of commitment to a community, and a sense of obligation to speak on its behalf, where the corporate mind of the community exercizes a restraint over the individual's perception of the truth. Doctrine is an *activity*, a process on the transmission of the collective wisdom of a community, rather than a passive set of deliverances.[16]

We have used the Islamic concept of *madhhab* to characterize doctrinal community in early Islam. Kevin Reinhart has stressed the importance of this concept with various hyphenated terms, such as "*madhhab*-chauvinism" and "*madhhab*-allegiance" that demonstrate that argument over doctrine in the early centuries of Islam was of social and political import.[17]

By contrast, Mu'tazilism is not for Nasution a body of communal doctrine. There is not much that can be identified as a Mu'tazili madhhab in Indonesia, nor is there corporate use of Mu'tazili doctrine to provide religious, intellectual, and social identity to a particular group. Ash'arism, and to a lesser extent Maturidism, are the official and acceptable kalam systems in Indonesia and in much of the modern Sunni world. The role of even these surviving madhhabs from medieval Islam as doctrinal communities is very limited, however. One does not find a renewal of Ash'arism or Maturidism, or read about the use of Ash'ari doctrine as a way to think through the problems of Islam and modernity in Indonesia. Following McGrath's sense of doctrines and their texts as social instruments for establishing group identity and defining what constitutes otherness (those who are not us), Nasution's *Kaum Mu'tazilah* lacks significant social extension in Islamic society. It does not define or have the "*madhhab*-allegiance" of a community. Instead, the text of *Kaum Mu'tazilah* represents the excavation of a text – or rather medieval kalam texts – by modern Muslim *and non-Muslim* scholarship. *Kaum Mu'tazilah* is the work of an individual intellectual, making a case in public, a text in search of a community. It is an instrument of criticism, not only of traditionalist Muslims as we have defined them, but even more so modernist Muslims, as we have argued earlier in this chapter.

In addition to the number of pages devoted to the origins and early history of the Mu'tazila, the reader will notice that Harun Nasution devotes a number of paragraphs to discussing the issue of divine attributes (III, I), far more than he devotes to the Prophet and the Qur'an. As we have seen, Qadi 'Abd al-Jabbar devoted ten paragraphs to the problem of attributes. The Mu'tazila, it will be recalled from earlier chapters, advanced a hard doctrine of divine unicity (al-tawhid) that denied attributing to God knowledge, vision, power, hearing, and the like as separate entities or qualities that made up God's being. Thus, in chapter 5 (¶ 19) the interlocutor asks: "What is the proof that God is knowing ('alim)? Say to him: Because skillful acts, such as writing and craftsmanship, can only be done by one who knows how. And since it is valid for God, in creating human beings, to exceed the wonders of crafts, therefore He must be knowing." In other words, God is "knowing" in His essence; He is not in possession of the attribute of knowing. 'Abd al-Jabbar's text treats of several qualities attributed to God by adducing arguments that explain how one knows that God is knowing, living, hearing, etc. Nasution explains in section III, I that the Mu'tazila emphasized the attribute of unity, al-tawhid:

> In an attempt to present the teaching of the unity of God in the purest form possible, they rejected all forms of thought which approach *shirk* or polytheism. If it is said that God has attributes, then it follows that God consists of many elements . . . To assign attributes of God implies that a large number of things are eternal, while in a theological sense eternalness is equated with unity. In the general sense of faith: there is no god other than Allah. In the language of theology: there is nothing eternal other than Allah.

The problem of divine attributes (*sifat*), we have already seen, was sharply debated between the Mu'tazila on the one side, and the traditionalists on the other, both the *ahl al-hadith* and the Ash'ariya. As Nasution notes, the problem for pious Muslims has always been that if one takes the Qur'an literally one must conclude that God has vision, hearing, the quality of mercy (*al-rahman*), and be in possession of the power to act, e.g. create (*al-qadir*), and so on, because He is so described in the Qur'an. He explains that the Mu'tazila sought to avoid the inevitable shirk this implied by arguing that "*al-Rahman, al-Rahim, al-Qadir*, and *al-'Alim* are not attributes distinct from, but rather aspects of God's *zat* (Ar. *dhat*) or essence." That Nasution gives so much attention to the problem of attributes is an indication of its continuing importance as a major marker of difference between traditionalists and their theological critics.

If the two Mu'tazili texts differ greatly with respect to style, arrangement of topic, and emphases, their intent is remarkably consistent: they each make a strong case for rational procedures in theological reflection and they each argue for communal inclusiveness and hence tolerance of differences within the community. Each opposes the kind of madhhab-chauvinism that often takes root in traditionalist worldviews. The similar in content, but differently arranged, outlines of Mu'tazili doctrine which we presented at the beginning of this section are the tool boxes used to construct a rationalist response to traditionalist conceptions of sin, faith and membership in the community (and hence the grounds for relations to non-Muslims and heterodox Muslims). The dispute in Qadi 'Abd al-Jabbar's time as well as in modern Islam turned largely on the respective tasks assigned to reason and revelation. That dispute took different forms in different times and places of *dar al-Islam*. It is a dispute that cannot achieve closure so long as different visions of community and identity are at stake within the Muslim *umma*. What will be important in the continuing recovery and use of Mu'tazili texts by modernists is the concomitant recovery of a manner of managing the dispute that is reminiscent of, or the modern equivalent of, the ritual and poetics of conflict that traditional kalam required. Do modernists and traditionalists have the will and the cultural means both to continue and to manage the debate productively? We turn now to a translation of Harun Nasution's text, *Kaum Mu'tazilah dan Pandangan Rasionalanya*.

Notes

1. Fazlur Rahman, *Islam and Modernity: Transformation of an Intellectual Tradition* (Chicago: University of Chicago Press, 1982).
2. Rahman, *Islam and Modernity*, p. 126.
3. Rahman, *Major Themes of the Qur'an*, p. 15.

4. The following biographical sketch is based on an autobiography included in a volume prepared in commemoration of Nasution's seventieth birthday, *Refleksi Pembaharuan Pemikiran Islam: 70 Tahun Harun Nasution.* (Jakarta: Lembaga Studi Agama dan Filsafat, 1989). Like many such Indonesian works, it was edited by a committee, in this case Panitia Penerbitan Buku dan Seminar 70 Tahun Harun Nasution Bekeriasama dengan Lembaga Studi Agama dan Filsafat. We have supplemented this material with information gained from interviews with Nasution himself and with Charles J. Adams, one of his professors at McGill University in Montreal.

5. Questions concerning ritual purity and the proper way to perform purification rites were important themes of Islamic discourse in traditionalist Muslim circles, including Indonesia, in the early decades of the twentieth century. Both traditionalist and modernist ulama were of the opinion that only Islamic scripture provided guidance in these areas. More secular-minded, Western-educated Indonesian Muslims often argued that the use of soap and disinfectants could be used to remove the polluting qualities of substances such as dog saliva. Nasution finds arguments about such ritual matters extremely frustrating because they detract from what are, for him, more important issues, including the development of modern Islamic education and functionally rationalist economic and political thought.

6. Informal mentoring among students outside the "classroom" is described and analyzed (in the North African context) in Eickelman, "The Art of Memory."

7. Nasution, "Filsafat Hidup Rational: Prasyarat bagi Mentalitis Pembangunan" (A rational philosophy of life: a precondition for a development mentality), p. 139, under the heading *Manusia: Makhluk Rasional* (Humanity: the rational creation).

8. As we saw in chapter 7, Geertz first set forth this concept in *Islam Observed*, p. 60, referring to Indonesia in particular on pp. 65–70.

9. Nasution, *Akal dan Wahyu dalam Islam* (Reason and revelation in Islam), p. 25

10. We are indebted to Professor Adams for sharing with us his recollections of Nasution and his student days at McGill. The difference between Nasution's thinking and Adams' is illustrative of the fundamental difference between committed and detached scholarship in the study of Islam and in Religious Studies more generally. Both men are meticulous scholars with deep understanding of Islamic history and the text of the Qur'an. Adams' understanding of Islam is rooted in the paradigmatic structures of Western post-Enlightenment scholarship. Nasution, on the other hand, is engaged in a quest for religious truth and uses the Qur'an as a "proof text" for his theological positions. See Woodward, "Talking Across Paradigms," in *Toward a New Paradigm*, pp. 1–46, for a fuller discussion of the distinction between detached and committed paradigms in the study of Indonesian Islam.

11. In many parts of the Muslim world, newspapers and magazines are important venues for the ideas of scholars and intellectuals.

12. *Refleksi Pembaharuan Pemikran Islam: 70 Tahun Harun Nasution* (Jakarta: Lembaga Studi Agama dan Filsafat, 1989).

13. Publishing is a highly competitive business in Indonesia. A senior editor at the

Surabaya daily *Surya* explained to us that the regular publication of articles on Islam by prominent Indonesians and virtually any foreign expert contributes greatly to his paper's circulation. Newspapers and magazines sometimes sponsor seminars featuring scholarly presentations for which admission is charged — a practice once described to us as "selling your name."

14. We once spent several hours rendering a single paragraph into readable English. For examples of this more technical, traditional genre, see Hasyim and Hamidy, *Syara Riyadhush Shalihin*, a translation and commentary on al-Nawawi's compendium of Hadith, *Riyad al-salihin*. For a discussion of this genre and its significance in Indonesian discourse, see Woodward, "Textual Exegesis as Social Commentary."

15. The political history of Mu'tazili origins was essayed by H. S. Nyberg in the substantial entry he authored on "al-Mu'tazila" in the first edition of the *Encyclopaedia of Islam*, which appears also in the *SEI*.

16. McGrath, *The Genesis of Doctrine*, p. 11, cited above in chapter 1, p. 17.

17. Reinhart, *Before Revelation*, pp. 9, 45–46, et passim.

nine

Kaum Mu'tazilah dan Pandangan Rasionalanya
(The Mu'tazila and Rational Philosophy)
A Translation[1]

[I. The Problem of Major Sin]

[A. The First *Fitna*]

The murder of 'Uthman, the third caliph, in 656 C.E. in Medina and the controversy that erupted as a result of the coming of the army from Egypt was a theological as well as a political problem. In a political sense this affair divided the Muslim community [*umma*] into two groups: the Sunni and the Sh'ia. In the unfolding of Islamic history, in religious and philosophical as well as in the political sense, the conflict between these major groups has been extremely influential. The conflict between the groups has begun to be resolved only in the twentieth century.

[B. The Question of Faith (*iman*)]

In a theological sense, the 'Uthman affair raised the question of the problem of faith [*iman*] and unbelief [*kufr*]. An attempt was made to settle the war between 'Ali, the fourth caliph, and Mu'awiyah, the governor of Damascus, which began as a result of questions concerning 'Ali's accountability for the murder of 'Uthman, by peaceful means, i.e. through arbitration [*hakam*] which was commonly employed in the pre-Islamic period. A portion of 'Ali's force did not agree with this procedure because they were close to achieving a military victory. This would have meant that they would have received a share of the spoils of war, which would have been divided among the victorious party. They were not satisfied with the situation and deserted the party of 'Ali, forming their own force which was subsequently known as the Khawarij. The name Khawarij is derived from the Arabic term *kharaja* which means "to go out," in this case to go out from the party of 'Ali, the fourth caliph.

[C. The Khawarij (Seceders)]

[The Khawarij] quickly elevated this political problem to the level of theology, confusing it with the problem of faith and unbelief, or in other words, of whether a person is or is not a Muslim. Verse 44 of sura al-Ma'ida states: "Who ever does not dispense justice according to what has been fixed by Allah is an unbeliever."[2] 'Ali and Mu'awiya settled their dispute not by turning to theology, but rather by following the pre-Islamic tradition of arbitration. From the perspective of the Khawarij this made them *kafir*. This judgment also applied to 'Amr bin al-'As and Abu Musa al-Ash'ari,[3] who mediated between the two parties.

According to the Khawarij, not to dispense justice according to principles laid out by Allah in the Qur'an is a major sin. From this they drew the conclusion that anyone who commits a major sin is a *kafir*, and what is more, that one who has left Islam is also *murtadd* [an apostate] who must be killed. Among the deeds considered to be major sins are adultery and killing a person without just cause. The Khawarij maintain that only those who uphold these views can be considered Muslims. Other Muslims are *kafir* and *murtadd* who must be struggled against. In addition to their political opponents 'Ali and Mu'awiya, the Khawarij identified all Muslims with whom they had theological differences as enemies.

[D. The Murji'a (Postponers)]

The Murji'i position developed in reaction to the narrow views of the Khawarij. While the Khawarij maintain that actions may lead to the loss of faith, the Murji'i position is that actions do not have any influence on faith. They were given the name Murji'a because they "postpone" the question which, they maintain, will be resolved by Allah on the Day of Judgment. If a person who has committed a major sin is pardoned by Allah he will go to Heaven. If Allah does not pardon him, he will suffer in Hell in accordance with the nature of the sin he has committed. After his punishment is completed he will be released from Hell and enter Heaven.

According to the Murji'a, what is important in the problem of faith and unbelief is what is in the heart, not the actions of the body, as the Khawarij maintained. For the Murji'a, actions do not have any effect on faith. They are given the name Murji'a because they "postpone" the problem of major sins to the Day of Judgment and probably also because they offer the hope of Heaven to those who have committed major sins, something the Khawarij do not do. The name Murji'a is derived from the Arabic term *arja'a* which means to "postpone" and "to give hope."[4]

[E. The Compromise Position in the Circle of Hasan al-Basri]

The problems of major sin and the major sinner were frequently and hotly debated in the first century of the Islamic era. These questions were raised by many of the *ulama* of the day. Among them was Hasan al-Basri (642–728) a famous *'alim* [Ar. sing. of ulama] from Iraq, who was asked the question by someone attending one of his lectures. Before he had time to answer the question Wasil ibn 'Ata' (699–748 C.E.) explained: "One who commits a major sin is neither a *mukmin* [Ar. *mu'min*] nor a *kafir*." He then left his teacher's school and established his own to expound this position. From Wasil's perspective the word *mu'min* is associated with worship. One who commits a major sin is not necessarily one who neglects worship. Consequently he is not a *kafir* because he accepts the two clauses of the confession of faith. Because one who commits a major sin is not a *mu'min* and not a *kafir*, he holds a position between the two and may be referred to as a Muslim.

The case of major sin can not be judged by the Muslim community, it rests with the one who commits it. If he has genuine remorse, Allah will pardon the sin and he will go to Heaven. But if he is not remorseful and dies before he has had the time to become remorseful, the sin will not be forgiven and he will go to Hell for a time. However, the punishment he receives will be lighter than that which Allah gives to a *kafir*. This position was known as the position between two positions, *mu'min* and *kafir*, both in this world and the next.[5]

[II. The Rise of the Mu'tazila]

[F. The Name "Mu'tazila"]

This event gave birth to the Mu'tazila, who arose in response to the theological positions of the Khawarij and the Murji'a. The name "Mu'tazila" is derived from the Arabic term *i'tazala* which means ["to withdraw" or] "to isolate oneself." According to one theory, this name was given on the instruction of Hasan al-Basri after he observed Wasil departing from his company. Hasan al-Basri is said to have given the following commentary: *"i'tazala 'anna"* [Ar. "he isolated himself from us"]. Those people who isolated themselves are known as Mu'tazila. "To isolate oneself" means here to isolate oneself from the school of Hasan al-Basri, or to isolate oneself from the positions of the Murji'a and the Khawarij.

According to another theory the term Mu'tazila is not based on the statement of Hasan al-Basri, but rather from the Arabic term *i'tazala* as it was used by those who distanced themselves from the political disputes which took place at the time of 'Uthman and 'Ali. According to the historians al-Tabari[6] and Abu al-Fuda[7] the term was already in use at that time. It was used to refer to the faction which did not wish to become involved in political controversies and who devoted themselves to ritual performance and the quest for knowledge. Among this group were individuals including the grandchildren of the Prophet Muhammad, Abu Husayn, 'Abdallah and al-Hasan ibn Muhammad ibn al-Hanafi[ya]. Wasil had a strong affiliation with Abu Husayn.

There is also an opinion that the term Mu'tazila has the meaning "to slip" and that because the Mu'tazila slip from the path of truth, they were given the name Mu'tazila, which means the faction which has slipped. In truth the Arabic term *i'tazala* is derived from the word *'azala* which means "to separate" and does not mean "to slip." In Arabic, the word for slip, *zalla*, sounds very much like *'azala*. However, the term Mu'tazila is not derived from *zalla*.

The Mu'tazila refer to themselves as *ahl al-tawhid wa ahl al-'adl*, "the People of the Unity of Allah and of Justice." They do not, however, reject the designation Mu'tazila. It is also clear from the statements of Mu'tazili scholars that they were the originators of the term.

According to al-Qadi 'Abd al-Jabbar, a leading Mu'tazili figure many of whose writings have come to light in the twentieth century, in a theological sense the Arabic term *i'tazala* means to distance oneself from that which is false, and in that sense it is associated with worship.[8] According to the explanation of another Mu'tazili thinker, Ibn al-Murtada, the term Mu'tazila was invented not by members of other groups, but by the Mu'tazila themselves.[9]

[G. The Mu'tazila are Misunderstood in Indonesia]

In Indonesia, Mu'tazili thought is not well known or appreciated, because, as was explained above, it is thought to be based on opinions which deviate from correct Islamic teachings. In their religious thought the Mu'tazila rely extensively on rationalism [Ind. *rasio*]. They sincerely believe in the power of reason [Ind. *akal*, Ar. *'aql*] which they consider to be among God's gifts to humankind. In the interpretation of Quranic texts they make extensive use of rational thought. Because of the great significance that they assign to rationality, some groups within the Muslim community have asserted that they value rationality more than revelation. It is this view which leads to the accusation that the Mu'tazila are the group within Islam that has departed from the straight and true path.

Not a small number within the Muslim community are of the opinion that [the Mu'tazila] do not believe in revelation at all, and therefore must be considered unbelievers [*kafir*] and not Muslims. In Orientalist circles, where much is written about the classical period of Islamic civilization, the Mu'tazila are referred to as Islamic rationalists.[10] D. B. MacDonald has called them "daring and absolutely free-minded speculators" and "deistic naturalists."[11] In order to understand the accusations leveled at the Mu'tazila, it is first necessary to examine their teachings and the results of their theological inquiries.

[III. Mu'tazili Teachings]

[H. Sin and Free Will]

As was touched on above, Wasil ibn 'Ata' was the founder and first spokesman for the Mu'tazili school. His first teaching was that of *al-manzila bayn al-manzilatayn*, the position between two positions concerning the case of one who commits a major sin. The second teaching is that of *qadariya*, which in English means *free will and free act*.[12] The attribute of God[13] that was valued most highly by the Mu'tazila was that of His justice. Wasil stated that God is both wise and just and cannot do evil or act in an arbitrary fashion. This understanding of God's justice requires us to accept the position that humans alone carry out acts in the sense that they possess the will and desire which brings acts into being. Human acts are not the result of the will of God as is maintained by the fatalistic *Jabariya*.[14] Because it is humans alone who, out of their own will and desire, do evil. God is justified in judging those who do evil and sending them to Hell. If humans did evil – not out of their own will and desire, but rather because of the will of or pressure from outside themselves – God would not be able to send them to Hell. The Mu'tazila's strong understanding of divine justice can only be maintained in conjunction with that of the freedom of human desire and action and is incompatible with the fatalistic perspective maintained by other Islamic schools. It is for this reason that the Mu'tazila are known for the teaching of *free will and free act*.[15]

[I. Divine Attributes]

Wasil's third teaching is the nonexistence of the attributes [Ar. *sifat*] of God. One of the attributes of God most strongly emphasized by the Mu'tazila is that of His unity. For them God is the great unity and the great justice.[16] In an attempt to present the teaching of the unity of God in the purest form possible, they rejected all forms of thought that approach *shirk* or polytheism. If it is said that God has attributes, then it follows that God consists of many elements: the element of His essence [Ind. *zat*; Ar. *dhat*] which is characterized by attributes and the elements of the attributes which are attached to His essence. If it is said that God has twenty attributes, God would consist of twenty-one elements. If there are forty attributes, His elements would number forty-one and if it is said that He has ninety-nine attributes God would consist of one hundred elements. To assign attributes to God implies that a large number of things are eternal [Ar. *qadim*], while in a theological sense eternalness is associated with unity. In the general sense of faith: there is no god other than Allah. In the language of theology: there is nothing eternal other than Allah. Therefore, the perspective that there are many eternal things[17] approaches *shirk*, which according to Islam is the most serious of sins and the one that Allah will not pardon.[18]

To overcome this version of *shirk*, Wasil claimed that God does not have attributes. This does not mean that Wasil and his followers rejected Quranic texts which describe the attributes of God such as *al-Rahman*, *al-Rahim* and *al-Qadir*. Like other Muslims, they believed that theology is based on the revelation of God to the Prophet Muhammad. However, their interpretation of these passages differs from those of other Muslims. For the Mu'tazila, *al-Rahman*, *al-Rahim*, *al-Qadir*, and *al-'Alim* are not attributes distinct from, but rather aspects of God's *zat* [Ar. *dhat*] or essence. For God knows them not by virtue of the attribute of knowing, but rather by virtue of His essence. In the words of [Abu] al-Hudhayl,[19] the second spokesman for the Mu'tazila:[20] "God the All-Knowing is associated with knowing, and God's knowing is His essence."[21] Other passages are interpreted in similar ways. God is all-powerful through the exercise of power and the power of God is His essence. God is all-merciful through the exercise of mercy and mercy is His essence. With this style of interpretation the Mu'tazila present a portrait of the unity of God that is not composed of the level of His essence and layers of attributes, but rather of a single essence which has various aspects. The intent of the Mu'tazili denial of the attributes of God is to emphasize the unity of God and to distance themselves from polytheism.

[J. Abu l-Hudhayl and Greek Influence]

Abu l-Hudhayl al-'Allaf (752–848)[22] was a prominent Mu'tazilite with strong connections with Greek philosophical thought. At this time there was an increasing level of interest in Greek philosophy and science. Greek books were translated into Arabic. At the time of Harun al-Rashid, emissaries were sent to Europe to purchase Greek manuscripts, which were collected and translated in Baghdad. During the reign of his son al-Ma'mun (813–833 C.E.) the work of translations was supported by the Bayt al-Hikmah [House of Wisdom][23] under the leadership of Hunayn ibn Ishhaq.

In Greek philosophical texts the *ulama* encountered the term *nous*.[24] The only Arabic term that approaches the meaning of this Greek word is *al-'aql*. According to Professor Izutsu, during the pre-Islamic period *al-'aql* meant *problem-solving capacity*.[25] However, in the Qur'an it has a religious meaning, i.e., the ability to understand the text of the Qur'an.[26] The term *al-'aql* acquires a greatly expanded meaning when it is used as a translation of the philosophical Greek term *nous*. It now means the capacity of thought, in which the brain is used as a tool for thinking.

[K. The Question of the Good (Theodicy)]

The high value given to [the notion of] *nous* or the *intellect* found in Greek philosophy has a great influence on Islamic philosophy, theology, law and textual exegesis from this time forward. The influence of Greek philosophy is readily apparent in the works of Abu l-Hudhayl.[27] He presented a philosophical explanation of Wasil ibn 'Ata's teaching of the non-existence of the attributes of God. From his perspective God is the completely perfect [one].[28] Because He is completely perfect, God *cannot* do that which is not good.[29] The actions of God as the completely perfect [one] are all necessarily good. God cannot will anything except that which is good for humanity. This is the origin of the Mu'tazili concept of *al-salih wa l-aslah*. The meaning of this term is that God must create that which is good, and particularly that which is best for humanity. Here the Mu'tazila use the Arabic term *wajib* [obligatory], a term which is not used by other theological schools in reference to God. In order to explain the meaning of this use of the term *wajib*, Abu l-Hudhayl states that God can not act tyrannically or lie to humanity. It is impossible for God to act in such ways because for Him to do so would be in conflict with His characteristics of complete perfection and perfect justice. The Mu'tazila distinguish between two understandings of the concept of *wajib*: *wajib shar'i* or necessity established by revelation and *wajib 'aqli* or necessity arising from reason. While the former is ultimately more important and difficult, the Mu'tazila employ the concept of necessity in the sense of *wajib 'aqli* in their discussions of God.

[L. The Role of Reason]

The Mu'tazila make extensive use of rationality in the development of their religious views. Abu l-Hudayl was the first to explain the extent to which human reason can be used in the resolution of religious problems. In his view reason can be used in seeking answers to two basic types of questions which arise in every religion: those concerning God and those concerning the problem of good and evil. He explains that human reason can:

1. discern the existence of God;
2. discern the duty for humans to give thanks to God;
3. distinguish between good and evil;
4. discern the duty for humans to do good and avoid doing evil.

In truth the totality of what can be known through reason, as summarized briefly above, constitutes two basic and important religious principles which include what is forbidden and what is required. Also included are issues of ethics, morals, and ritual, all of which are important components of religion.

[M. The Role of Revelation]

For this reason it is not surprising that opponents of the Mu'tazila often charge the Mu'tazila with the view that humanity does not need revelation, that everything can be known through reason, that there is a conflict between reason and revelation, that they cling to reason and put revelation aside, and even that the Mu'tazila do not believe in revelation. Such are the accusations of the opponents of the Mu'tazila. But is it true that the Mu'tazila are of the opinion that everything can be known through reason and therefore that revelation is unnecessary? The writings of the Mu'tazila give exactly the opposite portrait. In their opinion, human reason is not sufficiently powerful to know everything and for this reason humans need revelation in order to reach conclusions concerning what is good and what is bad for them.

It is true that reason can lead to the conclusion that it is necessary for humans to give thanks to God, but it cannot lead to knowledge of the ritual means through which this is to be accomplished. According to Abu Hashim,[30] ritual can be known not through reason, but only through revelation. It is the Prophet who explains ritual and whatever the Prophet says must be true.[31] Ibn Tufayl [d. 1185] comes to similar conclusions in *Hayy ibn Yaqzan*. Hayy grows up and lives alone on an island. He is capable of understanding his own environment and can understand the true way to carry out the duty of giving thanks to God, but only if an authority on *shari'a* explains it to him.[32]

Reason is also incapable of discerning everything concerning the problem of good and evil. According to Hilli, reason can lead to an understanding of only a portion of good and a portion of evil.[33] 'Abd al-Jabbar argues that while reason can be used to discern the broad outlines of religious duty, that it cannot comprehend the details.[34] According to Abu Hashim, this is why prophets are needed; they come to explain the details of what can be known through reason in a more general sense.[35]

While it is true that reason can discern that in the future there will be a Day of Judgment, it is not capable of determining the exact nature of the rewards and punishments that humans will be given at that time. 'Abd al-Jabbar's opinion is that these details can only be known through revelation.[36] This is also the opinion of al-Jubba'i.[37]

The explanation presented by the leading Mu'tazili thinkers confirms the view that not everything can be known through reason. Reason requires the aid of revelation to clarify the details of what can be known in general terms. Revelation is also needed to validate those things that can be known through reason; in other words to establish *wajib 'aqli* [rational necessity] as *wajib shar'i* [revealed necessity] and *haram 'aqli* [rational prohibition] as *haram shar'i* [revealed prohibition]. According to Abu Hashim, prophets come to validate [*taqrir*] that which can be known through reason. In the words of Albert Nader, *shari'a nabawiyah* [the law of the Prophet] validates and perfects *shari'a 'aqliyyah* [the law of reason].[38]

The Mu'tazilia do not believe that people can know how to live their lives only through the use of reason without the aid of revelation. Even though they give reason a very high place, the Mu'tazila consider revelation to be very important. It is not true that they consider reason to be more important than revelation. They maintain that it is necessary to accept the absolute truth of the text of the Qur'an. As Muslims they do not oppose or doubt the truth of the Qur'an.

[N. The Apparent Conflict of Reason and Revelation]

The question necessarily arises: what is the view of the Mu'tazila concerning conflicts between reason and the Quranic text? The Mu'tazila maintain that the text of the Qur'an does not have to be understood in a literal sense. The Mu'tazili view is that the Qur'an has metaphorical as well as literal meanings. Or to use the terminology of Islamic philosophy, it has external [Ind. *lahir*, Ar. *zahir*] and internal [*batin*] meanings. The Mu'tazila maintain that there is no conflict between reason and the true meaning of the Qur'an. If there appears to be a conflict it is in the external sense only. If the external or literal sense of the Qur'an is set aside and its internal meanings examined, the apparent conflict dissolves. For example, the Qur'an states that God has hands and [sits on] a throne. But reason demands that God cannot have hands and a chair because God does not have a physical body like humans. Therefore, the literal meaning of the hand and the chair acquires the metaphorical meaning of the authority and power of God. There is therefore no real conflict between reason and revelation. God certainly does not have hands and a chair, but He does have authority.

This method allows the Mu'tazila and other Islamic philosophers to overcome the apparent contradictions between reason and revelation. While this strategy is used to overcome the apparent differences and contradictions between reason and revelation, it does not entail rejection of the Qur'an or the claim that its verses do not come from God. On the contrary, they believe that the verses of the Qur'an are all genuine revelations. In cases such as these, they substitute metaphorical for literal meanings. This strategy is used by all Islamic legal, philosophical, theological and mystical schools to some extent. The Mu'tazila, Islamic philosophers, and Sufis use it to a greater extent than other Muslim groups.

[O. Mu'ammar and the Doctrine of Creation]

Mu'ammar ibn 'Abbad [d. 830] was a Mu'tazili thinker who lived at the same time as Abu l-Hudhayl. He established a naturalistic perspective in Islamic thought.[39] According to Ibn 'Abbad, God created only material elements. *Al-a'rad* or *accidents* are creations composed of material elements through the forces of nature, such as burning by fire, or heating by the sun, or the choice between movement [Ar. *haraka*] and stillness [Ar. *sukun*], or through collection and dispersion, and other actions carried out by animals.[40] 'Uthman Al-Jahiz offered the more profound explanation that every material element has its own nature. The Mu'tazila accepted the concept of natural law. They differed from the naturalist [school] in their belief that the laws of nature were created by God rather than being independent forces. Their position was that if God created the world, He also established the laws it must obey in its cycles of development. Through their own efforts humans can not exceed the boundaries of the laws of nature created by God. Consequently, according to al-Jahiz, human actions are limited by the laws of nature. Human freedom is limited to choices among those things that are possible according to natural law. Their position is that everything that happens in this world is in accordance with the laws of nature. Poverty is the law of nature, so is wealth. If a person follows that portion of natural law which produces poverty, he will be poor. However, in the opposite case, if he follows that portion of natural law which produces wealth, he will become rich.[41] The natural law created by God operates without reference to the religion of the individual. Natural law does not consider religion. A non-Muslim who follows the path of wealth will become rich, while a Muslim who follows the path of poverty will remain poor.[42] According to the Mu'tazila, there are no exceptions to the natural law that God has created. The Qur'an states: "You will never encounter an exception to natural law" (al-Ahzab, Q. 33:62).[43]

[P. The *usul al-khamsa* (Five Basic Teachings)]

The Mu'tazila have five basic doctrines that every follower of the school must accept:

1. *Al-Tawhid*, or the Unity of God. God is the Great Unity. Only if God has a unique essence is it true that there is nothing else with His form, [i.e., with Him]. The Mu'tazila strongly oppose theological positions according to which God is not unique including those which would give Him attributes [*sifat*]; anthropomorphism, *beatific vision*, or that there is anything eternal other than God.[44]

2. *Al-'Adl*, or the Justice of God. The doctrine of *al-tawhid* refers to the uniqueness of God in His essence. That of *al-'adl* refers to the uniqueness of the actions of God. None of the wishes or actions of God can conflict with His justice. The teaching of the justice of God is the point of departure for the rational religious thought of the Mu'tazila. [From this basic doctrine,] they derive their doctrines of freedom of human thought and action; the responsibility of humans for their own actions; the necessity of God doing that which is good for humanity; the necessity that He send Prophets to perfect that which can be known by humans in general terms through reason; the teaching that God does not give humans burdens they can not carry; and God's devotion to His promises.

3. *Al-Wa'd wa l-wa'id* [the promise and the threat], the doctrine that God would not be just if He did not reward those who do good and punish those who do evil. In the case of God's promise and threat we can see the application of the Mu'tazili formulation of the concept of God's justice. God necessarily rewards the good and punishes the evil in the afterlife. God has explained this in the Qur'an. It would not be just if God allowed sinners into Heaven and sent the good to Hell or did not carry out both His promise and His threat. According to 'Abd al-Jabbar, if God were to act in this way He would be a tyrant.[45]

4. *Al-Manzilah bayn al-manzilatayn* [the intermediate position], the doctrine according to which one who commits a major sin is neither a *mu'min* nor a *kafir*, but rather is a *muslim* who occupies a position between the two. He is not given either a place in Heaven or a heavy torment in Hell but rather a light torment located between the two. From the perspective of the Mu'tazila this is justice.

5. *Al-Amr bi l-ma'ruf wa l-nahy 'an al-munkar,* the doctrine of Commanding the Good and Prohibiting the Evil. The fifth basic teaching has a strong connection with the establishment of morality. The Mu'tazili understanding of this teaching must be understood from the perspective of their teaching of faith. As has been explained above, the Mu'tazili position is that faith does not consist in confession alone, as is argued by the Murji'a. For them confession must be accompanied by good deeds. They maintain that a person of faith who does evil can not escape Hell. Only those who have a combination of faith and good deeds will gain entrance to Heaven. To establish morality among the Muslim community it is necessary to *al-amr bi al-ma'ruf wa al-nahy 'an al-munkar* [that is, one must proactively command the good and prohibit evil].[46] This is a form of social control that we are obligated to carry out. It can take the form of verbal admonition if this is sufficient, but may also require harsh measures.

[IV. Conclusion: A Case for Modern Mu'tazilism]

These are some of the basic teachings of the Mu'tazila. In the analysis presented above, it is possible to discern a form of rationalism, but not a rationalism that opposes religion or rejects the absolute truth of revelation. It is rather a form of rationalism which is in accord with, and defines itself in terms of, the truth of revelation. It is also possible to discern a form of naturalism, but not an atheistic naturalism that denies the existence and greatness of God. It is rather a naturalism which accepts God as the Great Unity.[47] God created both the world and the natural laws that govern it. There is also human freedom and dynamism, but not absolute freedom from the design established by God. Rather, human freedom is a gift from God. In accordance with His wishes and through His revelation, God outlines good and evil, the true path and the path of error, and the nature of divine sanctions. On the Last Day good will be rewarded with happiness and evil with suffering. God gives humans the capacity to choose between good and evil, between the true path and the path of error. But with this freedom comes accountability. Humans will be held accountable for their actions on the Day of Judgment.

The doctrines of dynamism, human freedom and accountability, rationalism and naturalism taught by the Mu'tazila contributed significantly to the development of philosophy and the religious and secular sciences during the Classical Period of Islamic civilization. It is, however, ironic that the Mu'tazila, who profess human freedom, imposed their views on the Muslim community during the period in which they helped [those in] power. Their own harsh measures inspired a harsh and coercive response from their enemies. In the end, this led to the fall of the Mu'tazila. Their books went out of circulation. Knowledge of their teachings could be found only in the works of their enemies, who generally did not give an accurate potrait of Mu'tazili doctrine. It was not unusual for them to be described as *kafir*.

Begining in the nineteenth century C.E., leaders of the Islamic renewal movement began to return to Mu'tazili teachings and to search for the original works. They wanted to come to know Mu'tazili thought from the original sources. It became apparent that the depiction of the Mu'tazila presented in the works of their enemies was not congruent with their actual teachings.[48] With this knowledge came the reemergence of respect for the Mu'tazili school. In the twentieth century many scholars and *ulama* have come to defend the Mu'tazila. In response to the accusation that the Mu'tazili scholar al-Nazzam was an atheist, al-Nashshar wrote that the Mu'tazila were known for devotion to God [Ind. *takwa*, Ar. *taqwa*] and their devotion to ritual [*'ibada*].[49] [The modern historian] Ahmad Amin acknowledged the great value of the Mu'tazila and their defense of Islam from the attacks of atheists. He wrote: "If the Mu'tazili tradition had continued until the present time the position of the Muslim community in history would have been far different from what it is. Fatalism weakened the Islamic community and drained its energy while *tawakkul* [trust only in God] led to a static condition."[50] As has been explained, the Mu'tazili doctrine is dynamic. It is strongly opposed to the attitude which Ahmad Amin finds to be characteristic of the Muslim community. Shaykh Muhammad Yusuf Musa, an *'alim* from al-Azhar in Cairo, was also in agreement with the Mu'tazili position.[51] Shaykh 'Ali Mustafa al-Ghurabi of Mecca also defended the Mu'tazila and urged that "their valuable legacy be recovered."[52]

Throughout the Islamic world, and particularly in Egypt, the writings of the Mu'tazila are now being reprinted, read, and studied. Discussions of their teachings can now be found in many books and periodicals. In the Arab world, Pakistan and India, the attitude of the Muslim community about the Mu'tazila has changed significantly. Furthermore, among the reformers of Islam there are those who have perspectives identical to those of the Mu'tazila. Among these reformers are Jamal al-Din from Afghanistan, Muhammad 'Abduh of Egypt, and Sayid Ahmad Khan of India.[53]

Notes

1. The headings and subheadings have been added to the original text for easier reference to particular passages in the translation. Nasution's use of italics has been preserved in the translation. His original notations have been edited and supplemented to give fuller and more consistent reference information. In some cases we were not able to locate the editions of texts to which Nasution referred to check the accuracy of page references.

2. Pickthall translates: "Whoso judgeth not by that which Allah hath revealed: such are unbelievers" (Sura 5).

3. These two senior commanders of Muslim forces during the first decades of the Muslim conquests served as the representatives of Muʿawiya and ʿAli, respectively, during the fateful arbitration at Adhruh in 658.

4. The latter, "to give hope," is derived from the root r-j-a, not r-j-'. Watt also speculates that *irja'* bears the connotation of both roots (*Formative Period*, p. 137).

5. Nasution refers here to the Muʿtazili doctrine, *al-manzila bayn al-manzilatayn*, discussed by Qadi ʿAbd al-Jabbar in ¶ 14 in chapter 5.

6. *Al-Taʾrikh al-Tabari*, 4: 442.

7. Ahmad Amin, *Fajr al-islam* (Cairo, 1964), p. 290.

8. ʿAli Sami al-Nashshar, *al-Nash'at al-fikr al-falsafa fi l-islam*, 4th impression (Alexandria: Dar al-Maʿarif, 1966), pp. 430–431.

9. Nasution cites Subhi, *Fi ʿilm al-kalam* pp. 75–76.

10. Wensinck, *The Muslim Creed*, pp. 63 and 246.

11. MacDonald, *The Development of Muslim Theology*, pp. 141 and 160–161. The English quotation is embedded in the Indonesian text. The cited sentence reads: "[al-Jahiz] was a maker of books, learned in the writings of the Tabiʿiyun, deistic naturalists." The reference to the Tabiʿiyun is to a school known among early Muslims as Materialists, not to the atomistic occasionalism of most the Muʿtazila.

12. English and italics in the original.

13. Here Nasution uses the Indonesian term *sifat* (Ar. *sifa*) apparently in the very general sense that justice is inherent in God's nature. In the next paragraph he clarifies the Muʿtazili doctrine that God cannot have multiple attributes which are coeternal with Him, for that would compromise divine unity (*tawhid*). This is confirmed by his use of the Indonesian term *Tuhan* for "God" rather than the Arabic Allah. This is in keeping with the semiofficial Indonesian theological stance that one "God" is shared by all monotheistic faiths, which in Indonesia include Buddhism and Hinduism as well as Islam and Christianity. (See reference to the doctrine of *Panca Sila* in note 47 below.)

14. "Compulsionists," the label the Muʿtazila gave to the Ashʿariya and other madhhabs which held that creation is under the compulsion of (that is, foreordained by) the divine will. In kalam heresiographies, the Jabariya (or Mujbira) are the schematic opposite of the Qadariya – those who held that humans have power (*qudra*) over their own acts – which was often a nickname for the Muʿtazila.

15. English and italics in the original.

16. Rendered here literally from the Indonesian *maha esa* and the Indonesian/Arabic *maha 'adil*. The connotation is that humans possess some of the same qualities attributed to God, but not the divine perfection that the divine being enjoys.

17. That is, if divine unity is compromised by a plurality of attributes.

18. Shirk means associating other beings with Allah, which we have elsewhere in this volume translated as "polytheism."

19. Abu l-Hudhayl Muhammad b. Abi l-Hudhayl al-'Allaf al-'Abdi (d. ca. 841). Abu l-Hudhayl is discussed above in chapter 2, with additional references in   note 20 below.

20. Nasution probably means this in the sense that after Wasil, Abu l-Hudhayl was the next major figure. On the early history of the Mu'tazila, see above, chapter 2; *Formative Period* (passim); and *Theologie*, 3: 209–296.

21. Abu l-Fath Muhammad ibn 'Abd al-Karim al-Shahrastani, *Kitab al-milal wa al-nihal* (Cairo, 1851), pp. 1–49.

22. *Theologie*, 3: 209 gives only the date of death – 841 – followed by a question mark.

23. The Bayt al-Hikmah was a non-teaching research library and institute for translating and studying Greek and other foreign texts. See art. "Bait al-Hikma," *EI².*

24. Italics in the original.

25. English and italics in the original.

26. Izutsu, *God and Man in the Koran*, p. 66.

27. None of Abu l-Hudhayl's works have survived, although fragments exist and his writings are discussed by latter Mu'tazili writers, such as 'Abd al-Jabbar.

28. Here Nasution uses the Indonesian expression *Mahasempurna* to denote the complete perfection of God.

29. Italics in the original.

30. Abu Hashim ibn al-Jubba'i (d. 933). Nasution gives Abu Hashim's name in a variety of ways which we have standardized simply as "Abu Hashim" in the translation.

31. *Ta'liq*, p. 563.

32. Nasution refers here to Ibn Tufayl's (1105–1185) famous philosophical poem in which two islands or nodes of civilization are compared, one populous and governed by social conventions, the other with only one human, Hayy ibn Yaqzan, who develops a parallel body of human knowledge by pure reason, without the benefits of the conventions of culture. See Lenn E. Goodman, *Ibn Tufayl's Hayy ibn Yaqzan: A Philosophical Tale Translated with Introduction and Notes* (New York: Twayne Publishers, 1972).

33. Al-Hasan ibn Yusif ibn al-Muttahar al-Hilli, *Anwar al-malakut fi sharh al-yaqut*, 2nd printing (Tehran: Intisharat al-Rida, 1984) pp. 104–105. (The authors were not able to check this source.)

34. Abu Muhammad ibn Mattawayh, *al-Majmu' fi l-muhit bi l-taklif*, ed. 'Umar al-Sayyid 'Azma (Beirut, 1965), 1: 12.

35. Ibid., p. 22. The page to which Nasution refers bears only distantly on his point. In this passage, Nasution's general point is that reason and revelation are both necessary components of religion. His argument is that only the Mu'tazila have fully

appreciated this position.

36. Al-Shahrastani, *Kitab al-Milal wa l-nihal*, I: 120.
37. *Ta'liq*, p. 56 (reading more into the page than is actually there, though generally correct in his point about the position of al-Jubba'i).
38. Nader, *Falsafa al-mu'tazila*, II: 42.
39. On Mu'ammar's naturalistic theology, see *Formative Period* (passim); and *Theologie*, 3: 67–74. Mu'ammar was an important early member of the Baghdad branch of the Mu'tazila.
40. The meaning of the last phrase is not clear.
41. Here Nasution uses the concept of natural law in a sociological sense. His position is particularly important in light of the more deterministic position advocated by the Muhammadiyah and other Indonesian modernist groups, as well as traditional Muslim thinkers, according to which social position and wealth are determined by God. Nasution's position suggests that development, on the societal level, as well as individual attainment, are the consequence of human choices among the vastly different possibilities natural law presents. This is perhaps the key to understanding his devotion to Mu'tazili theology.
42. This passage offers a solution to the important religious problems posed by the combination of the economic characteristics of the modern world system with Islamic understandings of God's grace. Nasution suggests that Muslims, as individuals and societies, are poor because they have chosen the natural path of poverty, while the developed world is rich, despite its unbelief, because it has chosen to follow the natural path to prosperity. This position also offers a refutation of the modernist or Salafiyah position that there are religious causes for Western dominance and the poverty of the Muslim community. Nasution demands that Muslims accept responsibility for the social and economic conditions in which they find themselves. His position is, however, also clearly different from Marxist ideology because it emphasizes individual and collective choice rather than the operation of class-based modes of production as the determinant of individual and societal welfare.
43. Just how freely Nasution has translated this verse is apparent by comparing it with the more literal, but archaic, Pickthall translation: "thou wilt not find for the way of Allah aught of the power to change."
44. English and italics in the original. This is as close as Nasution comes to discussion of the Mu'tazili doctrine of the created Qur'an (*khalq al-qur'an*). While he accepts this teaching he does not emphasize it, because of its highly controversial nature and because it has little bearing on the social, economic and political aspects of his theological program. The recurring importance of khalq al-qur'an for modernists comes up again in chapter 10.
45. *Sharh* (= *Ta'liq*) p. 135 (the actual quotation is on p. 136).
46. Arabic and italics in the original.
47. Nasution uses the Indonesian expression *Tuhan Yang Maha Esa*, a term which, in the Indonesian national ideology of *Panca Sila*, is used as a generic, non-confessional

term for God, but which contemporary Muslim intellectuals generally interpret as an indirect, or localized reference to the doctrine of tawhid.

48. Nasution is referring to figures like Muhammad 'Abduh.
49. Al-Nashshar, *Nash'at al-fikr*, 1: 150.
50. Amin, *Fajr al-islam,* pp. 299-300.
51. Nasution, *Teologi Islam* (Theology Islam) (Jakarta, n.d.), p. 55.
52. 'Ali Mustafa Ghurabi, *Ta'rikh al-'iraq al-islamiya* (Cairo, 1958), p. 263.
53. Here Nasution restates his claim that Muhammad 'Abduh and other nineteenth- and twentieth-century reformers were advocates of the Mu'tazili school. His claims differ sharply from those of the Muhammadiyah and other Salafiyah thinkers who place the same group of reformers in the lineage of Ibn Taymiyah. We have tried to argue that in an important sense, both are right: Islamic modernism was inspired both by Mu'tazili rationalism and by the reformist project of Ibn Taymiya. Given the emphasis that Indonesian Muslims of all theological orientations place on intellectual lineages, Nasution's insistence on 'Abduh's Mu'tazili heritage must be understood as a direct assault on the religious legitimacy of the Muhammadiyah and other reformist organizations.

III

Mu'tazilism *and* (Post)Modernity

ten

Modern *and* Postmodern Glosses *on* Mu'tazilism

B y the mid-twentieth century, the transformation of European colonial governments into independent nation states across the Islamic world was more or less complete, if not entirely settled. The issues confronting Islamic modernists and traditionalists changed considerably once again, as we have already seen in the case of Indonesia. Indeed, the relationship of traditionalism and modernism to each other and to non-Muslims was to become more confrontational, as it had been from time to time throughout Islamic history. For all that, European specialists in Islamic studies at mid-century, such as Rudi Caspar, were anticipating the disappearance of traditionalism, which they often equated with medieval backwardness, as we saw in chapter 6. The Iranian revolution of 1979 made it clear that strident forms of traditionalism (including Shi'i forms), many of whose advocates called themselves "Islamists" (*islamiyun*) and fundamentalists (*usuliyun*) were in the ascendency. As Mary Douglas put it three years later:

> Events have taken religious studies by surprise. This set of university institutions devoted to understanding religion without the constraints of the divinity school has generally included change in its subject matter. No one, however, foresaw the recent revivals of traditional religious forms.[1]

The purpose of this chapter is to call attention to discussions among Muslim intellectuals about the more strident forms of Islamic traditionalism today. Since many of these critics are also critical of the influence of Western post-Enlightenment thought on Islam, we have adopted the term "postmodern" as a cautious, temporary label. In this chapter, the modernist and postmodernist thinkers we discuss do not identify themselves per se as Mu'tazilites, as Harun Nasution does. Rather, for most of them, Mu'tazili rationalism and free thinking is a symbol of the ability of Muslims to encounter change and external challenges in ways that can be construed as Islamic. It is their selective use of particular aspects of Mu'tazili doctrine and intellectual history that we shall foreground in this chapter. We begin by picking up the narrative where it was left off in chapter 6, in South Asia, with Fazlur Rahman, who also figured in our narrative about Harun Nasution.

Let us recall that Fazlur Rahman was a South Asian Muslim philosopher who was to have a considerable influence on young Asian-Muslim scholars in the North American diaspora, as well as on a younger generation of Western scholars. We shall not try to balance our selective coverage of twentieth-century Islamic modernism with equal treatment of Muslim traditionalists and Islamists. Indeed, our argument has been that the weight of modern scholarship has been disproportionately on the latter. Rather, the thrust of the argument in the following pages is that the modernism of Muhammad 'Abduh and Ahmad Khan, which we discussed in chapter 6, has evolved into postmodern expressions of Islam, some of which are virulently opposed to Islamist movements, and some of which are, in the spirit of the Mu'tazila, more open to dialogue. By use of the term "postmodern," we do not wish to engage in the debate between postmodernists and their critics. Rather, we simply refer to the growing number of non-European thinkers who are critical of the Eurocentrism of post-Enlightenment epistemologies, and who rebel at being construed academically as the "Other." Many have found in postmodern theories of texts strategies for subverting the control that Euro-Americans have exerted over the Islamic textual tradition.

The Modernist Encounter with Traditionalism: The Work of Fazlur Rahman (1919–1988)

Born in India (modern-day Pakistan), Fazlur Rahman was – as he often remarked – trained in the traditional Islamic subjects by his father and in life's virtues by his mother; of the enormous influence of both parents on his life he never failed to make mention in his writings. He also openly professed his appreciation of the contributions to his own understanding of Islam by some Western interpreters; the list often includes H. A. R. Gibb, Wilfred Cantwell Smith, and Kenneth Cragg.[2] In a manner reminiscent of the autobiographies of St. Augustine and al-Ghazali,[3] Rahman experienced an intellectual crisis as a young man, struggling with varied currents of the Greek philosophical heritage. Following a traditional education in his homeland, he went to Oxford to study Greek philosophy and its influence on early Islamic thought. His dissertation on Ibn Sina (Avicenna) indicated in its subtitle, "Philosophy and [Islamic] Orthodoxy," the two conflicting voices that Rahman heard when he tried to explore his own intellectual heritage.[4] He later remarked when he had established in his own mind why philosophical rationalism was a necessary, but not a sufficient, instrument of religion:

> The [Muslim] philosophers were intellectually clever, excelling in subtlety of argument, but their god remained a bloodless principle – a mere intellectual construct, lacking both power and compassion. Although intellectually less skillful, the theologians were nevertheless instinctively aware that the God of religion was a full-blooded, living reality who responded to prayers, guided men individually and collectively, and intervened in history: "He speaks and acts," as Ibn Taymiya so poignantly put it.[5]

Fazlur Rahman set out – first in Pakistan as an advisor to the government of Muhammad Ayyub Khan, and from 1969 until his death in 1988 as a scholar at the University of Chicago – to (re)define Islam in the context of modernity. In both of these phases, Rahman sought to establish the role of reason in religious thought. In the earlier phase in Pakistan, which is reflected in his 1966 work titled simply *Islam*, Rahman determined that the Mu'tazili *mutakallimun* went too far in their exaltation of reason alongside, and even superior to, revelation. Nonetheless, he pointed out that it was "undeniable that the Mu'tazila movement did a great internal service to Islam not only by attempting to erect an edifying picture of God for refined minds but, above all, by insisting on the claims of reason in theology." Rahman conceded that the early Mu'tazili mutakallimun had successfully rid the Muslim *umma* of what Schleiermacher would call much later, in a similar context for nineteenth-century Christianity, Islam's "cultured despisers." As Rahman put it for the early Mu'tazila, "they waged a relentless and successful struggle in defense of Islam against the outside attacks of Manichaeism, Gnosticism and Materialism. In so doing, they perforce produced the first systematically thought-out creed for Islam."[6]

The problem, Rahman concluded, was that although the Mu'tazila rendered a service in defense of Islam from outside attack, as constructive theologians they were unable to produce doctrines that were emotionally satisfying to orthodox Islamic piety. Ironically, he held that the Mu'tazila were not just the opponents of the Hanbali traditionalists; they were the cause of traditionalist extremism. It was his view that the extreme rationalism of the Mu'tazila was responsible, in part, for the extreme fideism and rigidity into which orthodox Islam developed by way of reaction. Hence, he also believed that orthodox Islam, as he called it, went to extremes, the opposite extreme of Mu'tazili rationalism, and thus that "Islam was launched on a career where its dynamic formulations had only a partial and indirect relationship to the living realities of the faith."[7]

On another matter where modernist Muslims like Shaykh 'Abduh have found contemporary relevance in Mu'tazili doctrine, Fazlur Rahman also articulated a *sic et non* "yes, but" judgment. The Mu'tazila held a theodicy – a doctrine of divine justice – that provided for the freedom of the human will (see ¶ 12 of the translation in chapter 5 below). This implied for the Mu'tazila, as Rahman put it, that

> God can neither pardon the evil-doer (and therefore violate His Threat) nor punish the good-doer (and violate His Promise). Taking the Qur'anic statements about the promise of reward and threat of punishment as categorical statements of future *facts*, they deduced that God would not only be unjust if He did not carry out His promises and threats, He would be a liar. Consequently . . . God *must* do the best for man; He *must* send prophets and revelations to mankind. If He did not do the best for man He would neither be just nor God.[8]

Rahman believed the Mu'tazila were correct in maintaining human moral freedom and responsibility. Nonetheless, by linking the idea of divine justice to that of human justice, Rahman concluded that the Mu'tazila again went to extremes (just as he believed the orthodox went to extremes in forfeiting the rationality of justice to the transcendent mind of God alone).[9]

Fazlur Rahman's confrontation with Islamic traditionalism came early in his career, in a passage on the nature of the Islamic revelation of the Qur'an. In *Islam*, which was first published in 1966 about the time of his arrival in the United States but was written in Pakistan, Rahman said the following about the Quranic revelation:

> But orthodoxy (indeed all medieval thought) lacked the necessary intellectual tools to combine in its formulation of the dogma of the otherness and verbal character of the Revelation on the one hand, and its intimate connection with the work and the religious personality of the Prophet on the other, i.e., it lacked the intellectual capacity to say both that the Qur'an is entirely the Word of God and, in an ordinary sense, also entirely the word of Muhammad.[10]

That which had been the unresolved problematic of divine/human encounter in the vessel of revelation for the great councils of early Eastern Christendom was quickly seen as challenge and insult to traditionalist Muslims, particularly in India and Pakistan. How can the transcendent and eternal divine exist in historical, human contexts? For Christians, the problem centered on a person, Jesus Christ. For Muslims, it centered on a book, the Qur'an. For Rahman, the die was cast for a life-long struggle over a single passage in a book read by a Western readership that would tend to be less intolerant of the paradox of the divine/human nature of revelation. In a certain sense, Rahman had once again raised the Mu'tazili issue of *khalq al-qur'an*, "creation of the Qur'an," as Shaykh 'Abduh had a generation earlier. And, as we saw in chapter 6, 'Abduh also encountered formidable resistance to his attempt to construe the Qur'an theologically as at one level being a human cultural production. In a larger and comparative sense in relation to Western theology, Rahman was criticizing what Christian theology has labeled the "Docetic" view of revelation, in this case the view that the Book (not the Son of God) was fully divine and only "appeared" in earthly form. Unqualified resistance to the Mu'tazili humanization of the Word of God, the reader will recall, was the occasion for Ahmad ibn Hanbal's enormous popularity, and it became a defining moment for Islamic traditionalism. Rahman's Muslim critics have been unforgiving because he was willing even to broach the subject of a historical, ordinary linguistic, and human nature for the Quranic text.

When we turn to Fazlur Rahman's later thinking in works such as *Major Themes of the Qur'an* (1980) and *Islam and Modernity* (1982), we find the use of reason in modern Islamic theology to be a prominent theme, but not the Mu'tazili heritage of rationalism. The Mu'tazili *madhhab* is mentioned by name in only a few passages in either book. More significantly perhaps, as Professor Hassan Hanafi of Egypt once remarked, we find little in works such as *Islam and Modernity* that shows us how Rahman would have constructed an Islamic critique of injustice visited upon Muslims by unjust regimes and colonial masters.[11] In short, Fazlur Rahman was a brilliant philosopher who could expose the failures of the classical Shi'i, Mu'tazili, and Sunni systems. He could envision a future in which reason could assist Muslims to live according to the Shari'a in the modern world. But Fazlur Rahman was a modernist theologian, a man of the Western Enlightenment as well as of the Islamic intellectual tradition. It was this that had brought him into conflict with Muslim traditionalists. Muslim postmodern challenges to Western modernity, on the other side, were not his principal interest. They were more the interest of such thinkers as Mohammed Arkoun, Fatima Mernissi, and Hassan Hanafi.

Rethinking Islam: The Poststructural Interpretations of Mohammed Arkoun

Like Muhammad 'Abduh, Fazlur Rahman, and other modernists, Mohammed Arkoun has labored to make Islam relevant to the modern world by encouraging self-criticism and the reappropriation of theological rationalism. Unlike Rahman the modernist, Professor Arkoun is a postmodernist. His project is inspired by the French school of poststructuralist deconstructionism which, like traditionalist Islam, has mounted a critique of post-Enlightenment modernity. The traditionalist Muslim attack on Western modernism is well known and need not detain us in this study. Post-Enlightenment secularism and modernity have habitually been seen in Islamic sectarian discourses as Western diseases, spread by colonialism, infecting and weakening the once great Islamic civilization. For the Egyptian theologian and critic Hassan Hanafi, whose work we shall discuss below, even postmodern criticism is seen as being antithetic to Islamic rationalism.

What makes Arkoun's writing interesting, with respect to Islamic responses to the West, is that his assessment of modernity and Islam is based not on traditional religious arguments but rather on postmodern critical theory. Arkoun is a North African Francophile who has studied and taught in Paris for most of his life. Whereas postmodern theory has played an influential role for both Western and Third World scholars in mounting critiques of colonialism and Orientalism, it was Arkoun's genius to begin seriously to apply postmodern theory to the classical Islamic textual tradition.[12] In this regard, Arkoun has attracted some Western scholars to experiment with postmodern methods of reading Islamic texts.[13] To be sure, like most other contemporary Muslim intellectuals, Mohammed Arkoun is critical – sometimes harshly – of European colonialism and Orientalism. On the other side, as a Muslim he is self-critical of Islamic responses to modernity. Like other critics, such as Edward Said, Fatima Mernissi, and Hassan Hanafi, Arkoun sees the production and reading of texts as political acts. Texts are instruments of power. In this respect, Arkoun has found in the Mu'tazila kindred spirits in rational criticism of religious texts and their interpretation.

On the classic point of Mu'tazili heterodoxy – the creation of the Qur'an (khalq al-qur'an) – Arkoun, too, has been critical of the orthodox Hanbali/Ash'arite doctrine of the eternal, uncreated Qur'an. In *L'Islam, morale et politique*,[14] he interpreted the decision of Caliph al-Ma'mun and his immediate successors, to require public belief that God had created the Qur'an in Arabic in history, as a political act that was directed against the interests of the ulama.[15] The ulama claimed authority over a closed, immutable, eternal text of the divine will. Mu'tazili mutakallimun sought to historicize the text and open it to criticism, which is to say, rational under- standing. On this point, Arkoun argues that:

> Psychologically, ever since the failure of the Mu'tazili school to impose its view of the Qur'an . . . as created by God in time, Muslim consciousness has incorporated the belief that all the pages bound together as *mushaf* contain the very Word of God. The Written Qur'an has thus become identified with the Qur'anic discourse or the Qur'an as it was recited, which is itself the direct emanation of the Archetype of the Book.
>
> This means that the phenomenon of writing as a means of transition to a different functioning of language and as an archival base linked to state authority is denied in the name of a theological position contradicted by numerous and explicit Qur'an verses.[16]

Arkoun comments further that "Holy Scriptures," such as the Qur'an and Bible, should be open to "historical, sociological, and anthropological" analyses, but that nonetheless to do so challenges "all sacralizing and tran- scending interpretations produced by traditional theological reasoning." He refers to the "demystification and demythologization of the phenomenon of the Book/book," but not in the way that nineteenth- and early twentieth-cen- tury biblical criticism destructed the sacred texts of Judaism and Christianity. He explains the concept of postmodern rationalism as follows:

> Modern rationality restores the psychological and cultural functions of myth and develops a global strategy of knowledge in which the rational and the imaginary interact perpetually to produce individual and historical existence. We must abandon the dualist framework of knowledge that pits reason against imagination, history against myth, true against false, good against evil, and reason against faith. We must postulate a plural, changing, welcoming sort of rationality, one consistent with the psychological operations that the Qur'an locates in the heart and that contemporary anthropology attempts to reintroduce under the label of the imaginary.[17]

One of the matters on which the Mu'tazili mutakallimun of the ninth to the eleventh centuries ran into trouble with their traditionalist and Ash'ari oppo- nents was the matter of scriptural exegesis. In ¶ 24 of *Kitab al-usul al-khamsa* in chapter 5 above, 'Abd al-Jabbar refers to the Mu'tazili argument against anthropomorphism (*tashbih*); if God had a body He would be limited in those ways that bodies limit ordinary beings, that is, He could only be in one place at any given time. Thus, as we have seen, the Mu'tazila argued on rational grounds for interpreting such passages metaphorically, not literally. Arkoun believes that not only the Qur'an as such, but also the great classical commentaries of al-Tabari (d. 922) and Fakhr al-Din al-Razi (d. 1209) should be analyzed by Muslims using modern textual linguistics and interpretive theory. This theme of challenging the traditionalist insistence on the sole right to interpret the text of the Qur'an (and the Hadith) is one that runs throughout the expressions of modernist and postmodernist Islamic rationalism, including most of the thinkers discussed in this and the next chapter. Indeed, as we have seen, it also has roots in Ibn Taymiya's fourteenth-century revival of Hanbalism.

In a work titled *Pour une critique de la raison islamique*,[18] Mohammed Arkoun discussed at length a concept characteristic of his thought in recent years, that of "Islamic Reason." The historical, theological and linguistic assumptions of traditionalist Muslims – such as the *ahl al-hadith* like Ahmad ibn Hanbal of old or the Islamiyun of today – lead to confusions about meaning and authority. Therefore, the task of Muslim intellectuals today is to mount a critique of traditional Islamic modes of reasoning because they confuse historically rooted traditional interpretations with the content of divine revelation. Whereas many traditionalist Muslims write about "Islamizing" the social sciences and other disciplines of the modern, secular university, Arkoun contends that it should be just the other way around: Islamic habits of reasoning should be deconstructed and sacred texts should be opened up to modern historical and linguistic study. Without the stimulation and discipline of open encounter with modern thought, Arkoun believes that the standards of knowledge about Islam among the traditional ulama as well as the Islamists will continue to decline.

Making a similar but even less compromising critique of Islamic traditionalism is the modernist, feminist critic Fatima Mernissi.

The Discourse against Islamic Irrationalism: Fatima Mernissi's Critique of Tradition

Like Fazlur Rahman and Mohammed Arkoun, Fatima Mernissi is a Muslim intellectual with a Western education, able to analyze and criticize Western thought on its own terms. Like the other two, she has written for Western audiences and for those Muslims who read Western languages and are acquainted with Western critical theories. Thus, her critique of traditionalist, male-oriented Islam has probably had more influence among Western, non-Muslim intellectuals than among Muslim intellectuals. Moreover, like Mohammed Arkoun, Fatima Mernissi is a Francophile North African Arab, trained as a social scientist (sociologist) in France. She is also familiar with postmodern criticism and themes, which she often uses to frame her analyses of Islamic social movements. For example, she refers to the Islamiyun and Usuliyun as "fundamentalists," with obvious reference to the general meanings that term now carries for Western readers of the social sciences. In the Introduction to the second edition of her popular book *Beyond the Veil*, the language shows the unmistakable influence of Michael Foucault, Edward Said, and their postmodernist followers in the social sciences.

> *Beyond the Veil* is a book about sexual space boundaries. It tries to grasp sex as it materializes, as it melts into and with space and freezes it in an architecture . . . [It] illustrates an important dimension of religion that is often ignored, since religion is usually confused with and reduced to spirituality: Islam is, among other things, an overwhelmingly materialistic vision of the world. Its field is not the heavens so much as terrestrial space and terrestrial power and access to all kinds of worldly pleasures, including wealth, sex, and power . . . *Beyond the Veil* . . . does not treat Islam and women from a factual point of view, but rather it identifies one of the key components of the system – namely, the way Islam uses space as a device for sexual control.[19]

As the preceding passage indicates, Fatima Mernissi is a feminist critic of modern Islamic societies. Her project is to wrest the sacred texts of traditionalist Islam from dominant male interpreters (the ulama and especially fundamentalists) and to liberate these texts for modernist and feminist readings. What is Mernissi's take on Mu'tazilism and rationalism?

In *Islam and Democracy: Fear of the Modern World*, Fatima Mernissi constructs a contrasting typology of formative trends in early Islam, Kharijism and Mu'tazilism, that have led, in her view, to the contemporary predicament of Islamic antimodernism. It is a post-Gulf War essay, and it raises the post-Gulf War question that many Western observers and not a few Muslim intellectuals have been raising about Islam: is Islam – a religion that requires total submission to the divine will as defined by religious elites – compatible with democracy? While many Muslims have tried to answer the question positively by broadening the Euro-American definition of democracy, Mernissi locates the problem primarily within the Islamic tradition.[20]

It is important to notice that Mernissi does not contrast Mu'tazili rationalism specifically with Hanbali fideism and traditionalism, as we have in these pages. Rather, she problematizes the issue politically. She contrasts the "rationalist tradition" (Mu'tazila) with what she calls "rebel Islam," Kharijism – those who seceded from 'Ali's camp in the seventh century because he neglected to take a hard line on what they regarded as the un-Islamic behavior of Caliph 'Uthman.[21] Her analysis comes much closer to that of the opening passage in Harun Nasution's text in the previous chapter. This was the divisive issue of the first *fitna*, discussed above in chapter 2, and it remained an issue in the political theology of the Mu'tazila three centuries later, as we saw in writings of 'Abd al-Jabbar (see ¶¶ 14, 45–46 of chapter 5 above).

Mernissi values the contribution of the Mu'tazila for two reasons in particular. First they "proposed reintroducing reason (*'aql*) and personal opinion (*ra'y*) into the political process" (this is one implication of ¶ 1 in chapter 5), and second they "raised the question of *qadar* (predestination), that is, the question of whether individuals are responsible for their own acts"[22] (see ¶¶ 12, 13, 62).

The importance of the Mu'tazila, according to Mernissi, is that they asked philosophically: "What is the purpose of our existence on earth, and to what use should we put 'aql, that marvelous gift from heaven?"[23] Beginning with 'Ali's caliphate (656–661), the rebel Kharijites fomented dissidence and terrorism against any ruler or imam who did not conform to their interpretation of Islam. Their importance, then, for Mernissi, was political. Mernissi draws out the Khariji/Mu'tazili contrast as a theme of Islamic political history and as a basis for understanding the fear Islamic fundamentalists have, she says, of rationalism and democracy:

> By introducing reason into the political theater, the Mu'tazila forced Islam to imagine new relationships between ruler and ruled, giving all the faithful an active part to play alongside the palace. Politics was no longer just a Kharijite dual between two actors, the imam and the rebel leader. A third element came on the scene: all believers who are capable of reasoning. The two conflicting trends within Islam appeared on the scene very early and continued, under various names, to be active throughout Muslim history. Although their approaches differed, they shared one basic idea: the imam must be modest and must in no way turn to despotism. It was only on the subject of methods of realizing this ideal of the imamate that they diverged.[24]

Thus, democracy would be quite possible in all Islamic societies, in Mernissi's view, if the rationalism and humanism of the Mu'tazila had not been politically suppressed by Khariji-like gangland politics. Kharijism, in this view, is just another name for, or perhaps a symbol of, extremist fundamentalism (or traditionalism) which continues to exist and even thrive,[25] and Mu'tazilism is the spirit of democracy, rationalism and humanism that the Khawarij throughout history, by whatever name, have feared and forcibly suppressed.

The condemnation of the Mu'tazili mutakallimun by Hanbali and Ash'ari traditionalists because they trafficked in foreign (Greek) and humanistic ideas had the effect of amputating a vital part of the body politic of Islamic civilization, according to Mernissi. Continuing the metaphor:

> Nevertheless, the fact that the rationalist, humanistic tradition was rejected by despotic politicians does not mean that it doesn't exist. Having an arm amputated is not the same as being born with an arm missing. Studies of amputees show that the amputated member remains present in the person's mind. The more our rational faculty is suppressed, the more obsessed we are by it.[26]

Fatima Mernissi's highly schematized version of early Islamic intellectual history is selective and unconventional in places. For example, she states mistakenly that "the activity of the *falasifa* (philosophers) was called kalam."[27] The methods of Muslim philosophers and mutakallimun, however, were quite distinct; the two groups were often in conflict. One may also question Mernissi's claim that reason, logic and theological open-mindedness were thoroughly eliminated by the "Kharijite rebel" and traditionalist movements in Islam. After the decline of the Mu'tazila in the eleventh century as a significant influence on Sunni intellectualism, *kalam* and *falsafa* continued to be studied and taught. With al-Ghazali (d. 1111) there was in fact both a critique of falsafa, and ironically, a trend to incorporate the Peripatetic tradition into Islamic theology.[28] Finally, there seems to have been considerable doubt among the mutakallimun themselves as to whether or not the common people should even be allowed to indulge in kalam – the form of rationalism they championed. The famed Mu'tazili theologian and littérateur, Abu 'Uthman 'Amr ibn Bahr al-Kinani, known as al-Jahiz "the Bug-Eyed" (d. 869), once remarked that kalam topics excite the masses into heated debate, despite the fact that ordinary Muslims are incompetent to discuss such matters.[29]

Nonetheless, Mernissi has touched on some of the themes we have noticed among modernist and postmodernist theologians. The view that human intellect ('aql) and independent reasoning (*ijtihad*) need to be cultivated in modern Islamic societies was stated by Shaykh 'Abduh, and has been restated by such modernist thinkers as Fazlur Rahman, Mohammed Arkoun, and Hassan Hanafi. Mernissi touches on another point in *Islam and Democracy* that we would like to note in closing this review of her critique of extreme forms of Islamic traditionalism. The early Mu'tazili mutakallimun were often accused of importing foreign ideas, such as Greek philosophy, into Islam. Mernissi and other modernists believe that in fact their discursive encounters with ideas outside Islam was an important ingredient of the vitality of what historians have called the "Renaissance" of Islam in the tenth century. A crucial part of the Mu'tazili paradigm of religious intellectualism is willingness, indeed eagerness, to debate the claims of religion and political theology with non-Muslims on their own terms, or on mutually agreed upon terms. Thus, as we saw in chapters 1 and 2 above, we find in medieval Islamic literature indications that the Mu'tazila in particular debated at length with Jewish, Christian, and even atheist thinkers, and this was often in the presence of rulers and large gatherings of intellectuals.[30] Mernissi argues relentlessly that openness to debate and new ideas is a necessary stance for Muslims in a world increasingly characterized by one form or another of political democracy, religious (and cultural) pluralism, and modernity.

The Renewal of *Kalam*: The Work of Hassan Hanafi[31]

Among contemporary Egyptian intellectuals, many have written constructive critiques of Mu'tazili kalam. For example, Husayn al-Muruwwa (d. 1987), like Harun Nasution, was particularly interested in the link between politics and religion in the early history of the Mu'tazila. In *al-Naza'at al-maddiya fi l-falasafa l-'arabiya l-islamiya* (Materalist trends in Arab-Islamic Philosophy), Muruwwa interpreted the rise of the Mu'tazila in the theological debates within Hasan al-Basri's circle in much the same manner as did Harun Nasution. He gives a Marxist economic historical analysis of the five principal doctrines (*usul*) of Mu'tazilism.[32] Another analysis of the rationalist/traditionalist debate in early kalam was by Hassan Hanafi, who has also been identified, particularly by his critics, as a Marxist and leftist thinker.

Hassan Hanafi was born in Egypt in 1935.[33] In secondary school in Egypt (1948–1952), he encountered the more strident form of Wahhabi traditionalism of the day expressed by al-Ikhwan al-Muslimun, the "Muslim Brotherhood."[34] He joined and supported the Ikhwan as an undergraduate at Cairo University, until the organization was banned by the government of Gamal Abdel Nasser. He earned a B.A. in philosophy at Cairo University in 1956. His intellectual horizons changed somewhat dramatically when he left Egypt to pursue his studies in Paris.

In 1966 Hanafi received the *doctorat d'état* from the Sorbonne for preparing three dissertations (on religious dialogue and revolution, the phenomenology of religion, and the existential interpretation of the New Testament). While earning the doctorate he taught Arabic at the École des Langues Orientales in Paris. He is an indefatigable writer, speaker, teacher and traveler. His works are read in many Islamic countries, and he is the subject of numerous studies and dissertations. Yet, for all that, Hassan Hanafi is comparatively less well known in Europe and North America than the other Islamic (post)modernists we have discussed. Nonetheless, it is important to review his ambitious reformulation of Islamic modernism, because Hanafi's work has had considerable influence in the Islamic world beyond the Middle East. This is especially true in Indonesia among contemporary Muslim modernists, such as Nurcholish Madjid. Moreover, despite his reputation as a leftist thinker, Hanafi believes the traditional Islamic texts are an important source of the Islamic dialectic with the conditions of modernity.

Hassan Hanafi is radical in his critique of both of the modern influences on his education – the Islamist movements on the one side and Western attempts to dominate Islam on the other. Yet, in a manner that we can now recognize as a calque on the Mu'tazili intellectual ethos of dialogic rationalism, Hanafi has sought to remain in communication with both camps. His intellectual ground is formed in part by postmodern trends in literary criticism and the social sciences, and he follows hermeneutical methods that reflect postmodern criticism. At the same time, he is critical of postmodernism, which he regards as another form of Western hegemony over modern Islamic thought. His thinking is also informed, as was Fazlur Rahman's, by a deep reading of European literature on philosophical and, in Hanafi's case, biblical hermeneutics. In an article written in 1988, Hanafi essayed an Islamic textual hermeneutic in the light of the theories of Martin Heidegger, Hans Georg Gadamer, and the New Testament exegete Rudolf Bultmann.[35]

Muhammad 'Abduh and Sayyid Ahmad Khan had recognized in the late nineteenth century that Islam would have to come to grips with modern science and Western control over the production of science. Hassan Hanafi's genius has been to realize that the European critique of religion, Christian and non-Christian, was rooted in Western concepts of history and text. That critique, which Muslim and non-Muslim scholars refer to as Orientalism, Hanafi recognized owed much to nineteenth- and early twentieth-century biblical criticism and *Religionswissenschaft*. He therefore set out to understand the philosophies of text and meaning that had been propounded by Continental philosophers and theologians.

At the same time, Hanafi made clear that this project, which began as his Sorbonne dissertation,[36] was to show that the hermeneutical act of "reading the text" was crucial to the political transition from traditionalism to modernism.[37] Following Heidegger and Gamader, Hanafi holds that meaning is not inherent in texts; meaning is produced in the contextual encounter between texts and human beings as political animals, in the social and political contexts in which texts are produced, read, and used. His position in hermeneutics is very close to that of Edward Said.[38] As texts are reread and reinterpreted from one generation and location to the next (Hanafi gives the example of the philosophy of Plato by Aristotle, and the philosophy of the Kant by Fichte, Hegel, Shilling, and Schopenhauer), meaning is reproduced by the individual (*fard*) and the social collective (*jama'a*).[39] There are three methods (*turuq*, sing. *tariqa*) or methodological fronts with which Third World interpreters, Muslims in particular, must come to grips in order to achieve authentic self-understanding in the modern world: (1) the Western intellectual and cultural heritage (*turath*), for that is an omnipresent condition of the modern world; (2) the traditional (Islamic) heritage; and (3) logical analysis of human social experience (which Hanafi terms "reality"), which find expression in any and all texts in the Western and Islamic heritage.[40] This presents the dialectical problematic of *al-turath wa l-tajdid*, "heritage and renewal," neither of which can or should be ignored by Muslims and other Third World peoples.[41]

With the first tariqa, the problem posed by the imposition of Western science, culture and politics on the Muslim world, Hanafi comes to the problem of Orientalism from a different angle from that of Edward Said's critique. The contribution of European and American scholars to the study of Muslim peoples and their texts was seriously questioned and problematized by Said in his 1978 book, *Orientalism*, as we saw in chapter 1.[42] In *Muqaddima fi'ilm al-istigrab* (Introduction to Occidentalism), Hassan Hanafi sets out to turn Orientalism back on its Western (and Muslim) proponents, much as Marx had done when he turn Hegelianism into a critique of European society.

In the *Muqaddima*, Hanafi identifies Orientalism as a product of post-Enlightenment thought, which reached its peak in the nineteenth century. His description of Orientalism as a conceptualizing term for Western scholarship on Islam does not depart significantly from the tone of Edward Said's analysis, although Hanafi's discourse is much more imbued with the language of Continental philosophy and Islamist criticism of the West. Occidentalism, on the other side, must necessarily arise from the growing need in the Islamic world to study the West. It is a normative field of study that Hanafi urges Muslims and other Third World communities to take seriously. For Hanafi, Occidentalism is an emerging discourse that will enable Muslims and others to recapture the rational knowledge of humankind and the world that Europeans and Americans have thought they owned since the sixteenth century.

Hanafi employs the geometric image of a circle, with Euro-Christian society at the center and Islam (and the Third World generally) on the periphery. The current phase of Orientalism is coming to an end, namely the

Eurocentric scientific and cultural hegemony that followed upon colonialism. Nonetheless, Western hegemony still exists in the form of technology transfer and other postcolonial means of maintaining economic, military, and cultural control over Muslim societies. The task of Occidentalism, *'ilm al-istighrab*, is to bring the injustice of Western ethnocentrism to an end and to help bring about an open, global, non-Eurocentric society – one that is receptive to the well-established cultural, ethical and intellectual contributions which have been kept on the periphery. Although he identifies the Third World generally with that periphery which is moving to replace the Euro-American center, the élan of Islamic rationalism is clearly his vision of a more just society in the future. An important implication of Hanafi's argument for "Occidentalism" is that Islamic intellectual history can now replace European Christian thought as an intellectual basis for comparative history of religions. The historical Mu'tazili practices of dialogue with Christians, Jews, and others, as well as the *dhimmi* system of Islamic protection of other recognized religions, carries the further implication for Hanafi, then, that traditional Islam is more open to other religious communities than Christianity, in particular, is theologically capable of being.

In keeping with the second tariqa or "method" of making the transition from traditionalism to modernism, Hassan Hanafi believes the Islamic philosophical and theological textual traditions should be preserved and studied by Muslims. When he was a younger scholar he and Muhammad Bekir collaborated with Muhammad Hamidullah to publish a critical edition of a Mu'tazili text by a pupil of 'Abd al-Jabbar: Abu l-Husayn al-Basri (d.1044), *Kitab al-mu'tamad fi usul al-fiqh* (Book of the reliable concerning the fundamentals of jurisprudence).[43] The third tariqa, the reality of both the Islamic Orient and the European Occident that is textual and must be analyzed by rationalism and hermeneutics, is the most important for the study of the Mu'tazila and classical kalam more generally.

Hassan Hanafi's greatest achievement to date in this regard is a five-volume work titled *Min al-'aqida ila l-thawra* (From creed to revolution).[44] In this work, Hanafi attempts to offer a modern "reading" of the classical kalam texts that is appropriate to the revolutionary political circumstances in which Muslims find themselves in the twentieth century. The five volumes are dedicated to themes we encountered when speaking about the Mu'tazila in Part I above, and especially in the translation of *Kitab al-usul al-khamsa*. The five volumes are titled: (1) *al-Muqaddima al-nazariyya* (Theoretical introduction), which reminds us of the first paragraphs of 'Abd al-Jabbar's *Kitab al-usul al-khamsa*; (2) *al-Tawhid* ([Divine] unicity), on the being of God, His attributes and operations as God; (3) *al-'Adl* (Justice), on the ethical condition of moral acts and the will to commit them; (4) *al-Nubuwwa – al-mu'ad* (Prophethood - reconsidered), on the development of revelatory inspiration (*wahy*) and the need for prophethood; and (5) *al-Iman wa l-'amal – al-imama* (Faith and works – the imamate), on the relation of belief and unbelief to ethical acts, especially political action in the world. The work juxtaposes on each page passages from the classical heritage of Islam (al-turath) with Hanafi's contemporary restatement of the problem in the modern world (*al-tajdid*).

Ironically, then, although Hassan Hanafi is perhaps politically the most radical intellectual we have considered in this chapter, in other ways he shares part of the more traditionalist agenda. By this we mean that, more than the others we have discussed, he seeks to conserve the Islamic textual tradition and the actual structure of its content by revivifying Islamic theology – kalam – in the modern context. In his role as professor and as General Secretary of the Egyptian Philosophical Society, Hassan Hanafi advances his project among students and colleagues. In June 1991 – just following the political and spiritual trauma of the Gulf War – he convened in Cairo, under the auspices of al-Azhar University and the Egyptian Philosophical Society, a national symposium on *'ilm al-kalam wa tajdiduhu*, "theology and its renewal." His emphasis on the "renewal" of 'ilm al-kalam reflects the spirit of Muhammad 'Abduh and Sayyid Ahmad Khan more than the other thinkers discussed in this chapter. For Hanafi, kalam is more than a symbol of rationalism; it is a textual tradition that must be reread in light of the present situation of Islam in the modern world. Characteristic of Hanafi's dialogical and irenic approach, a variety of Islamic theological viewpoints were represented in the papers that were read at the national symposium. Theologians representing Christian communities in Egypt were also invited to read papers. This earned him severe criticism from traditionalist Muslims.[45] This aspect of Hassan Hanafi's concern to promote an Islamic rationalism that is always in touch with opposing viewpoints was also demonstrated in the early 1980s when members of Islamic Jihad were arrested for the assassination of President Anwar al-Sadat. Hanafi publicly called for dialogue with Islamists – even the most radical – as the most productive and just way to avoid fitna. This, too, is a cultural reflex on the problems and solutions of Islamic theology in the early centuries, which have been discussed above, primarily in chapter 2.

Indeed, in *al-Usuliyya al-islamiyya* (Islamic fundamentalism) (Cairo, 1982) Hassan Hanafi held that Muslims mean something quite different from what the Western media mean by the phrase "Islamic fundamentalism." Rather than backwardness and the desire to cling to medieval religious mentalities, Hanafi says that the study of usul, "fundamentals," is a necessary occupation of intellectuals in every civilization. Capitalist, socialist and communist states, as well as Islamic societies, all seek legitimization on the basis of fundamental principles. The images that the Western media associate with Islamic fundamentalism – the hijab, bearded young men, militant cries for an Islamic state, and so on, are seen by Hanafi as superficialities. Real fundamentalism, in this view – the movements of Usuliyya and Salafiyya, are movements of reform, liberation and social justice responding to new challenges in each age and political circumstance. Thus, Hassan Hanafi agrees with the Western media and those scholars who believe that fundamentalism is the real essence of Islam, but he means something quite different by it.[46] For Hanafi, the value of fundamentalism for Islam is its dynamic revolutionary efforts to achieve social justice within the Muslim umma, which Hanafi, along with the Islamiyun, believes could be a model for the global society of the future. Although Hanafi, along with Islamiyun traditionalists, places Islam squarely in the middle of future global society, his vision of Islam is rationalist and modernist; like the Existentialist New Testament exegete Rudolf Bultmann, Hanafi wants to save the eternal humanizing message of the classical Islamic textual tradition, but not necessarily all of its ancient cultural forms.

Among Hassan Hanafi's many students is one in particular who has written about the Mu'tazila with a degreee of appreciation that reminds us of Harun Nasution. What makes the case of Nasr Hamid Abu Zayd important is the reaction to his writings among highly placed traditionalist thinkers. On 14 June 1995, the Appeals Court of Second Degree in Egypt ruled that Professor Abu Zayd, a younger colleague and former student of Hassan Hanafi at Cairo University, was a *kafir* (unbeliever). The ruling was based on the way that members of the court and those who pleaded the case against Abu Zayd read his academic writings about the Mu'tazila and other arguments for modernizing and rationalizing Islamic thought. The criticism against Abu Zayd's thought arose during the tenure process at Cairo University, which eventually went in his favor but not without lasting controversy. A consequence of the ruling was that Professor Abu Zayd's marriage to Dr. Ibtihal Yunis was ordered annulled. This was based on the ancient prohibition of Muslim women being married to non-Muslim men. In 1996 the couple was forced to live in exile in the Netherlands.

Ironically, in his ruling against Professor Abu Zayd, the presiding court judge cited an Islamic and Quranic principle that had been championed by the Mu'tazila – commanding the good and prohibiting evil. According to one account, the judge wrote: "Abandoning the Good is . . . a matter that harms every Muslim and spreads wrong-doing in society . . ."[47] The same report, confirmed by conversations with Professor Abu Zayd himself and his mentor, Hassan Hanafi,[48] indicates that modernists and traditionalists across Egyptian society are sorely divided by this ruling. For example, Dr. Muhammad 'Amara, the respected historian of Islamic theology, who has edited Mu'tazili texts and written about their doctrines, wrote in the Egyptian labor newspaper, *al-Sha'b*: "It is the Islamists who are going to lose if constraints are placed on freedom of expression."[49] Other intellectuals have feared that it is pro-Mu'tazilites like Abu Zayd and modernists more generally who are in the most danger of losing in the struggle with resurgent traditionalism at the present moment. More chilling for some Egyptians and Muslims outside Egypt who have watched this case develop is that many faculty and public leaders known to be sympathetic to modernist ideas have withheld from making any public statement. One thing seems clear in this particular case: the medieval articulation of Mu'tazili theology still has the power to generate bold modernist ideas and traditionalist reactions.[50]

It has been our aim in this chapter to show that the rational and critical spirit of the tenth-century Mu'tazili text translated in chapter 5 (and renewed for twentieth-century Indonesians by Nasution, chapter 9) resonates with trends found in the modernist theological projects of Muslim intellectuals in the Middle East and the West. The differences among intellectuals we have discussed – Muhammad 'Abduh, Sayyid Ahmad Khan, Fazlur Rahman, Harun Nasution, Mohammed Arkoun, Fatima Mernissi, and Hassan Hanafi – may seem at first striking and irreconcilable. It would seem that they hardly form a modernist madhhab such as the Mu'tazila or Ash'ariya had formed in medieval Islam. Yet, when we examine their texts and the issues they have debated with traditionalist Muslims, their differences are no greater than the differences among the Mu'tazili mutakallimun themselves on matters of doctrine. The one common thematic thread that runs through all the modernist Muslim thinkers we have discussed is their call to preserve the Islamic heritage by restoring reason ('aql) and independent judgment (ijtihad) to Islamic discourse. This much the modernists share with some Islamists. Their chief difference with the more hard-line Islamist intellectuals among the traditionalists is in the openness of the modernists to participate in critical dialogue with non-Muslim, Western, even secularist, intellectuals. The work of modernists and Mu'tazila reviewed in this chapter and throughout this book can be interpreted, we propose, as an invitation to dialogue. The need for productive theological disputation among Muslims is as important as dialogue between Muslims and non-Muslims. The rationalist/modernist contributors to this discourse have found in Mu'tazilism a spirit and symbol of an effective Islamic response to modernity.

The modernists differ among themselves as to how much of the traditional Islamic heritage is worth preserving in the modern world. They all believe, however, that the way to resolve the matter is to reread the ancient texts in light of the modern situation. In this sense, we suggest, they are implicitly Mu'tazili in their approach to theology.

Notes

1. Douglas, "The Effects of Modernization on Religious Change," p. 1. The issue in which her article appeared was devoted to the return of religion as a force in public life and politics.
2. See Rahman, "Review Essay," p. 193.
3. It is interesting to compare these autobiographical texts by two seminal medieval thinkers who reshaped their respective theological traditions: St. Augustine, *Confessions*, trans. Henry Chadwick (Oxford and New York: Oxford University Press, 1991 [1938]; and Muhammad al-Ghazali, *al-Munqidh min al-dalal* (Deliverance from error), trans. into English by W[illiam] Montgomery Watt as *The Faith and Practice of al-Ghazali* (Chicago: Kazi Publications, 1982).
4. Rahman, *Prophecy in Islam*. The reader will recall that Harun Nasution experienced much the same kind of conflict (chapter 8 above).
5. Rahman, "My Belief-in-Action," p. 155.
6. Rahman, *Islam* p. 88. Rahman took out the original copyright on *Islam* in 1966.
7. Ibid., p. 90.
8. Ibid., p. 89.
9. Ibid.
10. Ibid., p. 31.
11. Lecture to graduate students in Religious Studies at Arizona State University, November 1992, in which Professor Hanafi presented a critical review of Rahman, *Islam and Modernity*.
12. See, for example, Arkoun, "Logocentrisme et vérité."
13. See Carter, "Linguistic Science and Orthodoxy in Conflict"; and Martin, "Islamic Textuality in Light of Poststructuralist Criticism."
14. Arkoun, *L'Islam, morale et politique*, pp. 99–102. Cited by the translator and editor, Robert D. Lee, in Arkoun, *Rethinking Islam*, p. 40.
15. Interestingly, discussion of the Mu'tazili doctrine of the creation of the Qur'an does not appear in *Kitab al-usul al-khamsa*. Al-Ma'mun's *mihna* (inquisition) is discussed above in chapter 2.
16. Arkoun, *Rethinking Islam*, p. 36.
17. Ibid., pp. 36–37.
18. Arkoun, *Pour une critique de la raison islamique*.
19. Mernissi, *Beyond the Veil*, pp. xv–xvi.
20. Mernissi, *Islam and Democracy*. Also on the debate about Islam and democracy, see Bullet, *Under Siege*.

21. Mernissi, *Islam and Democracy*, p. 26.
22. Ibid.
23. Ibid., p. 32.
24. Ibid., pp. 32–33.
25. On the modern accusation that radical Islamiyun are Kharijis, see the fatwa written by Shaykh al-Islam Gad al-Haqq; the fatwa is translated and analyzed in Jansen, *The Neglected Duty*; see p. 59 on the Khawarij in particular.
26. Mernissi, *Islam and Democracy*, p. 27.
27. Ibid., p. 36.
28. See, for example, Frank, *Creation and the Cosmic System*, p. 9 et passim.
29. See the passage on "Theology and the Common People" (*al-ʻawwam*) in al-Jahiz, *Kitab al-ʻuthmaniyya*, ed. Abd al-Salem Muhammad Harun Harun (Cairo, 1955), translated in Pellat, *The Life and Works of Jahiz*, p. 79. For al-Ghazali's view, see Watt, *Muslim Intellectual*, esp. chs. 5 and 7.
30. See van Ess, "Une lecture à rebours de l'histoire du Muʻtazilisme," pp. 210, 228, et passim.
31. The preferred spelling among many Egyptians of the name "Hasan" is Hassan.
32. A brief synopsis of Muruwwa's analysis of the Muʻtazila is given by Issa J. Boullata, *Trends and Issues in Contemporary Arab Thought*, pp. 35–40.
33. Biographical information on Hassan Hanafi is found in Boullata, *Trends and Issues*, pp. 40–45.
34. The Ikhwan was founded early in the twentieth century by Hasan al-Banna' (1906–1949), a follower of Muhammad ʻAbduh who became persuaded that the social and political problems of Egyptians and Muslims generally must be addressed by a return to the Qur'an and Sunna of the Prophet, the common agenda of Hanbali traditionalism. By mid-century the Ikhwan had become widely influential in the Arab world and heavily persecuted by state governments. The basic study on the Ikhwan is Mitchell, *The Society of the Muslim Brothers*.
35. Hanafi, "Qira'at al-nass" (Reading the text).
36. Hanafi, *La phénomenologie de l'éxègse: essai d'une herméneutique existentielle à partir du Nouveau Testament* (Cairo: Anglo-Egyptian Bookshop, 1988 [Sorbonne, 1966]).
37. Hanafi, "Qira'at al-nass," pp. 10–11.
38. See, for example, Said, "Opponents, Audiences, Constituencies, and Community."
39. Hanafi, "Qira'at al-nass," p. 10.
40. Ibid., pp. 7–8.
41. The problem and the three methodological fronts are explained further in Hanafi, *Muqaddima fi 'ilm al- istighrab* (Introduction to Occidentalism), pp. 9–22.
42. The thesis of the book is stated in the Introduction, and dramatically summarized on p. 239.
43. 2 vols. (Damascus: Institut Français de Damas, 1964).
44. 5 vols. (Cairo: Maktaba Madbuli, n.d.).
45. At one point in the meeting, traditionalist participants demanded that Professor Hanafi, one of the conveners, preface a session by pronouncing a religious formula,

Hanafi declined, taking the position that it was an academic meeting about religion, not a religious meeting as such. This was a troublesome point for the Islamiyun.

46. The work *al-Usuliyya al-islamiyya* is discussed by Juan Eduardo Campo, "The Ends of Islamic Fundamentalism: Hegemonic Discourse and the Islamic Question in Egypt," in a paper presented at the American Academy of Religion, Washington, DC, November 1993, and published in *Contention* 4 (1995): 167–194.

47. Lone, "Heresy in Egypt?" p. 8.

48. Personal communications by each scholar during separate visits to Emory University in November, 1996.

49. Quoted by Lone, "Heresy in Egypt?" p. 8.

50. In the spring of 1997, as this book entered the editorial process, Professor Hassan Hanafi was charged by Yahya Ibrahim, a professor at al-Azhar University and General Secretary of the Islamist movement known as Jabhat Ulama al-Azhar (the Azhar Ulama front), with being a *murtadd*, "apostate." The price for apostasy can be death. The Egyptian press (followed later by Middle Eastern, European and even American press coverage) immediately ran numerous articles on the charge and several interviews with the accuser. The Jabhat Ulama al-Azhar is also associated with Nasr Hamid Abu Zayd's case and with the assassination in 1991 of the anti-Islamist writer, Faraj Fuda. When we asked Professor Hanafi during a visit to Egypt in June 1997 whether or not he would leave Egypt, at least for a while, to avoid possible violence against him, he said he probably would not. "If I leave after a life of teaching and writing about interpreting Islam in the present circumstances," he said, "what message will that send to modern Muslims and especially to my younger colleagues and students who must learn to engage extremist Islamic forces in the public marketplace of ideas, or be forced to acquiesce?"

eleven

The Implications *of* Modernity: Deconstructing *the* Argument

We began this work with the observation that few modernist scholars have actually identified themselves as Mu'tazila. Harun Nasution is among the few in modern times who have. Nonetheless, many Muslim critics of Islamist traditionalism have appropriated selected aspects of Mu'tazilism, particularly the emphasis on rationalism, vague as that term has proved to be. This suggests that Mu'tazilism has come to serve not so much as a doctrinal resource for constructing particular arguments against contemporary forms of traditionalism, but, rather, as a symbol of the will to be Islamic in a modern, pluralist world in which Muslims share social and political space with other confessional communities, as well as with secularism. What are the implications of this looking backward, not with nostalgia for the pristine Muslim *umma* of the time of the Prophet and the first four "rightly guided" caliphs (*rashidun*) of Sunni Islam, as traditionalist reform has persistently envisioned, but rather to the intellectual ferment of *kalam* making the Islamic case boldly among non-Muslim scriptuaries, philosophers, and critics of religion? The purpose of this concluding chapter is to explore that question as a means both to conclude the present work and to suggest a need to go beyond it.

Fundamentalism, Mu'tazilism, and Modernity

One of the implications, we have argued, has been to interrogate the general proposition that Islamist reform movements (Islamic fundamentalism) should be understood primarily as contemporary Muslim responses to modernity and secularization. We are particularly concerned with the bolder claim that without modernity there can be no fundamentalism. We believe that many recent scholars of comparative religious fundamentalism have constructed a faulty *modus ponens* argument which runs something like the following: if there is modernity, then it will cause religions to react like X (fundamentalism); many religions react like X; therefore, they are reacting to modernity. Our move has been to try to show that fundamentalism is a species of what we have called "traditionalism" and that traditionalism historically has reacted to religious rationalism and pluralism, not just in modern times. In making this argument, we do not wish to deny that the Enlightenment and the social and intellectual processes of secularization have had an effect on world religions, or that fundamentalist movements can be fully understood without taking into account the effects of modernity. Rather, our purpose has been to focus attention on the role of theological rationalism, in particular Mu'tazilism, and more recently modernism, in Islamic thought.

We have offered as devices for rethinking these issues two Mu'tazili texts, 'Abd al-Jabbar's *Kitab al-usul al-khamsa* from the Middle Ages and Harun Nasution's *Kaum Mu'tazilah dan Pandangan Rasionalanya* from the past generation. These texts can be seen as expressions of a form of theological "rationalism" that throughout history has defined itself doctrinally in opposition to several theological stances, especially what we have called theological "traditionalism." We have shown that Mu'tazilism has had discernible influence on Islamic modernist and postmodernist thinkers, just as Hanbali traditionalism has greatly influenced premodern and modern reformist movements of a more fundamentalist type.

In concluding the present work, we are obliged to deconstruct, in order to modify, the rationalism/traditionalism dichotomy we have drawn for the sake of argument so sharply in previous chapters. Having presented a case for a rationalist/traditionalist struggle at various moments in Islamic history, including the present, to shape public theology in Islamicate civilization, we must now return to the question bracketed earlier: what influence has modernity had on this historical debate among Muslim intellectuals? To what extent does modernity make Harun Nasution's debate with opponents of Mu'tazilism in Indonesia today different from 'Abd al-Jabbar's dispute with the Ash'ariya and Hanbaliya in the late tenth century?

The Rationalism/Traditionalism Debate in a New Key

Marshall Hodgson has termed the historical moment of Western cultural transformation into modernity the "Great Western Transmutation" (G.W.T.).[1] His analysis bears upon this study, because he raised the question of the influence of modernity upon the Islamic world in comparative, global terms. In social and political terms, the G.W.T. was marked not only by the dramatic occurrences of the Industrial and the French Revolutions. More decisively for the Muslim world, he argues, "about 1800 the Occidental peoples (together with the Russians) found themselves in a position to dominate the lands of Islamdom. The same generation that saw the Industrial and French Revolutions saw a third and almost equally unprecedented event: the establishment of European world hegemony."[2]

Until the eighteenth century, the various agrarian civilizations of Africa and Asia had maintained a certain parity of economic, social and cultural development. By the end of the eighteenth century, Hodgson explains in the third volume of *The Venture of Islam*, "we come to changes that are qualitatively different from those we have studied hitherto. Henceforth the gap in development between one part of the world and all the rest becomes decisive, and we must understand its character in order to understand anything else."[3] Our concern here is with the impact of this "gap" on religion in particular. We do well to recall that the impact of modernity on traditional religion was not only seismic in the non-Western world, but also, and initially, in Christian Europe in the decades following 1800.

The impact of modernity on the world religions has been the focus of secularization theory in the social sciences. Peter Berger defines secularization as "the process by which sectors of society and culture are removed from the domination of religious institutions and symbols."[4] It began in modern times with the Treaty of Westphalia in 1648, when the brutality of religious wars between Protestants and Catholics resulted in the removal of property from the ecclesiastical control that had exacerbated the conflict. Secularization was also a term used to describe the process of a cleric leaving holy orders and returning to the "world." As the Enlightenment progressed, secularization took on the meaning, in Berger's words, of

> an overall decline in the importance and credibility of religion, both in the institutional order of society and within the consciousness of individuals. To some extent this [secularization] theory can be seen as a continuation of ideas rooted in the European Enlightenment of the 17th and 18th centuries, ideas that identified the progress of reason with the decline of religion.[5]

Finally, secularization took on constructive significance in the historical absence of God for theologians like Dietrich Bonhoeffer during the Holocaust, and later for theologians like Harvey Cox who, as Berger put it, "hailed it as a realization of crucial motifs of Christianity itself."[6]

For many secularization theorists, and hence for the concomitant development of modernization theory, the secularization of religious civilizations was seen as a necessary first phase of modern economic and social development. In order to become "modern" it was argued – and the history of Europe in the seventeenth and eighteenth centuries seemed to bear this out, especially in the analyses of Max Weber – societies governed by the institutions and traditional religious worldviews must ineluctably cede ground in large measure to secular institutions and scientific worldviews. Classical secularization theory can be described as the hypothesis of an inverse ratio of religion and tradition to science and modernity. Secularization theory has come under increasing criticism in more recent times by those scholars who argue that the data of Islam in modern times are remarkably resistant to explanation by secularization and modernization theory. Of course, as our quotation from Mary Douglas at the beginning of the last chapter suggests, social scientists (and we would add historians of religion) were largely unprepared to account for the resurgence of traditional religion globally during the past two decades.[7] They have been scrambling ever since to develop theories of modernity and secularization that can account for the existence, indeed the resurgence, of renewed religious identity among modern urban peoples. Nonetheless, the claim that Islam, or any religion, is unique in some particular regard and therefore resistant to explanation by comparison to others must always be suspect to the historian of religion.[8]

Ernest Gellner has given an interesting spin on this problem recently, arguing that Islam is, uniquely among the world religions, resistant to secularization. "[I]n Islam," Gellner stated, "we see a pre-industrial faith, a founded, doctrinal, world religion in the proper sense, which, at any rate for the time being, totally and effectively defies the secularization thesis."[9] During the onslaught of modernity, many nations and peoples have found themselves to be underdeveloped economically and weak militarily, e.g. France in the eighteenth century; Germany at the beginning of the nineteenth century, Russia later in the nineteenth century. "The dilemma such countries face is," as Gellner poses the question for Muslims, "should we emulate those whom we wish to equal in power (thereby spurning our own tradition), or should we, on the contrary, affirm the values of our own tradition, even at the price of material weakness?"[10] The national traditions he refers to are not religious ones as such – Christendom or Judaism – but local cultural ones that differentiate the French, Germans, Slavs, and so on, and that fueled various European nationalisms. Alone among the underdeveloped countries of the past two centuries (Gellner compares Islam as such to countries and nations in Europe and the Third World), Islam

> recommended neither the emulation of the West, nor idealization of some folk virtue and wisdom. It commended a *return* to, or a more rigorous observance of, *High* Islam. Admittedly this was linked to the historically perhaps questionable assumption that High Islam had once dominated and pervaded the whole society, and also that it was identical with *early* Islam, with the teaching and practice of the Prophet and his Companions.[11]

In other words, Gellner believes that Islamic reform movements and responses to modernity and the West, *alone* among the world religions, are driven by efforts to recover their own pristine success in world history. Secularization is not possible in this model of a response to economic and military challenges from the West. "Islam is the Answer," as the popular phrase announces on posters and graffiti throughout the Muslim world.

The weakness of Gellner's argument lies in his monolithic conception of Islam, a mistake he partly shares with Samuel P. Huntington, who is willing to abandon the political analysis of nationalisms in favor of focusing on the deep cultural fissures that separate world civilizations (religions).[12] Gellner is also not willing to differentiate among the Islamic reform movements in Iran, Egypt, Indonesia, and in countries like South Africa where Islam is an active minority in a pluralistic, secular society. More tellingly, in characterizing Islamic thought, Gellner only takes into consideration the Islamist reform movements that are driven by a putative model of "High" Islam in the Age of the Prophet and first three generations of righteous followers. On the other side, his view of "rationalist fundamentalism," which he favors, is formed entirely by post-Kantian, Western thought, not by any intellectual resources he finds in Islamic intellectual history, past or present. That Muhammad 'Abduh and other critics of Islamic traditionalism have drawn on Mu'tazilism in reinterpreting Islam for modern times seems to have been lost on Gellner, as it has been lost on all too many Western interpreters of modern Islam.

Let us recall that Shaykh Muhammad 'Abduh contended at the end of the nineteenth century that science and reason on the one side and religion and the Qur'an on the other could not be in essential conflict. In chapter 6, we quoted Shaykh 'Abduh on science and revelation in Islam – a statement that was made in the shadow of debates that had raged in Europe since the publication of Darwin's *Origin of Species*. Consider again 'Abduh's position:

[W]e Muslims are fortunately under no necessity of disputing with science or the findings of medicine regarding the corrections of a few traditional interpretations [of the Qur'an]. The Kur'an itself is too elevated in character to be in opposition to science.[13]

That most Muslims were not yet ready to accept this claim or all of its implications in the last decades of the nineteenth century is beside the point. Neither were most Europeans vis à vis Christianity and post-Darwinian assertions by the growing scientific community. The point is that 'Abduh and some of his followers saw the theological need to rescue religion from the dangerous position of challenging modernity, thus risking being destructed by it.

A growing tendency among modernist Muslims, following 'Abduh, has been to locate the source of the conflict of modern science with religion not in revelation per se, but rather in tradition (*taqlid*), that is, in the traditional interpretations of the Qur'an that have been given precedence by the ulama. Freeing Quranic truths (which equal scientific truths in the modernist construction) from traditional interpretations has amounted to challenging the authority of the traditional ulama. Contemporary traditionalists (Islamists, the Muslim Brotherhood, Hizbullah, Islamic Jihad) have also challenged the authority of the traditional ulama, as we have seen. Contemporary Islamists, like their medieval counterparts, have challenged those who would govern Muslim societies by anything but Islamic principles (*usul*), often accusing the ulama of political quietism and accommodation to governments run by lapsed Muslims and infidels.[14]

Thus, the rationalism/traditionalism debate in contemporary Islam, as in the ninth to eleventh centuries, is a deeply political one involving power and authority. In chapter 1 we characterized Mu'tazili rationalists and Hanbali traditionalists as "contrary and conflicting trends that formed on opposite edges of Islamicate society and sought to influence the religious, intellectual, and political center."[15] It would be wrong to conclude from such a schematized comparison, however, that the historical and political realities of these relationships have always been balanced and symmetrical. In the ninth century, Mu'tazili influence within the Abbasid court in Baghdad brought about a strong Hanbali populist reaction. That conflict was stabilized somewhat in the tenth and eleventh centuries, with the growing patronage and influence of Shafi'i (and Hanafi) *fiqh* and of Ash'ari and Maturidi kalam, but it was not resolved. An important claim of this book is that the theological conflict between rationalism and traditionalism has never been finally resolved, even with the decline of Mu'tazilism after the eleventh century.

The historic ability of traditionalism to appeal more broadly across Islamic society than rationalism could, especially in times of political instability, is evident in the Islamic world today. Nonetheless, as we have shown above, especially in chapters 6–10, the rationalist critique of extreme forms of traditionalism is also heard in the public marketplace of ideas in the Islamic world. It remains to be seen whether or not thinkers like Harun Nasution, Nurcholish Madjid, Hassan Hanafi and Mohammed Arkoun can spark a more popular neo- or post-Mu'tazili, rationalist theological and political movement that can successfully compete with traditionalism in Islamic public discourse. Clearly, the case of Nasr Abu Zayd does not bode well for the success of Mu'tazili ideas when they are used in direct confrontation with traditionalist ideas and with traditional institutions such as the ulama and some faculties at universities in Islamic states. Nonetheless, largely outside the purview of Islam "watchers" among pundits and public policy academics, the authors have found that the Nasr Abu Zayd case is being discussed with considerable interest among some Muslim intellectuals. There is considerable evidence that the relevance of Mu'tazilism for Islam today is debated far beyond the select works we have reviewed in earlier chapters.

Other People's Texts

In chapter 1 we located the *raison d'être* of this essay in the general context of modern scholarship, not only in relation to studies of comparative religious fundamentalism, but also in relation to nineteenth-century *Religionswissenschaft* and Orientalism. Together with nineteenth-century biblical criticism, these are among the most important intellectual influences that produced today's history of religions scholarship. In these final pages of the book, we want to return to the implications of post-Mu'tazili rationalism for history of religious scholarship. Modern Muslim defenders of the general spirit of Mu'tazili rationalism, such as 'Abduh, Hanafi, Mernissi and Arkoun, have read Western critical scholarship on sacred texts and the comparative study of religions. This leads us to wonder: what effect will modern literary and historical criticism in the hands of Muslim modernists have on history of religions scholarship? To answer that question definitively would require at least another book and other points of view than our own. This concluding chapter brings us to the recent scholarship on kalam which suggests that medieval Islamicate society developed what one scholar has called a "Muslim comparative religion." [16] Only the eleventh-century Cluniac reforms, which generated an impressive effort to translate the sacred Islamic Arabic corpus of texts into Latin on the eve of the Crusades, were at all comparable in medieval Christendom.[17] The role of the Mu'tazila in the ninth to eleventh centuries in studying, analyzing and disputing with other religions was more general and more open actually to entering into rule-bound disputes with non-Muslim intellectuals and religious leaders. In terms of a "theology of the other," the religious (but not secularized) pluralism of medieval Islamicate civilization was different from the relationship of Christianity to Judaism and other religions within the Holy Roman Empire.

If we compare the projects of Orientalism and *Religionswissenschaft* with Protestant scholarship in biblical textual and historical criticism,[18] an important difference emerges. Biblical critics like Hermann Gunkel and Julius Wellhausen were scholars within the Protestant Christian tradition. The texts they deconstructed and analyzed – the books of the Hebrew Bible – were in an important sense "their" texts, although many of their fellow religionists were critical of what they did with these texts. The considerable tumult that was caused within European and North American Christendom by biblical criticism was largely an intraconfessional debate: Christian (and eventually Jewish) intellectuals criticizing Christian and Jewish sacred texts.

Religionswissenschaft and Orientalism, on the other side, have dealt largely with the sacred texts of non-European religious traditions, such as Hinduism, Buddhism, Islam, and Confucianism. The great Sacred Books of the East project under the direction of Friedrich Max Müller, to which we referred in chapter 1, also sought to reestablish critically an *Urtext* behind the "uncritical" texts of scriptures that were employed by traditional believers in premodern (and modern) times for everyday liturgical purposes. In a sense, *Religionswissenschaft* and Orientalism took possession of the sacred texts of other peoples, dissected them, reassembled them in critical editions, and translated them into European languages, thus adding them to the libraries and curricula of universities throughout the Western and the colonial world. What seemed like a natural and important application of post-Enlightenment Western textual methods in one tradition (Western Protestant Christendom) to the texts of other religious civilizations turned out to be perceived in the Islamic world, as well as among postmodern critics like Edward Said, as an enormous act of hegemonic scholarship. Ironically perhaps, as van der Veer and others have contended (see chapter 1), Muslims and others have begun to repossess their sacred texts. As a result, the interpretation and political use of the Qur'an and the Sunna, in part as a result of Orientalist scholarship, is no longer under the complete control of the ulama, which may be an example of the law of unintended consequences.

The question we again raise at the conclusion of this study is this: was this act of hegemonic scholarship something new in the history of religion?

Was the appropriation and editorial transformation of other people's sacred texts – the project of Orientialism – simply another cultural byproduct of the condition of modernity, which Europe foisted on the rest of the world after 1800? The answer, we have argued in the earlier chapters of this book, is a qualified no. Other people's texts, we have shown, were also a concern of the Mu'tazili *mutakallimun*, but certainly not only the mutakallimun, in the history of the interaction of traditional religious civilizations. Al-Biruni's (d. 1050) widely acclaimed studies of Indian religions and cultures were written and circulated during the generation after 'Abd al-Jabbar.[19] The mutakallimun wrote extensive and detailed heresiographies of sects and religions they encountered across the vast territories under Islamic rule and beyond. The best known is that by the Ash'ari mutakallim Muhammad al-Shahrastani (d. 1153), *The Book of Religions and Sects*.[20] Our concern in these pages, however, has been specifically with the kalam genre and the engagement of the mutakallimun with theological issues.

Kalam, the general term for theological discourse in medieval Islamicate society, became a way of negotiating critical theological differences across confessional communities within Islamic society as well as among Muslims belonging to different *madhhabs*. The mutakallimun – far more than the jurists (*fuqaha*) and other members of the ulama – had created a discourse that effectively shaped the articulation of Jewish and Christian thought within Islamicate society. The dominant discourse had been defined by Muslim mutakallimun, primarily the Mu'tazila. The texts under examination in the kalam project included primarily, but not exclusively, those of Muslims, Christians, Jews, and Zoroastrians. The thrust of the kalam project was to make rational sense of other people's texts, in order to position one's own textual tradition authoritatively in relation to others. Utter rejection and complete acceptance of other people's texts were only the most extreme moves made by Muslims when they found themselves confronted by "Peoples of the Book" in medieval Islamicate civilization. Qualified acceptance of "the other" in order to dispute significant differences was much closer to the theological agenda of the mutakallimun.

Recently, Steven Wasserstrom has made this case with respect to the hermeneutical principle of *ta'wil*, the principle of interpreting sacred texts. Originally, ta'wil was a term for Gnostic and esoteric interpretations of the Qur'an employed by extreme Shi'i groups to subvert the more literal Quranic worldview purveyed by the caretakers of the Islamic textual tradition, the Sunni ulama. If ta'wil was originally esoteric and not open to unguided readings of the text of the Qur'an, it was nonetheless able to bridge some sectarian differences. Marshall Hodgson observed that "[w]hat *ta'wil* did accomplish was to replace what seemed a 'naive' Kur'anic worldview with a more 'sophisticated' intellectual system, one which seemed to go beyond the superficial differences among the quarreling religious communities with their incompatible dogmatic claims, to reach a profounder common truth." [21]

The Mu'tazila turned ta'wil into a polemical enterprise, as we explained in chapter 4 above (pp. 68f.), by using reason to establish allegorical interpretations. Among their aims was to avoid nonsensical meanings of passages interpreted literally by the traditionalists. The allegorical method was used to interpret those passages in the Qur'an designated by Muslim exegetes as obscure verses (*mutashabihat*). More generally, the Mu'tazila argued for the rational meanings of sacred texts, Qur'an and Hadith, as warrants for the doctrines such as *khalq al-qur'an* that distinguished them from their opponents. Again, ta'wil or allegorical meaning served this purpose well. Moreover, other theological communities within ninth-century Islamicate society were soon negotiating their identities and differences within this discourse. Wasserstrom argues:

> What is so striking about this form of "allegorical" interpretation is that it was actively used by established groups in their polemics against each other. So powerful was it found to be that Jewish, Muslim, and Christian leaders all used it. Indeed, there was a moment in the ninth and tenth centuries in which Rabbanite and Karaite Jews, Coptic Christians, and Zaydi and Twelver Shi'ites, along with Sunni theologians, all used Mu'tazilite ta'wil. All these establishment leaders utilized this technique to defend the rationality of their own scriptures and to attack the irrationality of their opponents' scriptures. [22]

As an essay in the history of religions, one purpose of this study of Mu'tazili rationalism has been to make the case that Orientalism and *Religionswissenschaft* should be viewed in a much larger comparative world history of theological and scholarly concern with other people's texts. Specifically, we have shown that in the ninth to eleventh centuries, the mutakallimun constructed a discourse for negotiating sectarian and confessional differences based on textual arguments. As the Mu'tazili kalam project went into decline in the eleventh century in the Islamic world, a medieval Christian theological interest in Muslim texts arose under the able guidance of Peter the Venerable in France.

Both the kalam and the Cluniac projects were rigorous by the standards of their local scholarly institutions, and both were deeply theological in intent and articulation. What made Protestant biblical criticism, and subsequently Orientalism, different, was the boldly secular and historicist worldview of nineteenth-century textual criticism. That was the new challenge, not only to Muslim (and Christian) traditionalists, but also to rationalists and modernists. Neither could avoid confronting this challenge. Contemporary scholars like Martin Marty and Bruce Lawrence have led the academy in the attempt to explain and interpret what they call fundamentalism(s) and what we have called traditionalism. The vital importance of also understanding the modernist/rationalist responses – to modernity and to traditionalism – is the burden of our project, to which we hope others will contribute, including their criticisms.

In one way or another, each of the modernists we have discussed has tried to assess the relevance of Mu'tazili theological rationalism to modern secular criticism. Is Islamic rationalism an authentic Islamic warrant for historical and literary criticism of the Qur'an and the Sunna? Are modernity, secularization, historical and textual criticism to be welcomed as means of religious liberation, or should they be feared as agents of the destruction of religion?

This last question, we suggest, is the heart of the debate. If the modern, and indeed postmodern, conditions of this debate are relatively new in the Muslim world, the debate itself is neither new nor particularly Islamic. The two cultural moods of the debate – rationalism and traditionalism – have been present throughout Islamic history; indeed, we would argue, in most civilizations in one form or another. That, we hope, has become more clear with respect to Islam in the pages of this book. What is unclear is how this age-old conflict will be resolved under the conditions of modernity and postmodernity. More research is needed on such questions. Certainly at this stage of our knowledge of present trends, one outcome seems plausible: that the legacy of Mu'tazili rationalism will continue to serve as a catalyst for mounting Islamic alternatives to strident forms of traditionalism.

Notes

1. Hodgson, The *Venture of Islam*, 3: 176–222.
2. Ibid., 3: 177.
3. Ibid, 3: 176.
4. Berger, *The Sacred Canopy*, p.107.
5. Berger, "Religion and Modernity," p. 2.
6. Berger, *The Sacred Canopy*, p. 106.
7. Chapter 10 above, p. 199 and note 1.
8. This point is argued cogently by Jonathan Z. Smith, *Drudgery Divine*, chapter 2, pp. 36–53.

9. Gellner, *Postmodernism, Reason and Religion,* p. 18.

10. Ibid., p. 19.

11. Ibid.

12. See Huntington, "The Clash of Civilization?" pp. 22–49. Huntington goes beyond Gellner in seeing civilizations more generally as replacing all nationalisms as the highest and broadest category of social allegiance and identity in post-Cold War conflicts.

13. From *al-Manar* 9: 334–335; quoted and translated by Adams in *Islam and Modernism in Egypt,* p. 138.

14. This is clearly stated in 'Abd al-Salam Faraj's radical traditionalist treatise, *al-Farida al-gha'iba* (The neglected duty [i.e., jihad]), and answered from a staunchly traditional point of view by the Chief Mufti of Egypt, Jadd al-Haqq 'Ali Jadd al-Haqq; translated and analyzed by Johannes J. G. Jansen, *The Neglected Duty.*

15. See above, chapter 1, p. 12.

16. Wasserstrom, *Between Muslim and Jew,* p. 14 and chapter 4 generally.

17. A good discussion of the reforms at Cluny on the eve of the Crusades is Kritzeck, *Peter the Venerable and Islam.*

18. A succinct discussion of the methods of "lower" (textual) and "higher" (historical) criticism in nineteenth-century Old Testament studies, which preceded New Testament criticism, is given in the Editor's Introduction by J. Coert Rylaarsdam to Tucker, *Form Criticism of the Old Testament,* pp. iii–viii.

19. See al-Biruni, *Alberuni's India.*

20. See the excellent study by Bruce B. Lawrence, *Shahrastani on the Indian Religions.*

21. Marshall G. S. Hodgson, "Batiniyya," *EI²,* cited in Wasserstrom, *Between Muslim and Jew,* p. 139.

22. Wasserstrom, *Between Muslim and Jew,* pp. 142–143.

Glossary

'adl, justice; in Islamic theology *al-'adl* is the technical term for divine justice or theodicy.

ahl al-kitab, People of the Book, scriptuaries, such as Christians and Jews, who are recognized in the Qur'an and in Islamic law as comprising acceptable confessional communities under Islamic rule.

Ash'ariya, Ash'arites; the orthodox *kalam madhhab* in Sunni Islam that traces its doctrines to Abu l-Hasan al-Ash'ari (d. 935).

'aql, reason; rationalism in Islam thought.

dar al-islam, the Abode of Islam, a legal concept in the Shari'a that denoted land under Islamic rule, as compared to *dar al-harb*, the Abode of War (lands potentially or actually in conflict with Muslim lands) and *dar al-sulh*, the Abode of Peace (lands with which Muslim rulers have temporary treaties of nonbeligerence).

da'wa, call, propaganda, proselytizing; the invitation to accept Islam that many traditionalist Muslims believe must be extended to non-Muslims.

fatwa, a nonbinding legal interpretation of the Shari'a.

fiqh, legal reasoning; disciplined reflection on the sources and foundations of the Shari'a (see *usul al-fiqh*).

fitna, disruption within the Muslim *umma* resulting from religious conflict.

Hadith, a saying or collection of sayings attributed to Muhammad that relates, on the authority of his immediate companions and the next two generations, what the Prophet approved or disapproved of in the behavior of the community. Along with the Qur'an, Hadith are considered to be sacred texts in Islam.

Hanbaliya, Hanbalites; the traditionalist followers of Ahmad ibn Hanbal (d. 855).

ijma', consensus within the community, especially among the ulama of a particular school of law, on the interpretation of the Shari'a.

ijtihad, independent reasoning; the exercise of the considered, independent judgment of individual Muslims, especially jurists, in interpreting the Shari'a; see also *taqlid*, its antonym.

'ilm, knowledge, science, discipline, such as *'ilm al-kalam*, theology.

imam, religious leader, such as one who leads the prayer or who is recognized as an authoritative teacher.

Imam, 'Ali ibn Abi Talib, the cousin and son-in-law of the Prophet Muhammad and those of 'Ali's descendants who are recognized among the Shi'a as sources of religious authority in addition to the Qur'an and Sunna (see Shi'a).

islamiyun, Islamists, contemporary traditionalist Muslims, sometimes referred to as fundamentalists, who seek to make the Shari'a the highest and most pervasive authority in Islamic states.

isnad, the chain of authorities who transmit religious information. An identifiable *isnad* of reliable oral transmitters is considered by traditional Muslims to be the condition *sine qua non* of an authentic Hadith.

kafir, an unbeliever, one who has *kufr*, lit., ingratitude toward God. The antonym is *mu'min*, believer.

kalam, speech, as in *kalam Allah*, the speech of God. In Islamic thought *'ilm al-kalam* or simply *kalam* means theological discourse.

madhhab, school or habit of thought and practice in Islam.

madrasa, school for educating Muslims in the religious sciences, such as law, Qur'an, Hadith and Arabic language. Madrasas are often associated with larger complexes that include a mosque, library, and sometimes dormitories.

mihna, trial; the inquisition instituted by Caliph al-Ma'mun in 833 and lasting until 850, in which state-appointed religious authorities, such as qadis, were required to subscribe to al-Ma'mun's view that the Qur'an was created or be imprisoned.

mu'min, a believer, one who has *iman*, "faith." Compare the term *muslim*, "one who submits to God." The antonym is *kafir*, unbeliever.

mutakallim/un, a speaker, one who speaks about divine matters, a theologian.

qada, divine decree; often used as a synonym of *qadar*.

qadar, God's power to determine events. The Qadariya or Qadarism held that human beings have the power (*qudra*) to perform their own acts and must bear responsibility for them in the eyes of God. This position, which was refined and defended by the Mu'tazila, was opposed by the Ash'ariya and orthodox *madhabs*, who held a doctrine of divine predestination.

qadi, judge; in early and medieval Islam, the qadi was appointed by the political ruler to administer Islamic law on behalf of the state.

qiyas, analogy, reasoning by analogy from the text of the Qur'an and/or Sunna to present circumstances; one of the four *usul al-fiqh.*

Salafiya, a movement among traditionalist Muslims that urges the emulation of the *salaf,* the first generations of Muslims, as opposed to urging that Islam be adapted to changing historical circumstances.

sharh, commentary on a text other than the Qur'an, such as legal (*fiqh*) and theological (*kalam*) works.

Shari'a, the sacred law for Muslims, derived from the divine revelation (Qur'an) and prophetic example (Sunna) through the interpretive activities of the ulama.

Shi'a, partisans; those who believe Muhammad passed on his authority to his cousin and son-in-law, 'Ali ibn Abi Talib. The three major Shi'i communities are Imami or Ithna 'Ashari (Twelvers), Isma'ili (Seveners), and the Zaydi (Fivers), named for the number of Imams each community believes belonged to the common 'Alid line.

Sunna, the path or example of the Prophet Muhammad, which all Muslims seek to emulate in response to the requirements of the Shari'a.

taqlid, blind acceptance of the authority of a religious teacher or school of thought; in modern Islam, *taqlid* connotes tradition, following tradition.

tafsir, commmentary on the Qur'an, usually verse by verse and traditionally written in the margins of the Qur'an texts. Cf. *sharh.*

tawhid, unity; the divine unicity of God's being; a fundamental doctrine of *'ilm al-kalam.*

ulama, a plural form of *'alim*; one who pursues knowledge in the religious sciences of Islam. The ulama are the religious notables of the Muslim *umma.*

umma, community, confessional community, where the Shari'a is recognized and enforced.

usul al-din, fundamentals of religion; the organization of Islamic theology or *'ilm al-kalam* around fundamental issues such as God's unity and justice.

usul al-fiqh, fundamentals of Islamic jurisprudence, accepted by most Sunni Muslims as Qur'an, Sunna, consensus, and reasoning by analogy; and by Shi'i Muslims as including the teachings of the Imams.

Bibliography

References

Brockelmann, Carl. *Geschichte der arabischen Literatur.* 2 vols., 3 supplements. Leiden: E. J. Brill, 1996 [1936–1942].

Encyclopaedia Iranica. Edited by Ehsan Yarshater. London and Boston: Routledge & Kegan Paul, 1982–.

Encyclopaedia of Islam, 2nd edition. Edited by J. Kramers et al. Leiden: E. J. Brill, 1954–.

Encyclopedia of Religion. Editor-in-chief Mircea Eliade. 16 vols. New York: Macmillan, 1987.

Nadim, Muhammad ibn Ishaq, al-. *Fihrist of al-Nadim: A Tenth-Century Survey of Muslim Culture.* Translated by Bayard Dodge. 2 vols. New York: Columbia University Press, 1970.

Sezgin, Fuat. *Geschichte des arabischen Schrifttums.* 9 vols. Leiden: E. J. Brill, 1967–.

Shorter Encyclopaedia of Islam. Ithaca, N.Y.: Cornell University Press, 1953.

Primary Textual Materials

'Abd al-Jabbar, Abu l-Hasan. *Fadl al-i'tizal wa tabaqat al-mu'tazila.* In one volume with section from Abu l-Qasim al-Balkhi, *Maqalat al-Islamiyin,* and al-Hakim al-Jushami, *Kitab sharh al'uyun.* Edited by Fu'ad Sayyid. Tunis: al-Dar al-Tunisiya lil-Nashr, 1986.

——*Al-Mughni fi abwab al-tawhid wa l-'adl.* General editor, Taha Husayn. 16 of 20 volumes to date. Cairo: Dar al-Misriyah li l-Ta'lif wa-l-Nashr, 1961-1974.

——*Al-Mukhtasar fi usul al-din,* 2nd edition. Edited by Muhammad 'Amara. Cairo: Dar al-Shuruq, 1988.

——*Bayan Mutashabih al-qur'an.* Edited by 'Adnan Muhammed Zarzur. 2 parts in 1 vol. Cairo: Dar al-Turath, 1969.

——*Sharh al-usul al-khamsa.* Edited by 'Abd al-Karim 'Uthman. Cairo: Maktaba Whaba,1965. (Identified by Daniel Gimaret as *Ta'liq 'ala sharh al-usul al-khamsa* and now attributed to Manekdim.)

——*Tathbit dala'il al-nubuwwa*. Edited by 'Abd al-Karim 'Uthman. 2 vols. Beirut: Dar al-'Arabiya, 1966.

'Abduh, Muhammad. *Hashiya 'ala sharh al-Diwani li l-'aqa'id al-'Adudiya*. Edited by Sulayman Dunya in *al-Shaykh Muhammad 'Abduh bayn al-falasifa wa l-kalamiyin*. 2 vols. Dar al-Kutub al-'Arabi: n.pl., 1958.

——*Risalat al-tawhid*. Beirut: Dar Ihya' al-'Ulum, 1986.

——*The Theology of Unity*. Translated by Ishaq Musa'ad and Kenneth Cragg. London: George Allen & Unwin, 1966.

'Amara, Muhammad, ed. *Rasa'il al-'adl wa l-tawhid*. 2nd edition. Cairo: Maktabat al-Shuruq, 1988. (A collection of kalam texts, including a longer Mu'tazili creed by 'Abd al-Jabbar.)

Amin, Ahmad. *Fajr al-Islam*. Cairo: Matba'at al-I'timad, 1928.

Ash'ari, Abu l-Hasan, 'Ali b. Isma'il, *al-Ibana 'an usul al-diyana* (see Klein, *The Elucidation of Islam's Foundation*).

——*Kitab al-luma'* and *Risala fi istihsan al-khawd fi l-kalam* (See McCarthy, *Theology of al-Ash'ari*).

——*Kitab maqalat al-islamayin*. Edited by Helmut Ritter. 2nd edition. Wiesbaden: Franz Steiner Verlag, 1963.

Augustine. *Confessions*. Translated by Henry Chadwick. Oxford and New York: Oxford University Press, 1991.

Baqillani, Muhammad ibn 'Abd al-Tayyib, al-. *Kitab al-tamhid*. Edited by Richard J. McCarthy. Beruit: al-Maktabat al-Sharqiya, 1957.

Basri, Abu l-Husayn, al-. *Kitab al-mu'tamad fi usul al-fiqh*. Edited by M. Hamidullah, M. Bakr, and H. Hanafi. 2 vols. Damascus: Institut Français de Damas, 1964.

Biruni, Muhammed ibn Ahmad, al-. *Alberuni's India: An Account of the Religion, Philosophy, Literatures, Geography, Chronology, Astronomy, Customs, Laws, and Astrology of India about A.D. 1030*. 2 vols. New Delhi: Atlanta Publishers and Distributers, 1989 [1964].

British Museum Oriental 8613 (Arabic manuscrpt without title or colophon).

Bukhari, Muhammed ibn Isma'il. *Sahih al-Bukhari*. 6 vols. plus indices. Edited with notes by Mustafa Dib al-Bugha. 3rd printing. Damascus and Beirut: Dar Ibn Kathir, 1987.

——*The Translation of the Meanings of Sahih al-Bukhari*. Translated by Muhammad Muhsim Khan. 9 vols. 6th revised edition. Lahore: Kazi Publications, 1983 [1979].

Drewes, G. W. J. *The Admonitions of Seh Bari: A Sixteenth-Century Javanese Muslim Text Attributed to the Saint of Bonan, Re-edited and Translated with an Introduction*. The Hague: Martinus Nijhoff, 1969.

Ghazali, Abu Hamid Muhammad, al-. *Al-Munqidh min al-dalal*. Translated in Watt, *The Faith and Practice of al-Ghazali*, pp. 19–85.

Ibn Hanbal, Ahmad ibn Muhammed. *Al-Musnad.* 19 vols. in 12. Edited by Ahmad Muhammad Shakir. Egypt: Dar al-Ma'arif, 1954.

Ibn Mattawayh, Abu Muhammed. *Kitab al-majmu' fi l-muhit bi l-taklif lil Qadi 'Abd al-Jabbar.* 2 of 4 vols. to date. Vol.1 edited by J. J. Houben (Beirut, 1965) and 'Umar al-Sayyid 'Azma (Beirut: al-Dar al-Misriyya, 1965).

Vol. 2 edited by J. J. Houben and Daniel Gimaret (Beirut: al-Dar al-Machreq, 1981).

——*Al-Tadhkira fi ahkam al-jawahir wa l-a'rad.* Edited by S. N. Lutf and F. B. 'Awn. Cairo, 1975.

Ibn al-Murtada, Ahmad ibn Yahya. *Kitab tabaqat al-mu'tazila. Die Klassen der Mu'taziliten.* Edited by Susanna Diwald-Wilzer. Wiesbaden: Franz Steiner Verlag, 1961.

Khayyat, Abu l-Husayn, al-. *Kitab al-intisar wa l-radd 'ala ibn al-Rawandi al-mulhid.* Edited and translated by Albert Nader. Beirut: Éditions Les Lettres Orientales, 1957.

Klein, Walter C. *The Elucidation of Islam's Foundation.* New Haven, Conn.: American Oriental Society, 1940. (A translation of al-Ash'ari, *al-Ibana 'an usul al-diyana.*)

Manekdin, *Ta'liq 'ala sharh al-usul al-khamsa.* See 'Abd al-Jabbar, *Sharh al-usul al-khamsa.*

Memon, Muhammad Umar. *Ibn Taimiya's Struggle Against Popular Religion.* The Hague: Mouton, 1976. (Includes a loose translation of Ibn Taymiya, *Kitab iqtida' al-sirat al-mustaqim mukhalafat ashab al-jahim.*)

Nashshar, 'Ali Sami, al-. *Nash'at al-fikr al-falsafa fi l-islam.* Cairo (4th impression at Alexandria): Dar al-Ma'arif, 1966.

Nasution, Harun. *Akal dan Wahyu dalam Islam.* Jakarta: University of Indonesia Press, 1986.

——"Filsafat Hidup Rational, Prasyarat bagi Mentalitis Pembangunan." Reprinted in Harun Nasution, *Islam Rasional: Gagasan dan Pemikiran,* pp. 139–146. Jakarta: Mizan, 1995.

——*Islam Rasional: Gagasan dan Pemikiran.* Jakarta: Mizan, 1995.

Nisaburi, Abu Rashid, al-. *Al-Mas'il fi l-khilaf bayn al-basryin wa l-bagh-dadiyin.* Edited by Ridwan al-Sayyid and Ma'n Ziyada. Beirut: Ma'had al-Inma' al-'Arabi, 1979.

Plato. *Euthyphro; Apology; Crito; Phaedo; Phaedrus.* Translated by Harold North Fowler. The Loeb Classical Library. Cambridge, Mass.: Harvard University Press, 1990 [1982].

Qur'an al-karim, al-. *The Meaning of the Glorious Qur'an.* Translated by Marmaduke Pickthall. Interfacing Arabic/English edition. Cairo: Dar al-Kitab al-Masri, 1970.

Shahrastani, Abu l-Fath Muhammad, al-. *Al-Milal wa l-nihal.* Edited by Muhammad Sayyid Kilani. 2 vols. Beirut: Dar Sa'b, 1986.

Subhi, Ahmad Mahmud. *Fi 'ilm al-kalam, dirasa falsafiya: al-mu'tazila, al-ash'ariya, al-shi'a.* Cairo and Alexandria: Dar al-Kutub al-Jami'iya, 1969.

Tafsir al-imamayn al-jalalayn. Cairo: Dar al-Hikma, n.d.

Tirmidhi, Muhammed ibn 'Isa, al-. *Sunan al-Tirmidhi, wa-huwa al-Jami' al-Sahih.* Edited by 'Abd al-Rahman 'Uthman. Medina: Muhammed 'Abd al-Muhsin al-Kibty Press, n.d.

Watt, William Montgomery. *The Faith and Practice of al-Ghazali.* Chicago: Kazi Publications, 1982 [1953].

Secondary Sources

'Abbas, K. H. Siradjuddin. *40 Masalah Agama.* 4 vols. Jakarta: n. p., 1985.

Abdullah, Abdel Rahman. *Pemikiran Umat Islam di Nusantara: Sejarah dan Perkembangannya Hingga Abad Ke-19.* Kuala Lumpur: Dewan Bahasa dan Pustaka Kementrian Pendidikan Malaysia, 1990.

Adams, Charles C. *Islam and Modernism in Egypt: A Study of the Modern Reform Movement Inaugurated by Muhammad 'Abduh.* New York: Russell & Russell, 1968.

Ali, Fachri and Bahtiar Effendy. *Merambah Jalan Baru Islam: Rekonstruksi Pemikiran Islam Masa Orde Baru.* Bandung: Mizan, 1986.

Allard, Michel. *Le problème des attributs divins dans la doctrine d'al-Ašari et de ses premiers grand disciples.* Beirut: Imprimeur catholique, 1965.

Arkoun, Mohammad. *L'Islam, morale et politique.* Paris: Desclée de Brouwer, 1986.

——"Logocentrisme et verité religieuse dans la pensée islamique." *Studia Islamica* 15 (1972): 5–51.

——*Pour une critique de la raison islamique.* Paris: Maisonneuve et Larose, 1984 [1989].

——*Rethinking Islam: Common Questions, Uncommon Answers.* Translated and edited by Robert D. Lee. Boulder, Colo.: Westview Press, 1994 [1989].

Audebert, Claude-France. *Al-Ḫattabi et l'inimitabilité du Coran: traduction et introduction au Bayan I'gaz al-Qur'an.* Damascus: Institut Français de Damas, 1982.

Berger, Peter L. "Religion and Modernity." Paper delivered at the Conference on Religion and Society in the Modern World: Islam in Southeast Asia. Jakarta, 29–31 May 1995.

——*The Sacred Canopy: Elements of a Sociological Theory of Religion.* Garden City: Anchor Books, 1969.

Boland, B. J. *The Struggle of Islam in Modern Indonesia.* The Hague: Martinus Nijhoff, 1971.

Bresnan, John. *Managing Indonesia: The Modern Political Economy.* New York: Columbia University Press, 1993.

Bosworth, E[dmund] C[harles]. *The Medieval Islamic Underworld: The Banu Sasan in Arabic Society and Literature.* 2 vols. Leiden: E. J. Brill, 1976.

Boullata, Issa J. *Trends and Issues in Contemporary Arab Thought.* S.U.N.Y. Series in Middle Eastern Studies. Albany, N.Y.: State University of New York Press, 1990.

Bulliet, Richard W. *Islam: The View from the Edge.* New York: Columbia University Press, 1994.

——*The Patricians of Nishapur: A Study in Medieval Social History.* Cambridge, Mass.: Harvard University Press, 1972.

—— ed. *Under Siege: Islam and Democracy.* The Middle East Institute Columbia University Occasional Papers, 1. New York: Middle East Institute of Columbia University, 1994.

Campo, Juan Eduardo. "The Ends of Islamic Fundamentalism: Hegemonic Discourse and the Islamic Question in Egypt." *Contention* 4 (1995): 167–194.

Carter, Michael G. "Linguistic Science and Orthodoxy in Conflict: The Case of al-Rummani." *Zeitschrift für Geschicte der Arabish-Islamischen Wissenschaft,* 1 (1984): 212–232.

Caspar, Rudi. "Un aspect de la pensée musulmane moderne: le renouveau du Mo'tazilisme." *Mélanges de l'Institut Dominicain d'Études Orientales du Caire* 4 (1957): 141–202.

Denny, Frederick M. "Exegesis and Recitation: Their Development As Classical Forms of Qur'anic Piety." In *Transitions and Transformations in History of Religions: Essays in Honor of Joseph M. Kitagawa.* Edited by Frank Reynolds and Theodore M. Ludwig, pp. 91–123. Leiden: E. J. Brill, 1980.

Dhofier, Zamakhsyari. *Tradisi Pesantren.* 4th edition. Jakarta: L3PES, 1985.

Douglas, Mary. "The Effects of Modernization on Religious Change." *Daedalus* 111/1 (1982): 1–19.

Eickleman, Dale F. "The Art of Memory: Islamic Education and its Social Reproduction." *Comparative Studies in Society and History* 20/4 (1978): 485–516.

Eickelman, Dale and James Piscatori. *Muslim Politics.* Princeton: Princeton University Press, 1996.

Esposito, John L. *The Islamic Threat: Myth or Reality?* New York: Oxford University Press, 1992.

Fachruddin, A. R. *Pak A.R. Menjawab dan 274 Permasalahan dalam Islam.* Edited by Abdul Mulkhan. Yogyakarta: S. I. Press, 1993.

Fakhry, Majid. *A History of Islamic Philosophy.* 2nd edition. New York: Columbia University Press, 1983.

Farrukh, 'Umar. *Ibn Taymiyyah on Public and Private Law in Islam, Or, Public Policy in Islamic Jurisprudence.* Beirut: Khayats, 1966.

Federspiel, Howard. *Muslim Intellectuals and National Development in*

Indonesia. New York: Nova Science Publishers, 1993.

Frank, Richard M. *Beings and Their Attributes: the Teaching of the Basrian School of the Mu'tazila in the Classical Period.* Albany, N. Y.: State University of New York Press, 1978.

——*Creation and the Cosmic System: al-Ghazâlî and Avicenna.* Abhandlungen der Heidelberger Akademie der Wissenschaften, Philosphisch-historische Klasse 1991. Heidelberg: Carl Winter, Universitätsverlag, 1991.

——"The Divine Attributes According to the Teaching of Abul Hudhayl al-'Allaf." *Muséon* 82 (1969): 451–506.

Geertz, Clifford. *Islam Observed: Religious Development in Morocco and Indonesia.* New Haven and London: Yale University Press, 1968.

——*The Religion of Java.* Glencoe: the Free Press, 1960.

Gellner, Ernest. *Postmodernism, Reason and Religion.* London and New York: Routledge, 1992.

Gimaret, Daniel. "Matériaux pour une bibliographie des Ğubba'i." *Journal Asiatique* 264 (1976): 313–317.

——"Matériaux pour une bibliographie des Jubba'i: Note complémentaire." In *Islamic Philosophy and Theology: Studies in Honor of George F. Hourani,* edited by Michael M. Marmura pp. 31–38. State University of New York Press, 1984.

——"Les Usul al-Ḥamsa du Qadi Abd al-Jabbar et Leurs Commentaires." *Annales Islamologiques* 15 (1979): 47–96.

Gochenour II, David Thomas. "The Penetration of Zaydi Islam into Early Medieval Yemen." Ph.D. dissertation, Howard University, 1984.

Griffith, Sidney H. "Comparative Religion in the Apologetics of the First Christian Arabic Theologians." In *Proceedings of the Patristic, Mediaeval and Renaissance Conference.* Villanova, Pa.: Annual Publication of the International Patristic, Mediaeval and Renaissance Conference, 1979.

Haddad, Yvonne Yazbeck and Jane Idleman Smith. *The Islamic Understanding of Death and Resurrection.* Albany, N.Y.: State University of New York Press, 1981.

Hadikusuma, Djarnawi. *Kitab Tauhid.* Yogyakarta: P.T. Percetekan Persatuan, 1987.

Hanafi, Hassan. *Min al-'aqida ila l-thawra.* 5 vols. Cairo: Maktaba Madbuli, n.d.

——*Muqaddima fi 'ilm al-istighrab.* Cairo: al-Dar al-Fanniya, 1991.

——*La Phénomenologie de l'exégèse: essai d'une herméneutique existentielle à partir du Nouveau Testament.* Cairo: Anglo-Egyptian Bookshop, 1988 (Ph. D. dissertation, Sorbonne, 1966).

——"Qira'at al-nass." *Alif: Journal of Comparative Poetics* 8 (1988): 7–29 (in Arabic).

Hasan, Muhammad Kamal. *Muslim Intellectual Responses to "New Order*

Modernization" in Indonesia. Kuala Lumpur: Dewan dan Pustaka Kementerian Pelejaran Malaysia, 1980.

Hasyim, Hasten and Mu'ammal Hamidy. *Syara Riyadhush Shalihin.* Surabaya: Pustäka Islam, 1988.

Heemskerk, Margaretha T. *Pain and the Compensation in Mu'tazilite Doctrine: 'Abd al-Jabbar's Teaching and its Adoption by Manekdim and Ibn Matawayh.* Nijmegen: Quickprint, 1995.

Hodgson, Marshall G. S. *The Venture of Islam: Conscience and History in a World Civilization.* 3 vols. Chicago: University of Chicago Press, 1974.

Hourani, Albert. *Arabic Thought in the Liberal Age, 1798–1939.* Cambridge: Cambridge University Press, 1983.

Hourani, George F. *Islamic Rationalism: The Ethics of 'Abd al-Jabbar.* Oxford: Clarendon Press, 1971.

Huntington, Samuel P. "The Clash of Civilizations?" *Foreign Affairs* 72/3 (Summer 1993): 22–49.

Hurgronje, Christiaan Snouck. *Mekka in the Latter Part of the Nineteenth Century.* Leiden: E. J. Brill, 1931.

Izutsu, Toshihiko. *God and Man in the Koran.* Tokyo: Institute of Cultural and Linguistic Studies, 1964.

Jones, W[illiam] T[udor]. *A History of Western Philosophy.* 2 vols. New York: Harcourt, Brace & Company, 1952.

Jansen, Johannes J. G. *The Neglected Duty: The Creed of Sadat's Assassins and Islamic Resurgence in the Middle East.* New York: Macmillan Publishing Company, 1986.

Kamal, Musthafa, Chusnan Yusuf, and Rosyad Sholeh. *Muhammadiyah Sebagai Gerakan Islam.* Yogayakarta: Penerbit Persatuan, 1988.

Khafaji, 'Abd al-Mun'im, al-. *Al-Azhar fi alf 'am.* 3 vols. 2nd edition. Beirut and Cairo: 'Alam al-Kitab, 1988.

Kramer, Joel L. *Humanism in the Renaissance of Islam: The Cultural Revival of the Buyid Age.* Leiden: E. J. Brill, 1986.

Kraus, Paul. "Beiträge zur islamischen Ketzergeschichte: Das Kitab al-Zumurrud des Ibn al-Rawandi." *Revista degli studi orientali* 14 (1933): 93–129; 14 (1934): 335–379.

Kritzeck, James. *Peter the Venerable and Islam.* Oriental Studies Series, 23. Princeton N. J.: Princeton University Press, 1964.

Langan, John. "The Western Moral Tradition on War: Christian Theology and Warfare." In *Just War and Jihad: Historical and Theoretical Perspectives on War and Peace in Western and Islamic Traditions,* edited by John Kelsay and James Turner Johnson, pp. 71–90. New York: Greenwood Press, 1991.

Laoust, Henri. *Essai sur les doctrines sociales et politiques de Taqi-d-Din Ahmad b. Taimiya.* Cairo: Imprimerie de l'Institut Français d'Archéologie Orientale, 1939.

Lapidus, Ira M. *A History of Islamic Societies*. Cambridge: Cambridge University Press, 1988.

Lawrence, Bruce B. *Defenders of God: The Fundamentalist Revolt Against the Modern Age*. San Francisco: Harper & Row, 1989.

——*Shahrastani on the Indian Religions*. Religion and Society, 4. The Hague and Paris: Mouton, 1976.

Livingston, John. "Western Science and Educational Reform in the Thought of Shaykh Rifa'a al-Tahtawi." *International Journal of Middle East Studies* 28/4 (1996): 543–564.

Lone, Saahir. "Heresy in Egypt?" *Civil Society* (August 1995): 8.

MacDonald, D[uncan]. B[lack]. *The Development of Muslim Theology, Jurisprudence and Constitutional Theory*. London: Routledge & Sons, 1903.

Madelung, Wilferd. *Der Imam al-Qasim ibn Ibrahim und die Glaubenslehre der Zaiditen*. Berlin: Walter de Gruyter, 1965.

——"Imamism and Mu'tazalite Theology." In *Le Shi'ism Imamite*, edited by T[oufic] Fahd, pp. 13–29. Paris: Presses Universitaires, 1979.

——"A Mutarrifi Manuscript." In *Proceedings of the VIth Congress of Arabic and Islamic Studies, Visby and Stockholm, 1972*, pp. 75–83. Leiden: E. J. Brill.

——"The Origins of the Controversy Concerning the Creation of the Qur'an." In *Orientalia Hispanica sive studia F. M. Pareja octogenari dicta*, edited by J. M. Barral, pp. 504–525. Vol. 1. Leiden: E. J. Brill, 1974. Reprinted in Madelung, *Religious Schools and Sects*.

——*Religious Schools and Sects in Medieval Islam*. London: Variorum Reprints, 1985.

——*Religious Trends in Early Islamic Iran*. Columbia Series in Iranian Studies, 4. Albany, N.Y.: Bibliotheca Persica, 1988.

——"The Spread of Maturidism and the Turks." *Actas de IV Congreso de Estudos e Islamicos Coimbra-Lisboa 1968*, pp. 109–168. Leiden: E. J. Brill.

——"The Theology of al-Zamakhshari," *Actas del XII Congreso de la U.E.A.I., Màlaga, 1984*, pp. 485–495. Madrid, 1986.

Madjid, Nurcholish. *Islam: Doctrin dan Peradaban*. Jakarta: Yayasan Wakaf Paramadina, 1992.

——*Islam, Kemodernan, dan Keindonesiaan*. 4th edition. Bandung: Mizan, 1992.

——"The Issue of Modernization Among Muslims in Indonesian Culture: From a Participant's Point of view." In *What is Modern Indonesian Culture?* edited by G. Davis, pp. 143–155. Athens, Oh.: Ohio University Monographs in International Studies, Southeast Asia Series. Athens, Oh.: Ohio University Center for International Studies, 1983.

——"Penetia Penerbitan Buku dan Seminar 70 tahun Harun Nasution

Bibliography

Berkerkajasama dengan Lembaga Studi dan Filsifat." In *Refleksi Pembaharnan Pemikiran Islam*, q.v.
——"Sekularisme Bertentangam dengan Islam." *Panji Masyarakat Magazine* 57 (January 1970).
Makari, Victor E. *Ibn Taymiyyah's Ethics: The Social Factor.* American Academy of Religion Academy Series, 34. Chico, Calif.: Scholars Press, 1983.
Makdisi, George. *The Rise of Colleges: Institutions of Learning in Islam and the West.* Edinburgh: Edinburgh University Press, 1981.
Malek, Anouar Abdel. "Orientalism in Crisis." *Diogenes* 44 (1963): 103–140.
Martin, Richard C. "Islamic Textuality in Light of Postculturalist Criticism." In *A Way Prepared: Essays on Islamic Culture in Honor of Richard Bayly Winder*, edited by Farhad Kazemi and Robert D. McChesney, pp. 116–131. New York: New York University Press, 1988.
——"The Role of the Basrah Mu'tazilah in Formulating the Doctrine of the Apologetic Miracle." *Journal of Near Eastern Studies* 39/3 (1980): 175–189.
—— ed. *Approaches to Islam in Religious Studies.* Tucson, Ariz.: University of Arizona Press, 1985.
Marty, Martin E. and R. Scott Appleby, eds. *Fundamentalisms Observed.* Fundamentalism Project, 1. Chicago and London: The University of Chicago Press, 1991.
McCarthy, Richard J. *The Theology of al-Ash'ari.* Beirut: Imprimatur Catholique, 1953. Texts and translations of *Kitab al luma'* and *Risala fi istihsan al-khawd fi l-kalam.*
McGrath, Alister E. *The Genesis of Doctrine: A Study in the Foundations of Doctrinal Criticism.* Oxford: Blackwell, 1990.
Mernissi, Fatima. *Beyond the Veil: Male–Female Dynamics in Modern Muslim Society.* Revised edition. Bloomington, Ind.: Indiana University Press, 1987.
——*Islam and Democracy: Fear of the Modern World.* Translated by Mary Jo Lakeland. Reading, Mass.: Addison-Wesley Publishing Co., 1992.
Messick, Brinkley. *The Calligraphic State: Textual Domination and History in a Muslim Society.* Berkeley, Calif.: University of California Press, 1993.
Miller, Larry Benjamin. "Islamic Disputation Theory: A Study of the Development of dialectic in Islam from the Tenth Through Fourteenth Centuries." Ph.D. dissertation, Princeton University, 1984.
Mitchell, Richard P. *The Society of the Muslim Brothers.* London: Oxford University Press, 1969.
Nader, Albert. *Falsafa al-mu'tazila.* Alexandria, 1950.
——*Le Système philosophique des Mu'tazila (premiers penseurs de l'Islam).* 2nd edition. Beirut: Dar el-Machreq, 1984.

243

Oberman, Julian. "Political Theology in Early Islam: Hasan al-Basri's Treatise on *qadar*." *Journal of the American Oriental Society* 55 (1935): 138–162.

Ormsby, Eric. *Theodicy in Islamic Thought: The Dispute Over al-Ghazali's Best of All Possible Worlds.* Princeton: Princeton University Press, 1984.

Pellat, Charles. *The Life and Works of Jahiz.* Translated from French by D. M. Hawke. Berkeley, Calif.: University of California Press, 1969 [1967].

Perlmann, Moshe. "Medieval Polemics Between Islam and Judaism." In *Religion in a Religious Age*, edited by S[olomon] D. Goitein, pp. 103–138. Cambridge, Mass.: Association for Jewish Studies, 1974.

Peters, Johannes Reinier Theodorus Maria Peters. *God's Created Speech: A Study in the Speculative Theology of the Mu'tazili Qadi l-Qudat Abu l-Hasan 'Abd al-Jabbar Ibn Ahmed al-Hamadani.* Leiden: E. J. Brill, 1976.

Puar, Yusuf Abdullah. *Perjuangan dan Pengabdian Muhammadiyah.* Jakarta: Antara, 1989.

Qadi, Ahmad 'Arafat, al-. "Falsafat al-tarbiya 'ind al-mu'tazila wa l-ash'ariya." Ph.D. dissertation. Cairo University, 1993.

Rahman, Fazlur. *Islam.* 2nd edition. Chicago: University of Chicago Press, 1979.

——*Islam and Modernity: Transformation of an Intellectual Tradition.* Chicago: University of Chicago Press, 1982.

——*Major Themes of the Qur'an.* Minneapolis: Bibliotheca Islamica, 1980.

——"My Belief-in-Action." In *The Courage of Conviction*, edited by Phillip L. Berman, pp. 153–159. Santa Barbara, Calif.: Dodd, Mead & Company, 1985.

——*Prophecy in Islam: Philosophy and Orthodoxy.* London: Allen & Unwin, 1958.

——"Review Essay." In *Approaches to Islam in Religious Studies*, edited by Richard C. Martin, pp. 189–202. Tucson, Ariz.: University of Arizona Press, 1986.

Rais, Amin. "The Muslim Brotherhood in Egypt: Its Rise, Demise and Resurgence." Ph.D. dissertation, University of Chicago, 1981.

Refleksi Pembaharuan Pemikiran Islam 70 Tahun Harun Nasution. Edited by Panitia Peneritan Buku dan Seminar 70 Tahun Harun Nasution Bekerjasama dengan Lembaga Studi Agama dan Filsifat. Jakarta: Lembaga Studi Agama dan Filsifat, 1989.

Reinhart, A. Kevin. *Before Revelation: The Boundaries of Muslim Moral Thought.* S.U.N.Y. Series in Middle Eastern Studies. Albany, N.Y.: State University of New York Press, 1995.

Rippen, Andrew and Jan Knappert, eds. *Textual Sources for the Study of Islam.* Chicago: University of Chicago Press, 1990.

Sachedina, Abdulziz Abdulhussein. *Islamic Messianism: The Idea of the*

Mahdi in Twelver Shi'ism. Albany, N.Y.: State University of New York Press, 1981.

Said, Edward W. "Opponents, Audiences, Constituencies, and Community." In *The Politics of Interpretation*, edited by W. T. J. Mitchell, pp. 1–32. Chicago: University of Chicago Press, 1983.

——*Orientalism.* New York: Random House, 1978.

Sayyid, Ayman Fu'ad. *Ta'rikh al-madhahib al-diniya fi bilad al-yaman hatta nihayat al-qarn al-sadis al-hijri.* Cairo: Dar al-Misriya al-Lubnaniya, 1988.

Schacht, Joseph. *An Introduction to Islamic Law.* Oxford: Clarendon Press, 1964.

Schwartz, Michael. "The Letter of al-Hasan al-Basri." *Oriens* 20 (1967): 15–30.

Sharpe, Eric J. *Comparative Religion: A History.* New York: Charles Scribner's Sons, 1975.

Sjadzali, Munawir. *Islam dan Tata Negara: Ajaran, Sejarah dan Pemikiran.* Jakarta: University of Indonesia Press, 1990.

Smith, Jonathan Z. *Drudgery Divine: On the Comparison of Early Christianities and the Religions of Late Antiquity.* Chicago: University of Chicago Press, 1990.

Stroumsa, Sarah. "The Barahima in Early Kalam." *Jerusalem Studies* 6 (1985): 229–241.

Thoyfoer, Zamakhsyari. *Mutiara Kittah Nahdatul Ulama* 1926. Surabaya: Persatuan, 1987.

Tucker, Gene M. *Form Criticism of the Old Testament.* Philadelphia: Fortress Press, 1971.

'Uthman, Abd al-Karim. *Qadi al-Qudat 'Abd al-Jabbar b. Ahmad al-Hamadhani.* Beirut: Dar al-'Arabiya, 1968.

van Ess, Josef. "Disputationspraxis in der islamischen Theologie: Eine vorläufige Skizze." *Revue des Études Islamiques* 44 (1976): 23–60.

——"Une lecture à rebours de l'histoire du Mu'tazilisme." *Revue des Études Islamiques* 46/2 (1978): 163–240; 47/1 (1979): 19–69.

——"The Logical Structure of Islamic Theology." In *Logic in Classical Islamic Culture*, edited by G[ustav] E. von Grunebaum, pp. 21–50. Wiesbaden: Otto Harrassowitz, 1970.

——*Theologie und Gesellschaft im 2. und 3. Jahrhundert Hidschra: Eine Geschichte des religiösen Denkes im frühen Islam.* 5 of 6 vols. to date. Berlin and New York: Walter de Gruyter, 1991–.

van der Veer, Peter. "The Foreign Hand: Orientalist Discourse in Sociology and Communalism." In *Orientalism and the Postcolonial Predicament*, edited by Carol A. Breckenridge and Peter van der Veer, pp. 23–44. Delhi: Oxford University Press, 1994.

Voll, John Obert. *Islam: Continuity and Change in the Modern World.* 1st edition. Boulder, Colo.: West view Press, 1982.

von Grunebaum, Gustav E. *A Tenth-Century Document of Arabic Literary Theory and Criticism: The Sections on Poetry of al-Baqillani's I'jaz al-Qu'ran.* Chicago: University of Chicago Press, 1950.

Wahid, Abdurrahman. *Teologi Pembangunan, Meinbangun Teologi: Delam Peliti Hati.* Jakarta: Pustaka Kartini, 1986.

Wasserstrom, Steven M. *Between Muslim and Jew: The Problem of Symbiosis under Early Islam.* Princeton: Princeton University Press, 1995.

Watt, William Montgomery. *The Formative Period of Islamic Thought.* Edinburgh: Edinburgh University Press, 1973.

——*Muslim Intellectual: A Study of al-Ghazali.* Edinburgh: Edinburgh University Press, 1963.

Wensick, A[rendt] J[an]. *The Muslim Creed: Its Genesis and Historical Development.* London: Frank Cass, 1965.

Wolfson, Harry Austryn. *The Philosophy of Kalam.* Cambridge, Mass.: Harvard University Press, 1976.

Woodward, Mark. "Talking Across Paradigms: Indonesia, Islam and Orientalism." In idem, *Toward a New Paradigm,* pp. 1–45.

——"Textual Exegesis as Social Commentary: Religious, Social and Political Meanings of Indonesian Translations of Arabic Hadith Texts." *The Journal of Asian Studies,* 52/3 (1993): 565–583.

—— ed. *Toward a New Paradigm: Recent Developments in Indonesian Islamic Thought.* Tempe, Ariz.: Arizona State University Program for Southeast Asian Studies, 1966.

Zebiri, Kate. *Mahmud Shaltut and Islamic Modernism.* Oxford: Clarendon Press, 1993.

Index

Index